GREAT BATTLES OF THE CIVIL WAR

CONTRIBUTING WRITERS:

MARTIN GRAHAM

GEORGE SKOCH

CONSULTANT:

WILLIAM C. DAVIS

PUBLICATIONS INTERNATIONAL, LTD.

Contributing writer Martin Graham is co-author of *Mine Run: A Campaign of Lost Opportunities* and has written extensively about the Civil War for *Civil War Quarterly* and other magazines. He has also made presentations on Civil War figures Stonewall Jackson and James E. Taylor. Mr. Graham is a past president of the Cleveland Civil War Round Table.

Contributing writer George Skoch is an associate editor at *Blue & Gray Magazine* and co-author of *Mine Run: A Campaign of Lost Opportunities*. Mr. Skoch has also written extensively for such magazine as *Civil War Times Illustrated, America's Civil War,* and *Civil War Book Exchange & Collector's Newspaper.*

Consultant William C. Davis has been nominated for Pulitzer Prizes for his books *Breckinridge: Statesman, Soldier, Symbol* and *Battle at Bull Run.* He has written numerous other books and articles on the Civil War as well as contributed to various history anthologies. Mr. Davis has consulted for such television programs as ABC's *North and South* and Columbia Pictures' *The Blue and the Gray.* Mr. Davis is president of Museum Editions, Ltd., a division of Historical Times, Inc.

PICTURE CREDITS:

Manufactured in Yugoslavia.

h g f e d c b a

ISBN: 0-88176-641-0

Library of Congress Catalog Card Number: 89-63242

Lieutenant General
Ulysses Grant, USA

CONTENTS

General
Robert E. Lee, CSA

INTRODUCTION:
A HOUSE DIVIDED

THE STAGE IS SET

A crowd gathered around the steps of the Montgomery, Alabama, capitol on February 18, 1861, to witness an historic occasion. The secession of South Carolina from the United States less than two months earlier had set off a chain of events that culminated in this moment, the inauguration of Jefferson Davis as the provisional President of the Confederate States of America.

A convention of 37 representatives from the states that had seceded from the Union met in Montgomery on February 4, 1861, to form their new government. This group of determined men set about the business of creating a new nation with great resolve and commitment to the belief that a state had the inherent right to decide its own destiny. From the beginning, this conviction hindered the development of a national government, since states' rights were often put above the decisions of the Confederate government. The delegates to the convention elected Howell Cobb of Georgia as the president of the convention. "The separation is perfect, complete, and perpetual," Cobb addressed the delegates. "The great duty is now imposed upon us of providing for these States a government for their future security and protection." The convention adopted a provisional Constitution on February 8 and chose Jefferson Davis as President on February 9.

In his inaugural address, the 52-year-old former United States senator made no mention of the events over the past decades that seemed to predestine the dissolution of the Union. The issues of slavery and states' rights were not on the minds of Davis or those he addressed that day. The new President took the occasion to inform those states that had not yet joined the formation of this new nation that all the Confederacy desired was to be left alone. If attacked, however, "the suffering of millions will bear testimony to the folly and wickedness of our aggressors."

Less than two weeks later, on March 4, 1861, another President assumed office several hundred miles northeast of Montgomery. Abraham Lincoln's election as President of the Unites States of America on November 6, 1860, was a primary cause of South Carolina's secession from the Union and the subsequent creation of the Confederacy. Lincoln took the opportunity of his inaugural address to try to reduce some of the frenzy that had taken grip of the citizens of both the North and South. Although he felt states did not have the right to secede, Lincoln vowed to avoid war if at all possible. "In your hands, my dissatisfied fellow-countrymen, and not in mine, is the momentous issue of civil war," he stated in his address. "You can have no conflict without being yourselves the aggressors." He also reaffirmed his commitment to enforce all Federal laws, which included maintaining possession of all Federal property in Confederate states.

The North and South had been on a collision course over the issue of states' rights since the United States was formed in 1787. As a compromise between states economically dependent on slavery for survival and states opposed to slavery, the Founding Fathers gave each state the right to decide its own stance concerning slavery. Congress struggled with the free/slave issue throughout the nation's early years, and various factions fought over whether to allow slave states to enter the Union.

By 1820, Congress had assumed the authority to decide the free/slave issue for each new state admitted to the Union. The terms of the 1820 Missouri Compromise admitted Maine as a free state and Missouri as a slave state. But the Compromise prohibited further expansion of slavery into other northern territories.

The delicate balance in Congress between abolitionists and slave staters was severely tested as each western territory petitioned to be admitted to the Union as a state. Kentucky Senator Henry Clay's Compromise of 1850 admitted California as a free state and left the choice of free/slave to each new southwestern territory as each applied for admission to the Union. The compromise also contained the Fugitive Slave Law, which gave the Federal government the authority to capture and return escaped slaves. This last provision caused great discontent throughout the North.

The Kansas-Nebraska Act of 1854, wrought by Senator Stephen Douglas of Illinois, repealed provisions of the Missouri Compromise that restricted the expansion of slavery into northern territories. The citizens of Nebraska and Kansas were given the opportunity to choose free or slave status "as their constitution may prescribe at the time of their admission." This act caused open hostilities in Kansas between pro-slavery advocates and free staters. Many innocent men, women, and children died in this bloody border war.

In 1857, the United States Supreme Court entered the slavery debate when it handed down its controversial Dred Scott decision. Scott, an elderly black man and slave, had lived intermittently in free territory for a number of years with his owner, an army surgeon. While in Missouri in 1846, Scott sued for his freedom on the grounds that he had lived in free territory. A Missouri district court ruled in Scott's favor, but the judgment was overruled by the state supreme court. The United States Supreme Court ruled that Scott was not a citizen of the United States and therefore could not present a suit in a Federal court. The decision further stated that slaves were property, giving their masters the right of possession even in free territories and states.

In October 1859, radical abolitionist John Brown and 21 followers briefly held the United States Arsenal at Harpers Ferry. They intended to arm the

Abraham Lincoln's election in 1860 sparked the start of secession. Lincoln was determined to keep the nation united at any cost.

thousands of slaves they believed would join in their rebellion. But a small contingent of U.S. Marines, commanded by Robert E. Lee, stormed the firehouse in which Brown's men were trapped. Ten of the raiders were killed, and seven, including Brown, were captured. The abolitionist leader was executed for murder and treason about two months later.

This series of events, from the creation of the Union in 1787 to the winter of 1860, inflamed public opinion to the point where further compromise was impossible. Secession from the Union and creation of a new nation seemed the only alternative to the citizens of the South.

SECESSION AND MOBILIZATION

South Carolina seceded from the Union on December 20, 1860, followed in January 1861 by Mississippi, Florida, Alabama, Georgia, and Louisiana. By the time delegates met in Montgomery, Alabama, to form the provisional government of the Confederate States of America and elect a President, Texas had joined the fold.

Most secessionists realized that if fighting started, the Confederacy would be at a disadvantage. The resources of the industrialized North far outweighed those of the predominantly agricultural South. By June 1861, when Tennessee became the last of the 11 states to join the Confederacy, the population of the North was more than 19 million. The population of the South was a little more than 9 million, about 3.5 million of whom were slaves. At the start of the war, the Union had about 110,000 manufacturers compared with 18,000 in the Confederacy. The North also had a much larger and better maintained railroad system than the South. Although the South's principal industry was agriculture, the North boasted a much more productive agricultural system.

Fort Sumter

Since December 26, 1860, Federal troops had occupied Fort Sumter in Charleston Harbor, South Carolina. An expedition to resupply the garrison failed on January 9, 1861, when Confederate troops turned a Federal relief ship, *Star of the West,* back to sea before it reached the fort. Lincoln refused to abandon this outpost to the Confederacy.

The integrity, resolve, and strength of the Confederate government put to the test, Davis had no other choice than to order the fort taken by force. On April 10, the Confederate President directed Confederate Brigadier General Pierre G.T. Beauregard, commanding the provisional troops in Charleston, to demand the immediate evacuation of Sumter, and if rejected by the Federals, to "proceed in such manner as you may determine, to reduce it." Rebuffed by Sumter's commander, Beauregard's troops fired the opening shots of the war on April 12, 1861.

The bombardment lasted about 35 hours before Sumter finally surrendered. During the shelling, no one on either side was killed or seriously wounded. Ironically, the only serious casualties occurred on April 14 as the Federals were firing a salute before abandoning the fort. A spark landed on a pile of powder cartridges, causing an explosion that killed one soldier, mortally wounded another, and seriously wounded four others.

The fall of Fort Sumter electrified the emotions of the populace, both North and South. On April 15, Lincoln issued a call to Northern governors to furnish 75,000 men to put down the rebellion. A Virginia state convention, interpreting Lincoln's call as an act of war, voted to join the Confederacy on the

The early Confederate Stars and Bars flag flies above Fort Sumter, where the first shots of the war were fired on April 12, 1861. Confederate General Beauregard subdued the fort with a 35-hour bombardment.

17th of April. Although the popular vote to secede did not take place until May 23, Virginia militia seized the Federal arsenal at Harpers Ferry on April 18 and the Gosport Navy Yard at Norfolk two days later. The stage was now set for the struggle that both sides had earnestly wished to avoid but now just as avidly wished to win.

Military Policy
Lincoln issued a proclamation on April 19 blockading all Confederate ports. He directed his naval commanders to first warn ships trying to leave or enter Confederate ports. If they ignored the warning, Federal ships were to capture and confiscate ships and cargo. Lincoln received much criticism for this attempt to halt shipping along the 3549 miles of Confederate coast. Initially ineffective, by the end of the war the blockade had placed a stranglehold on the Confederate economy. Lincoln's land strategy was as basic as his sea strategy: take the offensive and destroy all Confederate armies in the field.

Meanwhile, Jefferson Davis and his new government began the necessary steps to preserve their new nation. Davis welcomed Virginia into the fold with open arms. To ensure the continued support of the citizens of Virginia, by far the most industrialized of the seceding states, the provisional government voted on May 20, 1861, to move the capital of the Confederacy to Richmond. Davis also did what he could to influence Arkansas, Tennessee, North Carolina, Maryland, Kentucky, Delaware, and Missouri to join the Confederacy. Within months, Arkansas, Tennessee, and North Carolina seceded, but the others remained part of the Union throughout the war.

Davis had few choices in developing his military policy. The tremendous resource advantages enjoyed by the North precluded any thought of establishing an offensive policy. Instead, Davis set out to defend his extensive borders in the hope that either the North would eventually weary of the war and recognize the Confederacy or that European nations, Davis thinking their markets would be dependent on Southern-produced cotton, would intervene on behalf of the South for economic reasons. By April 29, more than 62,000 men had answered the Confederacy's call to arms, and another 15,000 were moving toward key points along the Northern border. On May 9, Davis signed a bill giving himself authority to accept those volunteers into military service he considered necessary to defend the Confederacy.

The leaders of each secessionist state were also busy mobilizing their citizens to face invasion. The task was particularly pressing for Virginia Governor John Letcher. The Potomac River was the sole barrier between his state and the Federal capital. Letcher realized that Virginia would be a prime target for invasion by Federal troops. He quickly acted to mobilize volunteers to meet any such action by Union troops. To train and lead these inexperienced recruits, Letcher chose a native son who had recently resigned from the Federal army— 54-year-old Colonel Robert E. Lee. Lee eventually became military adviser to Jefferson Davis and finally commander of the Army of Northern Virginia.

While Davis and his governors mobilized troops to defend the Confederacy's borders, Lincoln and the governors of the Northern states were actively engaged in appointing officers to lead the many men who were answering the President's call to arms. In many cases, junior officers of the Regular Army resigned their commissions and were placed in command of volunteer regiments, brigades, divisions, and armies. In many other instances, men with little military experience but great political influence were given prestigious, important commands. The race to gain a significant military commission was intense, and many capable men were initially ignored. One such individual was a former Regular Army captain who had resigned in 1854 with the reputation as an irresponsible drunk. His name was Ulysses S. Grant.

1861: THE FIGHTING BEGINS
Virginia and Missouri were the two major theaters of operations throughout 1861. Although the Federals experienced setbacks for control of Missouri with defeats at Wilson's Creek and Lexington, they were able to muster enough military support to prevent the takeover of the state by secessionists.

In the east, attention was also focused on the Virginia plain south of Washington, D.C., where a Confederate force, commanded by Brigadier General Pierre G.T. Beauregard of Fort Sumter fame, threatened the Federal capital. The Federal army sent to meet this threat, commanded by Brigadier General Irvin McDowell, was routed. The Federals called this action the Battle of Bull Run, while the Confederates named it the Battle of Manassas, setting early on a tendency for some battles to have two names.

The casualty figures reported from the action, 2900 Federal and 2000 Confederate, had a sobering effect on the citizens of the North and South. Wives and parents began to realize that they were not sending their loved ones off to a pageant but rather to a struggle where soldiers could die or be maimed for life. The rout of the Federal army at Bull Run instilled a great confidence in the people of the South that they would ultimately win the war, but it also strengthened the resolve of the citizens of the North to commit all the resources necessary to put down the rebellion and reunite the divided nation. Having learned some valuable lessons from their first fight, both armies spent the remainder of 1861 preparing for a prolonged conflict.

1862
Throughout the winter of 1861–1862, thousands of Federal and Confederate volunteers were sent by their respective states to staging areas in both the eastern and western theaters. Regiments poured into Washington and were assigned to brigades, which were then detailed to divisions. By spring 1862, Major General George McClellan, now commanding Federal troops at Washington, had an army numbering more than 120,000 men. Under McClellan's direction, these raw troops, from the smallest rural communities to the largest Northern cities, were incessantly drilled by officers as green as the recruits.

Meanwhile, the Confederates had not been idle while McClellan's army was being shaped into an effective fighting unit. As troops arrived in Richmond, Jefferson Davis, with the guidance of military adviser General Robert E. Lee, sent them to key points along the defensive perimeter of Virginia. Under the guidance of Major General Thomas "Stonewall" Jackson in the Shenandoah Valley and General Joseph Johnston on the northern Virginia border, these recruits were drilled in the fine art of war. By the spring of 1862, they were ready to defend their new nation.

The Soldier's Life
Northern and Southern males, anxious to take part in the fighting before it ended, flocked to recruiting stations in the early months of the war. But their romantic visions of the military were quickly dispelled by the boredom and routine of camp life. Hours of drilling and idleness led many soldiers to yearn for the action of combat. Participants of the Battle of Bull Run and several lesser engagements told of the horrors of battle, but after months of

ABRAHAM LINCOLN

"This morning, as for some days past," Federal President Abraham Lincoln wrote on August 23, 1864, "it seems exceedingly probable that this Administration will not be re-elected. Then it will be my duty to so co-operate with the President elect, as to save the Union between the election and the inauguration; as he will have secured his election on such ground that he can not possibly save it afterwards." By August 1864, the Federal war effort was at perhaps its darkest moment, and with the November presidential election looming, Lincoln felt that the Democratic peace candidate, George McClellan, could possibly defeat him. But the capture of Atlanta and victories in the Shenandoah Valley enabled Lincoln to win the November election.

Lincoln was born near Hodgenville, Kentucky, on February 12, 1809. His education was primarily self-taught, and in 1836 he was licensed to practice law. Lincoln was elected to the United States House of Representatives in 1847. In 1858, he lost the race for Senator but drew national attention during his debates with his opponent, Stephen A. Douglas. That attention helped launch his successful bid for the presidency in 1860.

The strength of Lincoln's character and his resolve to save the Union has often been credited for holding the Federal government together throughout its most difficult crisis. Throughout four years of war, Lincoln was always affable and an excellent administrator. After several early mistakes, he turned military control over to the professionals while he paid closer attention to public matters. Although he found it personally painful to support the mounting cost in human lives that the war inflicted on citizens of the North and South, his commitment to the vigorous prosecution of the war was rewarded with the defeat of the Confederacy.

Lincoln's opportunity to savor the initial steps in the restoration of the Union was short-lived, however. On April 14, 1865, he was shot by John Wilkes Booth. His death the next morning sent shock waves throughout the North and South and marked the beginning of the long, difficult road to national reconciliation.

inactivity even these soldiers were anxious to get on with the war in the spring of 1862.

By the war's end, more than 110,000 blue-clad soldiers had died as a result of wounds sustained in battle. Although precise Confederate figures are unknown, it is estimated that some 94,000 Confederates were killed or mortally wounded in battle. But the respite between battles was often more treacherous and deadly than combat itself. Sanitary conditions were poor, and soldiers were subject to camp epidemics, particularly diarrhea and dysentery. During the course of the war, 225,000 Federal and 164,000 Confederate troops died as a result of disease.

The Peninsula Campaign

As the winter of 1861 drew to a close, Lincoln became increasingly concerned that his young General in Chief had not yet submitted plans for a spring campaign. With Johnston's Confederate army still encamped near Manassas, Virginia, Lincoln was anxious for McClellan to seize the initiative and drive the Confederates from the doorstep of the Federal capital. Finally, after an ultimatum from Lincoln forced the start of the campaign, McClellan took the initial steps that would result in his ill-fated Peninsula Campaign.

With Washington and Richmond less than 100 miles apart, the defense of the capitals became the primary concern of the opposing governments. Transporting Federal soldiers by water to the Virginia Peninsula and then marching up the Peninsula would threaten Richmond with capture. Lincoln and Secretary of War Edwin Stanton, however, expressed concern that McClellan's Peninsula Campaign would leave Washington defenseless. When Lincoln learned that McClellan intended to take his entire Federal army south, Lincoln held back almost 40,000 men. McClellan's disregard for the concerns of the President would be one of the factors leading to his dismissal later that year.

While the Federal Army marched up the Peninsula, Confederate General "Stonewall" Jackson conducted a successful campaign in the Shenandoah Valley, occupying more than 60,000 Federal troops. On May 31, 1862, the first day of the Battle of Seven Pines on the outskirts of Richmond, General Joseph Johnston was severely wounded. Davis turned to General Robert E. Lee to replace Johnston. Lee took advantage of Jackson's success in the Valley to drive the Federals from the gates of Richmond during the Seven Days' Campaign. By the end of summer 1862, the situation in the eastern theater had improved for the Confederacy. Lee was preparing to cross the Potomac into Maryland after the victory at Second Bull Run, and the morale of the people of the South had received a boost from Lee's victories.

Shiloh and Antietam

By September 1862, while the Federals had yet to experience a significant victory in the east, Union armies in the west had experienced nothing but success. The string of victories began in February 1862 with the capture of Forts Henry and Donelson by Brigadier General Ulysses S. Grant.

As a result of the fall of Forts Henry and Donelson, Confederate troops were forced out of Kentucky. The Federals needed only two more months to drive the Confederates from most of Tennessee. In a desperate attempt to stop the Union

advance, Confederate General Albert S. Johnston launched a surprise attack on April 6 against Grant's army encamped near Shiloh, Tennessee. Although Grant emerged victorious, he lost more than 13,000 men. Casualty figures for both sides were never truly exact; they were often determined during the confusing aftermath of a battle. But there was no mistaking the fact, Shiloh had been the costliest action by far for both sides since the start of the war. While civilians were appalled at the losses, the figures would be eclipsed in many future battles. Lincoln was pressured to replace Grant because of these high casualty figures, but Lincoln realized that the cost of winning the struggle would be heavy. The President resisted replacing Grant. "I can't spare this man," Lincoln proclaimed, "he fights!"

The Union continued to make headway in the west through the autumn of the year. Federal armies experienced victories at Perryville, Kentucky; Corinth, Mississippi; and at the turn of the year, at Stones River, Tennessee. Along the Mississippi River, Ulysses Grant began his campaign against the Confederate bastion at Vicksburg, Mississippi, in November.

Meanwhile, in the east, Lee's invasion of the North not only provided relief from the ravages of war for the citizens of Virginia but also allowed Lee and Davis to hope that a victory on Federal soil would have international implications for the Confederacy. Several European nations, including England and France, seemed poised to formally recognize the Confederacy and send it much-needed military and financial support. Both Davis and Lee felt a significant Confederate victory was necessary to sway the European nations. The opportunity for that victory arose along a meandering stream outside the sleepy hamlet of Sharpsburg, Maryland.

President Lincoln once again turned to McClellan to stop the Confederate invasion. After McClellan's disappointing performance on the Virginia Peninsula, Federal Major General John Pope, fresh from victories along the Mississippi River, had been brought east to assume command of all troops other than those with McClellan. But Pope's defeat at Second Bull Run left Lincoln no one else to turn to in this time of national emergency. McClellan and the vast army he had painstakingly assembled and trained would soon have another opportunity to prove themselves in battle. McClellan's army clashed with Lee's along Antietam Creek on September 17, 1862. A single day of fighting resulted in combined casualties of more than 25,000. The following evening, Lee crossed back into Virginia, ending his invasion of the North.

Abraham Lincoln took advantage of the Federal "victory" at Antietam to issue his Preliminary Emancipation Proclamation. "That on the first day of January in the year of our Lord, one thousand eight hundred and sixty-three," the proclamation read, "all persons held as slaves, within any state, or designated part of a state, the people whereof shall then be in rebellion against the United States shall be then, thenceforward, and forever free."

This pronouncement had been much discussed in the halls of Congress and among members of Lincoln's cabinet. Lincoln had intended for several months to issue this preliminary proclamation, but he felt a major Federal victory was necessary or the proclamation would seem a desperate effort to gain international support for the Union cause. The decree

was as much a political as a moral measure, raising the Federal cause to more than just a fight to preserve a nation. It now became a struggle to free a people. Recognition of the Confederacy by European nations would put them in the position of condoning slavery. This bold and brilliant move by Lincoln effectively negated Europe as a factor in the war.

1863

While Lincoln was satisfied with the progress of the war in the west, the situation in the east was his most pressing concern. After the devastating defeat at Fredericksburg and the subsequent "Mud March," which ended with the Army of the Potomac bogged down in a sea of mud during an attempt to outflank Lee's army, Lincoln replaced General Ambrose , Burnside, who had earlier replaced McClellan, with Major General Joseph Hooker. The new commander instilled a renewed confidence in his army and by spring 1863 thought the army ready to destroy the Confederate force camped across the Rappahannock.

Two Great Battles: Chancellorsville and Gettysburg

The winter months had been hard on Lee's troops camped around Fredericksburg. While the winter respite always served to amply replenish the manpower and supplies of the Federal army, the Confederate army received only limited amounts of supplies from the dwindling resources of the Confederacy. Many soldiers were forced to do without shoes or adequate clothing during the long winter months. Confederate soldiers maintained a perpetual state of hunger because of these shortages, and Lee had even found it necessary to send two divisions to southeastern Virginia on a foraging expedition.

Confederate President Jefferson Davis, a wealthy Mississippi plantation owner, had much to lose in this war, and he did not prove to be the best executive officer for the difficult job ahead.

JEFFERSON DAVIS

"The South did not fall crushed by the mere weight of the North," observed Pierre G.T. Beauregard several years after the war, "but it was nibbled away at all sides and ends because its executive head never gathered and wielded its great strength." Such was the feeling of many of those who had followed Jefferson Davis for the duration of the war. Following the war, the Confederate President became to many citizens of the North and South a symbol of defeat, the leader of the "Lost Cause."

Davis was born on June 3, 1808, in Christian County, Kentucky. He graduated from West Point in 1828, 23rd in a class of 33 cadets, and served in the army for seven years before retiring to a Mississippi plantation. Davis first married the daughter of future President Zachary Taylor, but three months later she died of malaria. Ten years later, in 1845, Davis married Varina Howell.

Davis entered public service in 1845 with his election to the United States Congress, becoming a staunch advocate of states' rights. During the Mexican War, Davis served as colonel of the 1st Mississippi Rifles. Wounded at the Battle of Buena Vista, Mexico, he returned home a hero and was selected by the Mississippi governor to fill a vacant seat in the Senate. He resigned in 1851 to make an unsuccessful run for governor of Mississippi. President Franklin Pierce selected Davis in 1853 as his secretary of war, a position he filled with distinction during a period of national and military expansion. He returned

to the Senate in 1857 but resigned four years later when Mississippi seceded from the Union. Following his appointment as major general of the state's militia, the provisional Confederate Congress elected Davis provisional President of the Confederacy on February 9, 1861. He was formally elected President of the Confederate States of America on November 6, 1861.

Davis has been described as a man unable to get along with people, a poor administrator, and a leader too involved in military concerns at the expense of civil affairs. As the fortunes of the Confederacy ebbed, those closest to Davis saw him gradually change from a confident, poised statesman to a stubborn chief executive, increasingly withdrawn at a time when leadership and guidance were desperately needed.

Just before the fall of Richmond, Davis and his cabinet fled south to escape the Federals. Davis evaded capture until May 10, when he was seized in Irwinville, Georgia. He was imprisoned in Fort Monroe, Virginia, for two years under the threat of trial for treason. Finally released on bail, Davis spent several years traveling overseas before returning to Mississippi.

Davis died on December 9, 1889, without ever having his United States citizenship restored. His place in American history was well-recognized at the time of his death, however, for his obituary in the *New York World* stated, "A great soul has passed away."

From left to right: the uniforms of a Union brigadier general, a Union infantry private, a Confederate infantry private, and a Confederate general.

Meanwhile, Hooker had devised a plan to outflank Lee, thereby forcing Lee to either abandon his position and fall back toward Richmond or attack the Federal column over terrain chosen by Hooker. Hooker's movement began on April 27, and by May 1, Lee's outmanned army was caught between two Federal forces roughly as large or larger than his own.

Although a portion of his army was absent, Lee didn't hesitate to seize the initiative. In one of the boldest moves by any army commander in the history of warfare, Lee divided his outnumbered command and struck Hooker's column in the Wilderness of Virginia around the tiny hamlet of Chancellorsville. The Confederate victory was costly for the South: "Stonewall" Jackson was wounded by fire from his own troops. Within eight days, Jackson died of pneumonia.

Lee took advantage of the victory at Chancellorsville to launch a second invasion of the North on June 3. By June 24, the leading column of Lee's army was marching into Chambersburg, Pennsylvania.

With reports of Confederate activity north of the Potomac River arriving in Washington and Northern newspapers stirring the citizens of Pennsylvania with disturbing accounts of Confederate destruction and looting, Hooker's army left Washington in pursuit. But Lincoln lacked trust in Hooker's ability to defeat Lee, and when Hooker offered his resignation in the midst of a disagreement with the Federal War Department, the President readily accepted. Lincoln chose Major General George G. Meade as Hooker's replacement. Hesitant to assume such overwhelming responsibilities, particularly during this national emergency, Meade only reluctantly accepted the command.

Neither Meade nor Lee had intended to fight at the crossroads town of Gettysburg, Pennsylvania, but by the time they reached the field, the decision had been made for them. On the morning of July 1, a division of Confederate infantry and a division of Federal cavalry collided west of Gettysburg, starting three days of the bloodiest fighting of the war. After the disaster of "Pickett's Charge," with supplies dwindling and his overstretched lines of communication threatened, Lee turned his army around on the evening of July 4 and headed back to Virginia. Lincoln later likened Meade's failure to pursue Lee to "an old woman shooing geese across a creek." Little occurred in the east during the remainder of 1863.

Fighting in the West

As in 1862, when Lincoln needed to find some signs of success to bolster his sagging spirits, he looked to the west and the army commanded by Ulysses S. Grant. Despite the difficulties of late 1862, Grant did not abandon his plan to capture Vicksburg, Mississippi. Instead, in the spring of 1863 he renewed his campaign. After a long siege that was marked by starvation and disease, Vicksburg surrendered to Grant's forces on July 4, 1863. Word of Grant's great victory echoed loudly throughout the North.

Federal General Rosecrans's Army of the Cumberland remained inactive for almost six months after its victory at Stones River, Tennessee. Finally, on June 24, the Federal commander moved his army against Confederate General Bragg. Rosecrans conducted a series of brilliant maneuvers to outflank Bragg, forcing Bragg's army into upper Georgia. Chattanooga was in Federal hands, and Rosecrans believed the Confederates were retreating all the way to Atlanta.

Unknown to Rosecrans, however, Bragg's army had withdrawn only a short distance into northern Georgia to regroup. Bolstered by the arrival of reinforcements, Bragg struck the Federals at Chickamauga, Georgia, on September 19. On the second day of intense fighting, the Federal army was routed and fled back to Chattanooga.

Bragg's Army of Tennessee followed the Federals back to the outskirts of Chattanooga and deployed on the heights to the east and south of the town. Rosecrans's army was virtually placed under siege. Since possession of Chattanooga was essential to maintaining Federal control of Tennessee, Ulysses Grant, commander of the district, began taking steps to lift the siege. After three days of assaults against Confederate positions on Lookout Mountain and Missionary Ridge, the Federals finally drove Bragg's army from its strategic position.

Black Troops

Throughout the war, the Union tightened the blockade of Confederate ports by capturing key positions along the Atlantic and Gulf coasts. One such strategic location was Fort Wagner, near the mouth of Charleston Harbor, South Carolina. A Federal force that included the black troops of the 54th Massachusetts unsuccessfully attacked the fort on July 18.

Toward the end of 1862, Lincoln had authorized the recruitment of black troops to make up for shortages in military manpower. Throughout the war, more than 178,000 black troops served in the Federal army. Segregated from whites, blacks were formed into their own units, which were then placed under the command of white officers. In response to the use of black troops to bolster the Federal army, Jefferson Davis approved a policy that called for the execution of all white Union officers commanding black soldiers. But in an ironic attempt to bolster its own manpower shortage, the Confederate Congress passed legislation in March 1865 calling for the enlistment of 300,000 black soldiers, but it proved too late to save their cause.

Reports of massacres of black troops by Confederate soldiers surfaced throughout the later stages of the war. The most notable episode was during the capture of Fort Pillow, Tennessee, on April 13, 1864, where only 58 of 262 black soldiers were taken prisoner.

The Home Front

While the military fortunes of both North and South rose and fell during 1863, the citizens were becoming greatly disillusioned with the war as thousands of families on both sides were touched by the death of a loved one. In the South, the Federal blockade combined with the limited resources of the Confederacy had a devastating effect on the Confederate economy. By June 1863, the Confederate paper dollar was worth only $.08 in gold, increasing the cost of goods astronomically. By April 1865, the Confederate paper dollar was worth only $.015. Jefferson Davis was under constant pressure to do something to bolster the economy, but there was little he could do to halt the rise in costs. As the war progressed, basic staples of life became increasingly difficult to obtain. In addition, discouraging news from the front during the later part of the war did nothing to bolster the morale of Southern citizens. But the resolve of the men and women of the Confederacy carried them through the many deprivations of the war.

During the spring of 1862, with the hardships many citizens in the Confederacy were beginning to face, it seemed an inopportune time for the Confederate Congress to pass, and Davis to sign, a bill permitting the draft of men aged 18 to 35 to bolster sagging military enlistments. It was apparent

ROBERT E. LEE

"To save useless effusion of blood, I would recommend measures be taken for suspension of hostilities and the restoration of peace." Thus ended an appeal by General Robert E. Lee on April 20, 1865, to Confederate President Jefferson Davis to give up any idea of continuing hostilities through guerrilla-type warfare. Over the years, Lee has come to represent a model of honesty, integrity, and principle—a military genius whose campaigns are studied in all corners of the world.

The "Marble Man," a sobriquet given to Lee due to his larger-than-life legend, was born on January 19, 1807. His father, "Light Horse Harry" Lee, was a Revolutionary War hero and friend of George Washington. On June 30, 1831, Lee solidified his standing in the Virginia aristocracy by marrying Mary Anne Randolph Custis. Her father, George Washington Parke Custis, was the adopted son of George Washington.

The future Confederate general graduated from West Point in 1829, second in his class of 46 cadets. He then served the Union with distinction for 32 years. Lee was a staff officer during the Mexican War, and Federal Lieutenant General Winfield Scott considered Lee "the very best soldier I ever saw in the field." Lee also served as superintendent of West Point from 1852 to 1855.

Lee was on cavalry duty in Texas when Virginia seceded from the Union. Offered the command of the Federal army, Lee declined. As with many Federal officers with Southern roots, the decision to resign from the Federal army was a difficult one for Lee. Even though he had taken an oath to defend the Union and was fundamentally opposed to slavery and secession, Lee realized he could not take part in an invasion of Virginia or any other Southern state.

From the time Lee accepted command of the Confederate Army of Northern Virginia, he faced the unenviable challenge of confronting a larger, better supplied force on many fields of battle. The lack of resources and manpower against Ulysses S. Grant's war of attrition in 1864-1865 literally wore Lee and his army out. Lee surrendered at Appomattox Court House, Virginia, on April 9, 1865.

Lee's success in battle has often been attributed to his ability to both discover his enemy's weakness and seize the initiative. His leadership and personal example were the primary sources of the admiration his troops felt for him throughout the war. Never were those qualities more important, however, than after the war, during the struggle to reunite the nation. Although citizenship in the reunited nation was denied him, Lee encouraged all to take the loyalty oath and submit to the laws of the United States.

He accepted the post of president of Washington College in September, 1865, holding that position until his death on October 12, 1870.

Freedom for black slaves was one of the major issues of the war. Here a black family, their goods loaded in one cart, enter Union lines on their way to freedom.

to the Confederate lawmakers, however, that a draft was necessary to keep pace with the growing Federal army. This law was met with mixed reactions throughout the South, but most realized its necessity to preserve the cause. As the need for manpower increased, the law was amended to include all men aged 17 to 50. On December 28, 1863, the Confederate Congress also abolished the use of substitutes, a method used by many draftees to avoid service by supplying a replacement. During the last year of the war, almost one-third of Confederate soldiers in the east were draftees.

Although the citizens of the North did not suffer as much as their Southern counterparts from inflation or limited resources, by mid-1863 they were becoming tired of the human cost of the war. For some time after the bombardment of Fort Sumter, recruits had flocked to enlist in the Federal army. By the end of 1862, however, Congress was forced to enact draft laws to bolster sagging enlistments. Opposition to conscription was so hostile in many Northern cities that riots broke out. The most serious riot began in New York City on July 13, 1863. For three days fires were set in various parts of the city, resulting in property losses of more than $1.5 million. Blacks and Federal officials were special targets for rioters. Lincoln immediately transferred seasoned troops from the front to squelch these violent protests in New York. By the time the rioting ended, some 100 persons had been killed or wounded.

On February 1, 1864, Lincoln expanded his call for troops, ordering that 500,000 men be drafted on March 10 to serve for three years or until the end of the war. With these new men, the Federal government was able to furnish the manpower necessary to replenish the ranks decimated by the battles of Fredericksburg, Chancellorsville, and

Gettysburg. By the end of the war, the names of almost 250,000 men had been drawn in the draft, but few of them actually served, due to a policy allowing draftees to hire substitutes. Some men made a living being paid as a substitute, only to desert to begin the process over again.

1864

With wartime disillusionment growing throughout the North, Lincoln realized changes in the military fortunes of the Federal armies in the east were necessary. To lead the army in this renewed effort to end hostilities, Lincoln turned to the only man who had consistently given him victories, Ulysses Grant. With the approval of Congress, Lincoln promoted Grant to the rank of lieutenant general, a position previously held only by George Washington and Winfield Scott, and named him commander of all Federal armies. Grant formulated a military policy to put pressure on every Confederate command, thereby stopping the Confederacy's practice of transferring troops to bolster threatened positions. To execute this strategy in the west, Grant placed William Sherman in command of all western troops and assigned him the tasks of destroying the Confederate Army of Tennessee, commanded by General Joseph Johnston, and capturing the rail center of Atlanta, Georgia.

Sherman launched his campaign on May 7, 1864. A series of flanking maneuvers around Johnston's army and battles in northern Georgia forced the Confederates to a position less than seven miles from Atlanta. When Johnston had to withdraw to the defenses of Atlanta itself, Jefferson Davis replaced the Confederate commander with the much more aggressive Lieutenant General John Hood. But Hood's desperate attacks failed to check the Federal advance, and he was forced to abandon Atlanta late in

the evening of September 1. Word of the capture of Atlanta gave the Northern war effort a much-needed boost for, as in the past, the Federal campaign in the east had met with only limited success.

When Grant assumed command of all Federal armies, he decided to personally oversee the campaign of the Army of the Potomac. Thus began a series of battles and flanking movements known as the Overland Campaign. Several times Grant attempted to pass around the right flank of Robert E. Lee's Army of Northern Virginia and place the Federal army squarely between Lee and Richmond. But Lee reacted quickly each time. Battles at such places as the Wilderness, Spotsylvania, and Cold Harbor finally led to the long, grinding siege of the city of Petersburg. Casualties during the campaign were high: Grant had lost almost 50,000 men while Lee suffered losses amounting to more than 21,000. While Grant received a stream of reinforcements, there were very few men left to send to Lee's embattled army.

Prisons and Prisoners

While Grant's war of attrition caused concern in the North because of heavy casualties, it was having a marked effect on the Confederacy's ability to maintain its defenses in Virginia and Georgia. With limited manpower resources available, Jefferson Davis and his generals were particularly concerned over Grant's cessation of the prisoner exchange policy. Throughout most of 1862 and 1863, prisoner exchange had been a common practice between North and South. This policy benefited the South

since it enabled the Confederacy to use returned prisoners to beef up depleted ranks. Recognizing this fact, Grant ordered the policy stopped on April 17, 1864. "Every man we hold," Grant wrote, "when released on parole or otherwise, becomes an active soldier against us....If a system of exchange liberates all prisoners taken, we will have to fight on until the whole South is exterminated."

The cessation of prisoner exchange, aside from cutting off a steady supply of reserves to the Confederacy, also increased the number of prisoners held in camps throughout the North and South. The most infamous Confederate prison camp was at Andersonville, Georgia. The first Federal prisoners were interred there in February 1864, and by July 32,000 men were crowded into the 26-acre stockade. About 13,000 prisoners died in less than a year. At the worst, more than 100 men died each day. Prisons existed throughout the South where men were subjected to conditions similar to those in Andersonville. The poor treatment of Federal prisoners was partly due to the fact that by the summer of 1864 the Confederacy could spare few resources for Federal prisoners.

Word of the poor treatment of Union prisoners caused Federal authorities to retaliate in kind against Confederate soldiers interred in Northern camps. Treatment of Confederate prisoners in such camps as Camp Douglas in Chicago, Elmira in New York, and Johnson's Island in Ohio was not much better than that experienced by Federal prisoners at Andersonville. By the war's end, 26,000 Confederates and 30,000 Federals had died while imprisoned.

ULYSSES S. GRANT

"He was possessed of a moral and physical courage which was equal to every emergency in which he was placed. He was calm amid excitement, patient under trials, sure in judgment, clear in foresight, never depressed by reverses or unduly elated by success....His singular self-reliance enabled him at critical junctures to decide instantly questions of vital moment without dangerous delay in seeking advice from others, and to assume the gravest responsibilities without asking any one to share them." This portrait of Ulysses S. Grant was sketched by Horace Porter, an aide and friend.

From the time his name first catapulted into national headlines with the capture of Fort Donelson, Tennessee, Grant's character has probably been more closely scrutinized than that of any other personality of the time. Described as a butcher and drunkard by some and a humanitarian and great military leader by others, Ulysses S. Grant has been the focal point of discussion and controversy for generations.

Born April 27, 1822, in Point Pleasant, Ohio, Grant was baptized Hiram Ulysses. He assumed Ulysses Simpson after a congressman mistakenly listed it on Grant's admission papers to West Point. Graduating from the academy in 1843, 21st in his class of 39 cadets, he entered the infantry and served with distinction during the Mexican War as a regimental quartermaster. After the war, he was assigned to the Pacific Northwest. The isolation of his remote post and the loneliness he felt being away from his wife, Julia, and two children, se-

verely depressed Grant and compelled him to turn to drink. This would mark the beginning of his reputation as a drunkard, which would haunt him throughout his career. When he failed to secure a transfer east, he resigned his commission in 1854. The next six years were extremely frustrating for Grant. He proceeded from one failed business venture to another, finally ending up as a clerk in his father's leather goods store before reentering the service as colonel of the 21st Illinois Volunteers Infantry Regiment at the start of the war.

Grant rode the crest of his fame after the war to the presidency in 1868. He served two terms that were marked by corruption and scandal. Following his tenure as President, Grant was again unsuccessful in business and was forced into bankruptcy. With only his military pension to subsist on, Grant began writing his memoirs to support his family. He finished the project shortly before his death from throat cancer on July 23, 1885.

Grant's reputation as a military commander has been eclipsed by that of Robert E. Lee and other generals of the war. Heavy death tolls resulting from Grant's disastrous charges at Vicksburg, Cold Harbor, and Petersburg have been cited as examples of his inability as a tactician. But no one can dispute his success as a strategist. During the course of the war, three major armies surrendered to him, a feat unparalleled by any other Union or Confederate general. He also had the foresight and moral strength to initiate a war of attrition that finally ended the Confederacy's ability to fight.

Wounded soldiers in the field after the Battle of Chancellorsville. The man on the stretcher has lost his foot. Amputation was one of the more common "treatments" received by casualties in the days of less-advanced medicine.

Sherman's March to the Sea

While the Federal Army of the Potomac was bogged down on the outskirts of Petersburg, victories in Georgia and the Shenandoah Valley provided impetus to the Northern war effort. Further Federal victories at Franklin, Tennessee, on November 30 and Nashville, Tennessee, on December 16 provided additional jubilation and encouragement for Lincoln and the North.

Nothing, however, brightened the Federal President's Christmas more than the following message from Sherman on December 22: "I beg to present you as a Christmas gift the city of Savannah." Sherman's army had reached the Atlantic coast, having cut a wide swath of devastation and destruction through the state of Georgia. Meeting little resistance, Sherman turned his army north with the intent, as he wrote Grant, to "punish South Carolina as she deserves."

Sherman's march through Georgia and South Carolina in late 1864 and early 1865 did much to dishearten Confederate civilians. By carrying out Sherman's policy of total war, his soldiers brought the effects of war to those who had been sheltered from it. Sherman's march had a debilitating impact on the Confederate economy and destroyed the resolve of the citizens of the South. "If it is as the newspapers say," Southern diarist Mary Chesnut wrote in the dark days of early 1865, "why waste our blood? Why should we fight and die when it is no use?" Another Southerner wrote, "Would that the men would take matters in their own hands, and end the war. Let every man in both armies desert and go home!"

1865: THE END IS NIGH

By the end of March 1865, Sherman's army had passed through South Carolina, brushing aside opposition led by such Confederate generals as Pierre Beauregard, Braxton Bragg, and Joseph Johnston. The last organized assault against Sherman was launched on March 19, and a Federal counterattack on March 21 routed the Confederates. On April 26, Confederate General Johnston surrendered his army of about 29,000 men at Durham Station, North Carolina.

Throughout the remainder of 1864 the siege of Petersburg continued. While Sherman was taking Atlanta and marching to the sea, Grant slowly extended his lines south and west of Petersburg, cutting off vital supply lines to the city. Lee realized it was only a matter of time before Grant cut off all supply lines to Petersburg.

The winter of 1864–1865 was extremely hard on Lee's troops in their trenches around Petersburg. Suffering from starvation, exposure, disease, and desertion, the Confederates valiantly but unsuccessfully attempted to stop the Federals from cutting Petersburg off from the rest of the Confederacy. With their victory at Five Forks on April 1, Union troops cut the last supply line into Petersburg. The next evening, after a Federal attack, Lee abandoned Petersburg. Richmond fell the next day as the remnants of Lee's once great Army of Northern Virginia fled west. On April 9, Lee surrendered near Appomattox Court House.

The formal surrender of the Confederate Army of Northern Virginia on April 12 at Appomattox was later described in a moving account by Federal Brigadier General Joshua Chamberlain. "[W]hen the head of each [Confederate] division column comes opposite our group," Chamberlain wrote, "our bugle sounds the signal and instantly our whole line from right to left, regiment by regiment in succession, gives the soldier's salutation, from the 'order arms' to the old 'carry'—the marching salute....[Confederate Major General John Gordon's] successive brigades... pass us with the same position of the manual,—honor answering honor. On our part not a sound of trumpet more, nor roll of drum; not a cheer, nor word nor whisper of vain-glorying, nor motion of man standing again at the order, but an awed stillness rather, and breath-holding, as if it were the passing of the dead!"

AFTERMATH OF WAR

News of Lee's surrender spread quickly throughout the North and South. But Lincoln's exultation that the war was finally coming to an end was short-lived. On April 14, five days after Lee's surrender, the Federal President was shot by John Wilkes Booth at Ford's Theater in Washington, D.C., while watching the comedy *Our American Cousin.* Lincoln died at 7:22 A.M. the next morning. After an extensive manhunt, Booth was killed on April 26.

Born in Maryland in 1838, Booth had deep Southern sympathies and saw Lincoln as a man bent on the destruction of the defeated states. Booth and his small band had originally planned to kidnap Lincoln and hold him for the ransom of thousands of Confederate soldiers held in Federal prison camps. When this scheme failed, Booth's intentions turned to Lincoln's assassination. On June 30, 1865, eight persons were found guilty of conspiring with Booth to assassinate the President; four were hanged on July 7.

Thousands mournfully filed past Lincoln's casket in the White House and the Capitol Rotunda from April 18th to the 21st before it began a 1700-mile journey back to Illinois. The train stopped in many cities, where thousands more paid final homage to the man who successfully led the nation through its greatest test. One observer accompanying the casket noted, "The intensity of feeling seemed to grow deeper as the President's remains went further westward." His body was interred in Springfield, Illinois, on May 4, 1865.

While Northerners and Southerners alike shared in the grief over Lincoln's death, the citizens of the South were most affected by his death. On December 8, 1863, Lincoln had issued a Proclamation of Amnesty and Reconstruction that restored practically full rights to any Confederate who took an oath of allegiance to the Federal government. It also offered liberal terms to reestablish home rule by state voters loyal to the Union. Lincoln's second inaugural address on March 4, 1865, reaffirmed his commitment to a peaceful reconciliation. "With malice toward none; with charity for all;...to do all which may achieve and cherish a just, and a lasting peace, among ourselves, and with all nations."

When Lincoln's vice president, Andrew Johnson, assumed the presidency, he also assumed a reconciliatory approach to reconstruction. But radical elements in Congress ended Johnson's reconstruction program. Lincoln's influence most likely would have pushed through a reconciliatory plan for reconstruction, but Johnson was no match for congressional radicals.

Northern "carpetbaggers" attempted to gain control of state governments through the black vote, and Southern "scalawags," Southern Republicans, attempted to influence the course of events in the South after the war. They met with much resentment from the citizens of the South, and hostility continued for many years as a result of the antagonism raised by Radical Reconstruction. Finally, home rule was returned to state governments in 1877, finishing the job of reuniting the nation so many men had fought and died to preserve.

KURZ AND ALLISON

Louis Kurz and Alexander Allison, two Chicago lithographers, formed their partnership in 1880. While little is known of Allison's life and career, Kurz's story has been well-chronicled.

Kurz was born in Salzburg, Austria, in 1833. His family moved to Milwaukee, Wisconsin, in 1848 to escape political upheavals in Europe. Kurz polished his artistic skill in Milwaukee and Chicago, working primarily in theaters as a scenery painter. He became interested in lithography in 1860 and was a founder of the Chicago Lithographic Company in 1863. One biographical sketch in *Chicago und sein Deutschtum* states that Kurz was sent by President Abraham Lincoln to make battlefield and camp-life sketches. His obituary in the *Chicago Tribune,* March 23, 1921, stated, "Mr. Kurz was a friend of [John A.] Logan, Lincoln, [Ulysses S.] Grant.... During the civil war Lincoln asked him to make sketches of the battlefields and his pictures were the first to be issued after the close of the war."

Kurz's reputation as an artist and lithographer flourished throughout the 1860s, particularly with the publication of *Chicago Illustrated* in 1865, which presented 52 of his lithographic views of public buildings and points of interest around Chicago. He was one of the founders of the Chicago Academy of Design in 1866.

When the Great Chicago Fire of 1871 destroyed the Chicago Lithographic Company, Kurz moved back to Milwaukee. His stay was brief, however, and he returned to Chicago in 1878. Two years later he established his partnership with Allison. The firm was dissolved in 1903.

Kurz and Allison were primarily engaged in creating and marketing finely detailed lithographs on varying subjects. Throughout the 1880s and 1890s, they printed a series of chromolithographs of American battle scenes from the Revolutionary War, the Civil War, and the Spanish-American War. A chromolithograph is a colored picture created from several lithographer's stones of different colors. Thirty-six of those prints are reproduced here.

The battle scenes in this book represent a romantic vision of war still commonplace at the end of the 19th century. Although the pieces depict a comprehensive and somewhat fanciful view of the 36 battle scenes, the true value in these lithographs lies in the fine detail of the works, which adds to our understanding of the war as it was remembered years later by those who fought in and depicted it.

BATTLE OF BULL RUN
(FIRST MANASSAS)
July 21, 1861

**Brigadier General
Irvin McDowell, USA**

About three months after the surrender of Fort Sumter, 37,000 Federal soldiers under Brigadier General Irvin McDowell clashed with the 35,000 Confederate forces of Brigadier Generals Pierre G.T. Beauregard and Joseph E. Johnston near an obscure Virginia creek. It was thought that this battle would determine the fate of the Confederacy. Ten hours of bitter fighting resulted in 2900 Federal and 2000 Confederate casualties. Both sides realized ultimate victory would require more than a single battle.

**Brigadier General
Pierre G.T. Beauregard, CSA**

"On the hill beside me there was a crowd of civilians on horseback and in all sorts of vehicles, with a few of the fairer if no gentler sex. A few officers and some soldiers, who had straggled from the regiments in Reserve, moved about among the spectators and pretended to explain the movements of the troops below, of which they were profoundly ignorant."

This scene along the heights southwest of Centreville, Virginia, was observed by English journalist William H. Russell on July 21, 1861. These civilians had traveled more than 25 miles from the environs of Washington to watch the pageantry of war and the "triumph of Union arms" along the banks of an obscure, meandering Virginia creek named Bull Run.

Ripples of excitement circulated through the crowd with each Federal movement. "That is splendid. Oh, my! Is not that first-rate? I guess we will be in Richmond this time tomorrow." They watched as the Federal army of Brigadier General Irvin McDowell maneuvered before Brigadier General Pierre G.T. Beauregard's Confederate force. Few spectators expected the show to last long, and they savored every moment and cheered every Federal achievement.

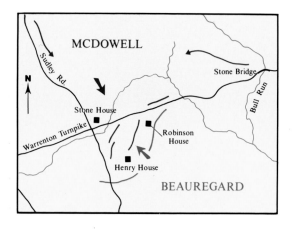

The politicians of Washington, many of whom were in the crowd that day, had been impatient in their desire to see the Confederate force driven from a position so close to the Federal capital. Since assuming command on May 28, McDowell had been pressured to attack the "Rebels" and end the hostilities as soon as possible. Both he and General in Chief Winfield Scott were reluctant to plan an attack with raw, undisciplined troops. President Lincoln, however, reminded them, "You are green, it is true, but they are green, also; you are all green alike." The President was particularly anxious for his generals to act since the expiration of service of the 90-day men (volunteers who had enlisted for only 90 days) who had answered his initial call to arms in April was fast approaching.

While Lincoln pressed his generals to take the offensive, Confederate President Jefferson Davis and his generals prepared to meet any Federal thrust into Virginia. Since May, Davis had gradually assembled a force of about 22,000 men along Bull Run near Manassas Junction to block the most direct overland route from Washington to Richmond. The Confederate President placed Beauregard, the "Hero of Sumter," in charge of this force. An additional 12,000 troops under Brigadier General Joseph E. Johnston were stationed at Harpers Ferry, Virginia, protecting the approaches into the strategic Shenandoah Valley from Federal forces under Major General Robert Patterson. Although each Confederate force was outnumbered by the Federals facing them, Beauregard and Johnston were linked by the Manassas Gap Railroad. This gave both Confederate generals the ability to quickly reinforce each other if necessary.

As the first celebrity of the war, Beauregard had delighted in the attention he had received in the Confederate capital upon his triumphant

arrival there on May 31, fresh from his victory in Charleston Harbor. Many, himself included, viewed Beauregard as the savior of the Confederacy. Beauregard's appearance, stature, and background inspired confidence in his ability to bring the war to a quick, successful conclusion, and he had come to Virginia to fulfill that expectation.

Joseph Johnston did not have Beauregard's flair, and he had not yet captured the attention of the people of the South. But Johnston was a competent officer who had established an excellent reputation during his 32 years in the Regular Army of the United States. Jefferson Davis was confident that his northern defensive line was in very capable hands.

Across the battle lines was Irvin McDowell, who had been a West Point classmate of Pierre Beauregard. Before the outbreak of the Civil War, McDowell had served as a staff officer in an adjutant general's office. Through the influence of such notables as Secretary of the Treasury Simon P. Chase, Secretary of War Simon Cameron, and Governor William Dennison of Ohio, McDowell was promoted to the rank of brigadier general of the Regular Army on May 14, bypassing several officers who had been senior to him in rank and length of service. McDowell did not lack confidence in his ability, but he did lack confidence in the ability of his newly created army. "This is not an army," he confided to a friend. "It will take a long time to make an army." McDowell did not have a long time, however, for Lincoln was pressing him to act.

Through June and July, McDowell and Scott reluctantly began to develop a plan of attack, having little choice but to give in to the desires of the President. They decided to use the distance between Beauregard's and Johnston's commands to McDowell's advantage. The 18,000 Federal troops under Major General

Patterson were to keep Johnston occupied in the Shenandoah Valley while McDowell advanced with his 37,000 troops against Beauregard.

In his 69 years before April 1861, Patterson had seen only five years of military service, but he had made the most of his opportunity. He fought with distinction during the War of 1812 and the Mexican War, winning praise from Winfield Scott for his service in Mexico. At the start of the Civil War, Scott commissioned him major general of the Pennsylvania Volunteers, followed by his appointment to command the Army's Department of Pennsylvania. While Patterson may have earned a reputation as an effective fighter during those earlier wars, it would soon be clear that he was not up to the responsibilities of his present position.

McDowell began advancing into Virginia on July 16. Due to extreme straggling and the fear of enemy attack, his army needed more than two days to march approximately 20 miles to Centreville. After examining the terrain north of Bull Run for two more days and testing the disposition of Confederate troops by a small engagement at Blackburn's Ford on July 18, McDowell decided to feign an attack against both enemy flanks while sending two divisions around the enemy's left to strike their line from the rear. It was an ambitious, relatively complex plan for the inexperienced troops and officers of the Federal command since it depended on coordinated movements of troops along a front more than three miles long. The plan was even more difficult because neither McDowell nor any member of his staff had any experience in directing large commands. Before his promotion to brigadier general, McDowell had never commanded more than a squad of troops in the field. Since it would be three days before the attack was launched, Beauregard had plenty of time to act.

Beauregard learned of the Federal advance from Washington practically the moment it began and wired Richmond requesting reinforcements. Meanwhile, Patterson did not carry out his orders as aggressively as intended, thus failing to occupy Johnston in the Valley. Therefore, Johnston did not hesitate to send troops to assist Beauregard. Johnston sent his infantry by way of the Manassas Gap Railroad to join Beauregard, while Confederate cavalry commander Colonel J.E.B. Stuart masked the movement from Patterson. By July 20, Johnston and most of his command had reached Manassas Junction, unknown to either Patterson or McDowell.

That evening, Beauregard proposed that they take the offensive and attack McDowell at Centreville. Johnston, the senior of the two Confederate officers, approved Beauregard's plan. Since Johnston was unfamiliar with the terrain or Federal dispositions, he turned battlefield command over to Beauregard.

Early on the 21st, as civilians began to fill the heights southwest of Centreville, McDowell seized the initiative before Beauregard could act on his plan. The Federal feint against the Confederate right flank at Blackburn's Ford and the Confederate left flank at the Stone Bridge over Bull Run began about 6:30 A.M. The feints were desultory in nature, however, and failed in their attempts to create enough of a diversion to mask the Federal turning movement across Sudley Ford. The feints also proved to be premature. It would be almost four hours before the Federals finally managed to begin their main attack.

McDowell's turning movement was discovered by Confederate Captain E. Porter Alexander's signalmen before 9:00 A.M. To block the Federal turning movement, Colonel Nathan Evans shifted part of his lightly engaged brigade in front of the Stone Bridge northwest to Matthews Hill, less than a mile from Sudley Ford. No more than a half hour later, Colonel Ambrose Burnside's command, the lead brigade in the Federal flanking movement, charged across an open field toward Evans's hastily formed line. Confederate fire checked the Federal advance. Evans held his position against the steadily increasing enemy force for close to an hour before reinforcements finally arrived.

The combatants exchanged fire for another hour before the Federals, supported by three artillery batteries, proved too much for the Confederates, who were driven back to Henry Hill. Lacking the experience to follow up this initial success, the Federals stalled when they met the reformed Confederate line along the hill. The Confederate line was anchored by a brigade led by a former Virginia Military Institute instructor, Brigadier General Thomas J. Jackson.

Confederate Brigadier General Barnard Bee, the commander of one of the brigades beaten back by the Federals, rode up to Jackson exclaiming, "General, they are beating us back." Jackson responded, "Sir, we'll give them the bayonet." Bee rode off and tried to rally his broken columns by gesturing toward Jackson and referring to him as a "stone wall."

The exact wording of Bee's reference to Jackson has been lost to history. Bee's meaning has also been questioned because some evidence supports the claim that Bee had been upset with Jackson since the latter did not send support troops forward to help stem the Federal advance. Bee was never able to record his remarks or intent, however, for he was mortally wounded minutes later while at the head of his troops. What lived on was the nickname Jackson and his brigade would forever be associated with, "Stonewall."

While the musketry and artillery shelling intensified along Henry Hill, the Civil War claimed its first civilian casualties. Unable to escape to safety before the fighting reached the area around her home, Mrs. Judith Carter Henry, an elderly bedridden widow, was resting in her room when a Federal shell smashed through the wall of her home on the hill and shattered her bed. The widow was mortally wounded, and her servant, who had been hiding beneath the bed, was severely wounded.

There was a lull in the fighting of about an hour around 1:00 P.M. This gave both sides the opportunity to catch their breath after hours of fighting. The soldiers quenched their thirst and prepared for the renewal of combat that they knew would occur shortly. While their troops rested, the commanding officers on both sides reorganized their lines and moved reinforcements into position.

Fighting resumed at about 2:00 P.M. The Federals and Confederates charged and countercharged across the slopes of Henry Hill for more than two hours before Beauregard began his final attack. He struck at the exposed Federal right flank, sending McDowell's exhausted troops streaming to the rear. Panic soon spread throughout the Federal line, and a somewhat orderly retreat deteriorated into a chaotic rout.

Men and wagons congested the roads leading away from the battlefield. The bridge over Cub Run, the Federal's primary route of escape, was especially obstructed. A Confederate shell exploded on the bridge, turning a wagon over and blocking the span. Once across Bull Run, disorganized groups of Federal soldiers became entangled with panicked civilians who were trying to flee from the Confederate force they thought followed closely behind the demoralized Federal army.

William Russell described the scene in this dispatch to the *London Times*:

The runaways ran alongside the waggons [sic], striving to force themselves in among the occupants; who resisted tooth and nail. The drivers spurred and whipped and urged the horses to the utmost of their bent. I felt an inclination to laugh which was overcome by disgust and by that vague sense of something extraordinary taking place which is experienced when a man sees a number of people acting as if driven by some unknown terror.

The next day, as he watched the confusion along the streets of Washington, Russell wrote, "Why Beauregard does not come I know not, nor can I well guess....If the Confederates do not grasp that which will never come again on such terms, it stamps them with mediocrity." Beauregard's and Johnston's troops had been unable to press their victory to the Federal capital. Disorganized and exhausted, their men could only pursue the enemy as far as Centreville before halting. By the time Beauregard's inexperienced officers were able to regain some semblance of order, the opportunity to take Washington, if it ever really existed at all, had passed.

The Federals suffered about 2900 casualties, while the Confederates lost about 2000. What began with an air of pageantry and fun ended in terror and death, a fitting prelude to the four years of war that followed.

The battle served as a proving ground for many officers on both sides who would make names for themselves during the next four years. For the Federals, the list includes: Colonel William T. Sherman, Colonel Ambrose E. Burnside, and Lieutenant George A. Custer.

UNION ARMY OF THE POTOMAC

Following Abraham Lincoln's call to arms in April 1861, volunteer units from most Union states poured into Washington to begin the job of reuniting the Union. Few of the officers—military men, politicians, influential community leaders—had any large-scale military experience.

Less than two months before Brigadier General Irvin McDowell led these men into their first battle at Bull Run, they were organized into the Army of Northeastern Virginia. McDowell had been given the unenviable task of whipping this inexperienced group into an effective fighting force. He failed, as evidenced by the rout suffered by this army after Bull Run. In an attempt to restore order and discipline to these troops and the additional volunteers still streaming into Washington, Lincoln abolished McDowell's army and brought Major General George B. McClellan to the capital to reorganize the mob into a force that could successfully oppose the enemy in battle.

The Army of the Potomac was established August 15, 1861. During the first two years of its existence, the Army of the Potomac's failure on the battlefield was due more to mismanagement and ineffective leadership than the ability of its opponent.

The lessons the army learned were long and costly under the tutorship of McClellan, Ambrose Burnside, Joseph Hooker, and George Meade. By the time Ulysses S. Grant came to the eastern theater to personally supervise its campaigns, the Army of the Potomac had grown to more than 100,000 men. Its attitude had become more professional. Ineffective commanders had been replaced by such fighters as Winfield Hancock, Philip Sheridan, and Gouverneur Warren. The men of the Army of the Potomac had learned the lessons of war and had become a veteran force, one up to the task of defeating Robert E. Lee's Army of Northern Virginia.

The remains of Henry House on Henry Hill, where the fighting raged for hours. Widow Henry did not leave her house before the battle and died when a shell hit her home.

On the Confederate side, the list includes: Brigadier Generals Richard S. Ewell, James Longstreet, Thomas J. Jackson, and Colonels Jubal A. Early and J.E.B. Stuart.

While initially thankful for victory, many Southerners were disappointed over the Confederate failure to take Washington. A noted diarist of the day, Mary B. Chesnut, wrote, "Time and tide wait for no man, and there was a tide in our affairs which might have led to Washington. We did not take it, and so lost our fortune." In his official report of the battle, Beauregard tried to shift the blame for failing to capture the Federal capital to Jefferson Davis. The Confederate President had earlier rejected a plan that Beauregard felt would have resulted in the seizure of Washington. The general's claim helped cause a quarrel between the two that lasted the duration of the war.

The shameful defeat at Bull Run had a sobering effect on the Northern populace, particularly their President. Lincoln was at his best, however, during moments of trial and adversity, and he acted immediately to restore confidence in his government. The day after the battle he brought Major General George B. McClellan, fresh from his victories in western Virginia, to Washington to take command of the army. Lincoln also issued a memorandum of military policy on the 23rd that called for expansion of the war effort.

There were those on both sides, military and civilian alike, who thought the cost of war was far too high. Among this group was Wilmer McLean, whose residence near Blackburn's Ford had been partially destroyed by Federal shells while serving as headquarters for Beauregard during the battle. Wishing to escape from this strategic corridor between the opposing capitals, McLean moved his family to a quiet village west of Richmond, Appomattox Court House. Four long years later, Robert E. Lee and Ulysses S. Grant would use his home to discuss and agree upon the terms of Confederate surrender.

The ruins of the Stone Bridge over Bull Run, where the Federal retreat became a rout. Beauregard failed to follow up on this great victory for the South.

THOMAS J. "STONEWALL" JACKSON

"This is no ordinary war. The brave and gallant Federal officers are the very kind that must be killed. Shoot the brave officers and the cowards will run away and take the men with them." Such was Thomas Jackson's response to a report that one of his subordinates had attempted to save the life of a brave Federal officer during the heat of battle. The Civil War had a style of warfare far different from the chivalrous conflicts of earlier times, and Jackson recognized that the enemy's courage must be treated without emotion.

Jackson's lack of feeling toward anything but total victory often extended to the treatment of his own men. To a request from one of his officers to visit his dying wife, Jackson responded, "Man, man, do you love your wife more than your country?" When the colonel of one of his regiments objected to an attack on the grounds that his "regiment would be exterminated," Jackson responded, "Colonel, do your duty. I have made every arrangement to care for the wounded and bury the dead."

While his actions and decisions embittered some officers and enlisted men, most followed him with a devotion unmatched during the course of the war. Jackson led by example, and his victories made those who followed him proud to state they belonged to his command.

Jackson was born on January 21, 1824, in Clarksburg, Virginia. He graduated from West Point in 1846 and served in the Mexican War. Resigning his commission in 1852, he became a professor of artillery and natural philosophy at the Virginia Military Institute (VMI).

At VMI, Jackson gained a reputation for eccentricity that carried over to the war. His extreme religious beliefs, nonmilitary manner of dress, dietary habits (for example, he ate lemons during battle), and his reluctance to fight on Sunday are just a few aspects of his personality that helped create the aura of eccentricity. His eccentricities, however, added to his mystique.

Following First Bull Run, Jackson's presence would make a difference on many fields of battle for almost two years. His subsequent absence would affect the outcome of many other battles during the last two years of the war.

CONFEDERATE ARMY OF NORTHERN VIRGINIA

One of the first decisions made by Brigadier General Pierre G.T. Beauregard when he took control of the Confederate troops along Bull Run was to name this newly created command the Army of the Potomac. Following the battle on July 21, Joseph Johnston's Army of the Shenandoah merged with Beauregard's, taking the Army of the Potomac as its title.

It did not take Jefferson Davis long to realize that Johnston and Beauregard could not effectively function together as commander and subordinate in the same army. When Beauregard was transferred to the western theater, Johnston began the task of shaping his undisciplined command into the effective fighting force that would achieve unprecedented success over the next four years.

Throughout the Virginia Peninsula Campaign of 1862, the Confederate Army of the Potomac clashed with the Federal Army of the Potomac. On May 31, Johnston was wounded at the Battle of Seven Pines, and Robert E. Lee assumed command the next day. Lee changed the name to Army of Northern Virginia.

Under the imaginative, aggressive command of its new leader, this Confederate army successfully repulsed a much larger Federal force from the defenses of Richmond and finally bottled it up along the James River. This marks the beginning of a storied existence that would create for the Army of Northern Virginia a reputation matched by few commands in the annals of military history.

From June 1862 to July 1863, the much larger Federal army proved no match for the Army of Northern Virginia. Only the Battle of Antietam, which was at best a draw, marred the perfect record of the Confederate army. The tide began to turn with the Battle of Gettysburg in July 1863. By the start of the Wilderness Campaign in May 1864, the fate of the Army of Northern Virginia and the Confederacy was sealed.

It was not for want of effective leadership or fighting skill that the army's existence finally came to an end on April 9, 1865, at the hamlet of Appomattox Court House. Rather, time and resources finally ran out for the men who had fought for so long with so little.

BATTLE OF WILSON'S CREEK
(OAK HILLS)
August 10, 1861

Brigadier General
Nathaniel Lyon, USA

Brigadier General
Ben McCulloch, CSA

Federal Brigadier General Nathaniel Lyon, outnumbered more than two to one, launched a surprise attack on the Confederate forces commanded by Brigadier General Ben McCulloch along the banks of Wilson's Creek in Missouri. After about 1300 casualties on both sides, the Federals were driven from the field. The troops exhausted, disorganized, and low on ammunition, McCulloch could not pursue the fleeing enemy. This battle was to set the tone for the fight over Missouri.

Breakfast was already on the table in E. Ben Short's house at first light on August 10, 1861. It was probably like the start of most days on the southwest Missouri farmstead, located in a hollow just west of a meandering stream called Wilson's Creek. This day would be different, however. As E. Ben Short and his wife were about to sit down to their meal, a commotion outside made the couple glance out their kitchen window. They couldn't have been more surprised when they saw their yard full of blue-clad soldiers, on foot and horseback, moving quickly to the south.

Confederate cavalry pickets on the hill south of the Short house were as surprised as the Shorts to see Union soldiers suddenly emerge from the morning fog. One rider carried warning of the Union advance to the tent of Major General Sterling Price, commander of the Missouri Militia, where he and several army leaders breakfasted on roasted green corn.

"Oh, nonsense!" replied Brigadier General Ben McCulloch. "That's not true." Looking up from the table, however, the skeptical officers saw "a great crowd of men on horseback...mixed with wagons...in terrible confusion...rushing toward us."

The rattle of musketry and bark of artillery fire soon mixed with the clamor of the panic-stricken gray-clad men. Price mounted his horse and galloped up the hill hoping to rally his troops. McCulloch also climbed onto his horse and splashed across Wilson's Creek to where his troops were camped. As they hurried to join their commands, both Confederate officers knew that Union Brigadier General Nathaniel Lyon had stolen a march on them.

This wasn't the first time the aggressive, 42-year-old Lyon had bested his enemies during the young but bitter struggle for control of the border state of Missouri. Exactly three months to the day earlier, Lyon, then a Regular Army captain commanding the U.S. arsenal at St. Louis, Missouri, had surprised and captured several hundred secessionist militiamen he claimed had threatened to seize the arsenal for the Confederacy. Within days of the incident, two fledgling armies, composed largely of militiamen and home guard units, took to the field to battle for possession of the state. The campaign of these two armies would ultimately lead to the banks of Wilson's Creek.

All summer the pro-South state guardsmen were hard-pressed by the impetuous Lyon. Lyon commanded about 6200 troops, which included 1250 home guards led by a flamboyant German immigrant, Colonel Franz Sigel, and several battalions of U.S. Regular Army soldiers.

In July, 6000 pro-South state guardsmen, commanded by Missouri Governor Claiborne Jackson moved south to rendezvous with the 5400 strong Confederate army of Brigadier General Ben McCulloch just inside the Arkansas border. Now numbering more than 11,000 soldiers, McCulloch's force moved north again, anxious to destroy Lyon and win Missouri for the Confederacy. In addition to the state guardsmen, now under the command of Sterling Price, McCulloch's army consisted of troops from Louisiana, Texas, and Arkansas. After skirmishing at Dug Springs, Missouri, and forcing Lyon back to Springfield, McCulloch's force settled beside ripening cornfields along the rugged banks of Wilson's Creek.

From his bivouac near Springfield, about 10 miles north of the Confederate encampment, Lyon pondered his next move. Now outnumbered two to one by the combined forces of Price and McCulloch, Lyon's little army, comprised mostly of untried recruits, was tired and hungry from weeks of constant maneuvers. About 120 miles of bad roads separated Lyon from his supply base at Rolla, Missouri—the railhead from St. Louis. Expecting a Confederate attack any day, Lyon chose what he considered the only logical course. "A bold dash, skillfully made," Lyon claimed, "would astonish the enemy." Lyon decided, therefore, to divide his already slender force under the very muzzles of enemy guns.

After dark on August 9, Lyon sent Sigel with 1200 men and a six-gun artillery battery on a wide sweep east of the Confederate position to hit the enemy's right flank and rear. Sigel was to strike at the first sound of Lyon's main assault on the Confederate front.

Lyon roused his force at 4:00 A.M. on August 10. "Just as there was a slight flash of dawn in the east," recalled a Federal soldier, "somebody came along and woke us all up, and told us to keep still and fall in line." Advancing through fields and woodlots west of Wilson's Creek, Lyon quickly formed his troops into a battle line after striking Confederate outposts. Covering another mile and a half, the Federals slammed into Price's first line on a hilltop just south of the E. Ben Short farmhouse and put the startled Southerners to flight.

From the base of the first hill, the Confederates ascended the rise and joined a solid formation of their comrades three and four ranks deep amid scrub oak on the rock-ribbed slope. The "lines would approach again and again within less than fifty yards of each other," wrote a Confederate officer, "and then after delivering a deadly fire, each would fall back...reform and reload, only to advance again...."

Combat lulled occasionally on the slopes of "Bloody Ridge" while the two armies drew apart to catch their breath, only to intensify when battle resumed.

East and south of Wilson's Creek, equally savage fighting raged on McCulloch's front and rear when Sigel drove forward as planned. Sigel's success was brief, however. The Union flanking column opened fire on unsuspecting Confederate camps, drew enemy fire in return, but then suddenly collapsed and fled the battleground before the brute force of McCulloch's counterattack. After driving Sigel from the field, McCulloch's troops turned against Lyon on Bloody Ridge.

"The engagement at once became...almost inconceivably fierce along the entire line," recalled a Federal staff officer. Wounded in the head and leg, his horse having been shot out from under him, Lyon staggered along as his battle line began to buckle. Lyon mounted another horse, attempting to lead a desperate countercharge, when a bullet punctured his chest and knocked him to the ground. He died moments later.

Exhausted and their ammunition dwindling, the Federals managed to blunt one more Confederate attack before they withdrew from the battlefield during the following lull. They left behind about 1300 casualties.

The Confederates, as weary and bloodied as the Federals, and having suffered an equal number of losses, according to a general officer, "watched the retreating enemy through our field glasses, and were glad to see him go."

Despite the Confederate victory at Wilson's Creek, the fate of Missouri still hung in the balance. Seven months later, these same troops would meet at Pea Ridge, Arkansas.

BATTLE OF FORT DONELSON
February 12–16, 1862

Brigadier General
Ulysses Grant, USA

Brigadier General
Simon Buckner, CSA

After subduing Fort Henry, Tennessee, Federal Brigadier General Ulysses Grant turned to Fort Donelson, 11 miles east. For four days under miserable winter conditions, Grant's 27,000 soldiers laid siege to the Confederate stronghold of 20,000. After failing to break through Federal lines and having suffered 1500 casualties, the Confederates surrendered. Grant, whose army had 2800 casualties, accepted the surrender from Brigadier General Simon Buckner. The Mississippi Valley now lay open to the Federals, and the possibility of dividing the South became real.

The hotel refused to return "Sam" Grant's luggage until he paid for his room and board. It was the summer of 1854, and the former U.S. Army captain had just resigned from the Army to avoid a court-martial—reportedly for drunkenness and neglect of duty. Nearly penniless, Grant had stopped in New York on his way home. He appealed to a West Point friend and fellow Mexican War comrade, Simon Bolivar Buckner, for money to pay his hotel debt. Buckner lent his friend enough money to pay his debt and return home, a gesture Grant would remember more than eight years later.

Commanding a Federal army of 15,000 troops in early January 1862, Brigadier General Ulysses S. Grant embarked on a campaign to penetrate Confederate defenses in western Kentucky and Tennessee and gain control of those areas for the Union. Two keys to the region were Confederate Forts Henry and Donelson, standing just across the Kentucky state line inside Tennessee. Fort Henry was located on the east bank of the Tennessee River. About 11 miles east of Fort Henry stood Fort Donelson on the west bank of the Cumberland River.

In a joint operation with a flotilla of river gunboats commanded by U.S. Navy Flag Officer Andrew H. Foote, Grant planned first to descend the Tennessee River and capture Fort Henry. Accomplishing this, Grant would then march overland to attack Fort Donelson while Foote's gunboats returned to the Ohio River. The gunboats would then sail up the Cumberland to join Grant in his operation against Fort Donelson. With these two strong points in the hands of Union forces, Grant reasoned, "The enemy would necessarily be thrown back" to Mississippi and Alabama. This would be a giant step in the North's strategy to split the Confederacy along the Mississippi Valley.

Fort Henry proved an easy target for the determined Federals. The dirt fort, built at river level and vulnerable to flooding, was protected with antiquated cannons. Confederate Brigadier General Lloyd Tilghman surrendered the fort on February 6, 1862, after a short, token resistance that bought enough time to allow most of the garrison to escape to Fort Donelson.

The fall of Fort Henry prompted General Albert S. Johnston, the supreme Confederate commander in the western theater, to withdraw his forces from Kentucky to a new position south of the Cumberland River. To screen this move from Grant's army, Johnston needed to hold Fort Donelson as long as possible. Accordingly, he directed two infantry divisions, about 12,000 men commanded by Brigadier Generals John B. Floyd and Simon B. Buckner, to reinforce Fort Donelson.

Embracing about 100 acres of land, Fort Donelson was protected by rifle pits and heavy earthworks. The fort stood on steep bluffs as high as 100 feet above the Cumberland River. Broken, wooded terrain cut by many swollen streams surrounded the fort and made the land approaches difficult. About 20,000 Confederate soldiers occupied the garrison under overall command of Brigadier General John B. Floyd, a former governor of Virginia and Secretary of War under U.S. President James Buchanan.

"I was very impatient to get to Fort Donelson," wrote Grant in his memoirs, "because I knew the importance of the place to the enemy and supposed he would reinforce it rapidly." Advancing unopposed from Fort Henry on the morning of February 11, Grant settled outside Fort Donelson that afternoon.

Rough, wooded slopes protected Grant's men from Confederate gunfire but offered little shelter from the fickle weather. "It was mid-winter," recalled Grant, "and during the siege we had rain and snow, thawing and freezing alternately." With 6000 fewer troops than Floyd and only one gunboat available, Grant satisfied himself with long-range sniping at the fort until reinforcements arrived on February 13 and 14. Foote and several gunboats arrived with them.

Grant planned to hold the perimeter while Foote's heavy guns pounded the fort into submission. But two main Confederate river batteries, one dug in just above water level, the other behind ramparts 100 feet above the river, disabled two of Foote's vessels and severely damaged the others. "The gunboat [*St. Louis*] with Flag Officer Foote on board, besides having been hit about sixty times," observed Grant, "had a shot enter the pilot-house which killed the pilot, carried away the wheel, and wounded the flag-officer himself."

Grant visited the bedridden flag officer on the morning of February 15 and was informed that the disabled boats would be inactive for 10 days while they underwent repairs. Without close naval support, Grant decided on siege operations to subdue the fort. "But," wrote Grant, "the enemy relieved me from this necessity."

Convinced that the fort could not be defended, General Floyd decided on the evening of February 14th to abandon the garrison by fighting through Grant's line instead of holding on a few more days as General Johnston had expected. Attacking to the south early the next morning, the Confederates punched a hole in Brigadier General John McClernand's Union division during bitter fighting but failed to capitalize on that success. Indecision and bickering among the Confederate leaders forced Floyd to cancel the attempt. "General Floyd,...who was a man of talent enough for any civil position," observed Grant, "was no soldier and, possibly did not possess the elements of one." Having steadied his troops and sealed the gap in his line, Grant was confident of victory the next day.

That night the command of the fort devolved on the third-ranking Confederate leader, General Simon B. Buckner. Realizing the Confederates had no alternative but to surrender the garrison, Floyd turned command over to Brigadier General Gideon J. Pillow so that Floyd could escape. Pillow in turn passed command to Buckner so Pillow could escape. The two generals made their way across the river with 3000 troops. Confederate cavalry commander Lieutenant Colonel Nathan Bedford Forrest led another 1000 men out of the fort along the river bank around the Federal right flank. Both Floyd and Pillow were subsequently relieved of command for their actions.

Before daylight on February 16th, Buckner wrote his old friend "Sam" Grant requesting "terms of capitulation of the force and fort under my command." "Unconditional and immediate" was Grant's reply, the source of his nickname "Unconditional Surrender" Grant. White flags soon appeared above the Confederate rifle pits. About 12,000 soldiers were marched into captivity.

As the meeting to settle surrender terms ended, Buckner rose to leave when Grant said, "Buckner, you are, I know, separated from your people, and perhaps you need funds; my purse is at your disposal." Buckner graciously declined Grant's offer, though certainly recalling the scene in New York City eight years earlier.

BATTLE OF PEA RIDGE
(ELKHORN TAVERN)
March 7–8, 1862

Brigadier General
Samuel Curtis, USA

Major General
Earl Van Dorn, CSA

Approximately 11,000 troops under the command of Federal Brigadier General Samuel R. Curtis confronted the 14,000 troops of the Confederate army led by Major General Earl Van Dorn. In the cold of late winter, the fate of Missouri would be decided near Pea Ridge, Arkansas. After initial success on the 7th of March, Van Dorn's army was driven from the field the following morning. The Federals suffered almost 1400 in casualties while the Confederates left 800 casualties behind.

Jesse Cox brought his wife Polly and their seven children from Kansas to Benton County, Arkansas, in 1858 and bought a tavern with 313 acres at the foot of Pea Ridge. A God-fearing businessman, Cox added an outside stairway so local church folk could use an upstairs meeting room for services without disturbing downstairs guests. He named his tavern "Elkhorn." The Cox family lived prosperously and peacefully with their five slaves and their many patrons during the next four years while the slavery issue tore the world around them apart. However, the conflict would finally invade their tranquil existence in March 1862.

Two armies crossed from Missouri into Arkansas and clashed on the Cox property in an attempt to finally decide Missouri's fate. Strong, divided loyalties had prevented Missouri from embracing either the Union or Confederate cause at the outbreak of the Civil War. It also led to the creation of two separate state governments, one favoring the North, the other the South.

Following the Confederate victory at Wilson's Creek, former Missouri congressman and governor Sterling Price led his state militia north to Lexington, Missouri, where he forced the surrender of the Federal garrison there on September 20, 1861. This victory garnered weapons, supplies, and recruits for Price, but threats of a large Federal force approaching from St. Louis compelled him to retreat to southwest Missouri.

After Federal Brigadier General Nathaniel Lyon's death at Wilson's Creek, Brigadier General Samuel R. Curtis was appointed to the command of the Army's Southwestern District of Missouri on December 25, 1861. The 56-year-old Curtis quickly organized an army of about 12,000 men and began probing for the location of Price's army by the end of December. The newly named Army of the Southwest was organized into four

divisions under Brigadier Generals Franz Sigel and Alexander Asboth and Colonels Jefferson C. Davis and Peter Osterhaus. This Federal army began advancing on Price's army of 6800 men from Springfield, Missouri, on February 9, 1862.

Price conducted a fighting retreat across the Arkansas border in the face of Curtis's overwhelming numbers. Marching along Telegraph Road, the area's main north–south highway, Price joined forces with Confederate Brigadier General Ben McCulloch's small army of 6000. They finally settled deep within the Boston Mountains in northwest Arkansas. Bickering arose between Price and McCulloch over which of them was the ranking commander. The dispute was finally put to rest when Confederate authorities assigned Mississippian Major General Earl Van Dorn to overall command. Amidst rain and snow, Van Dorn arrived at the Arkansas campsite on March 2, 1862.

With the destruction of Curtis's army as his immediate goal, Van Dorn set out early the next morning. He headed north along Telegraph Road and skirmished with Federal cavalry as he advanced. Joining Van Dorn's offensive were 800 Cherokee Indians under Confederate Indian Commissioner Brigadier General Albert Pike. This brought the Confederate force to more than 14,000 men.

When he learned of Van Dorn's approach, Curtis concentrated his defense along bluffs on the north bank of Little Sugar Creek, five miles south of the Missouri state line. Curtis posted most of his troops in a position to block Telegraph Road where it crossed the creek, guessing that would be Van Dorn's route of approach.

Realizing the hazards of a frontal attack, Van Dorn planned to cross Little Sugar Creek a few miles west of Curtis's position and strike the Federal right flank and rear. With Price's

Missourians in the lead and campfires left burning to deceive the enemy, Van Dorn began his maneuvers about 8:00 P.M. on March 6. A Confederate marcher wrote, "The night was one of intense severity and the men suffered immeasurably."

Van Dorn directed McCulloch and Pike to hit the Federal right flank near Leetown, a hamlet about two miles behind Curtis's Little Sugar Creek line, by early morning on March 7. The Confederate commander ordered Price's troops to strike at the Federal rear located near Elkhorn Tavern. Serving as headquarters for a Federal provost marshal, the Elkhorn Tavern grounds were also stockpiled with equipment, food, and supplies.

In the cold, clear dawn of March 7, firefights erupted near Elkhorn Tavern when Federal pickets detected Sterling Price's force. Forewarned by the firing to his rear, Curtis about-faced and rushed two infantry divisions, artillery, and most of his cavalry to block the narrow valley that was Price's only avenue of approach from the north. Charge and countercharge swirled through the meadows and woodlots around Elkhorn Tavern while the Cox family remained sheltered in their basement. "A solid shot struck the house," wrote a newspaper correspondent who was near the tavern during the fight, "and passed completely through, injuring no one." Federal troops gradually retreated from the tavern area, which would become Van Dorn's headquarters and a hospital that night.

McCulloch and Pike briefly routed Federal troops at Leetown on the Federal right flank. Pike's Cherokees, on foot and horseback, captured several Union cannons in the assault but failed to turn them on the enemy. Soon afterward, counterfire from Union batteries drove the Indians into a grove where the Cherokees, unaccustomed to artillery fire—

calling the field pieces "wagons that shoot"— remained inactive.

In mid-afternoon, McCulloch and cavalry leader Brigadier General James McIntosh, McCulloch's second in command, were shot dead within minutes of each other. The loss of these Confederate commanders caused the attack on the Federal right flank to falter. Leaving a small force behind to hold Pea Ridge, Pike led the remaining troops to Van Dorn's position. By the time Pike's troops arrived, fighting had been suspended for the evening.

Curtis consolidated his forces during the night and opened a heavy artillery barrage on Confederate positions on the morning of March 8. Curtis launched a series of assaults on Van Dorn's overextended line, beginning with Franz Sigel's fresh division on the Federal left. The Federals pressed from their left to right toward Elkhorn Tavern as morning progressed. Short of ammunition and provisions and disarrayed by the loss of McCulloch, McIntosh, and several other key officers, Van Dorn's army was forced to abandon its line. By 11:00 A.M., the Confederates were driven from the battlefield in confusion.

Van Dorn's defeat was decisive, securing Missouri for the Union and ending any significant military activity in the state until 1864. Suffering 800 dead and wounded, and broken in spirit, Van Dorn's army was transferred to Tennessee on March 28. Curtis, victorious but at a cost of 1400 men, abandoned the battlefield on March 12 "to avoid the stench" of death. Curtis later conducted minor campaigns in Arkansas.

When the battle ended and the invading armies had deserted the fields littered with the debris of death and destruction, the Cox family crawled from their basement refuge to begin the job of disposing of the by-products of war and once again resuming the business of peace.

BATTLE OF THE *MONITOR* AND THE *MERRIMACK*
March 9, 1862

Lieutenant John Worden, USN

Lieutenant Commander Catesby ap R. Jones, CSN

On March 9, 1862, the C.S.S. *Virginia* (also called *Merrimack*) battled the U.S.S. *Monitor* at Hampton Roads, Virginia. What set this fight apart from the typical naval engagement was that both ships were ironclad, capable of withstanding enemy fire that would prove fatal to wooden ships. While neither ship achieved complete victory, the *Monitor* gained a tactical victory by saving the remaining Federal fleet at Hampton Roads. This engagement signaled the demise of the wooden battleship.

Sailors had sloshed buckets of pork fat over the thick wrought-iron sides of the C.S.S. *Virginia* before she weighed anchor and slowly steamed out of Gosport Navy Yard, off Hampton Roads, Virginia, on the afternoon of March 8, 1862. The fat, the Confederate seamen supposed, "would increase the tendency of the projectile to glance" once battle commenced with the Union blockade fleet near the entrance of Chesapeake Bay.

Making five knots, the 275-foot ironclad ship passed wharves full of curious, cheering spectators at Portsmouth and Norfolk. Confederate soldiers shouted encouragement as the vessel slid by harbor defenses built along the shoreline. Once it reached Hampton Roads, the *Virginia* bore directly upon several Union warships anchored off Newport News. Laundry hung from rigging aboard the Union ships. "Nothing indicated that we were expected," recalled a Confederate lieutenant.

Taken by surprise, the Federal ships reacted slowly at first. Finally, clusters of their smaller support craft darted toward the safety of Federal shore batteries, and faint strains of fife and drums aboard the warships called Union sailors to battle stations. In the *Virginia*'s path stood the U.S.S. *Congress,* a 50-gun sailing frigate, and the U.S.S. *Cumberland,* a 24-gun sailing sloop. Both ships were cleared for action, cannons manned and loaded.

Drawing on the events of the Crimean War (1853–1856), Confederate Secretary of the Navy Stephen Mallory had quickly realized the potential of iron warships. He regarded "possession of an iron-armored ship as a matter of the first necessity." Mallory envisioned such a vessel terrorizing the coastal United States and preventing the blockade of Southern seaports.

The cornerstone of Mallory's dream was the shattered, charred hull of the U.S.S. *Merrimack,*

a frigate partially destroyed when U.S. Navy facilities at Gosport Navy Yard in Portsmouth were evacuated and burned in April 1861. Confederate reconstructive work spanned nine months. Stripped of her masts and upper works, she was fitted with a 172-foot slope-sided superstructure of thick wood and iron casements, which enclosed 10 heavy cannons. Afloat in February 1862 and commanded by Flag Officer Franklin Buchanan, she had a crew of 350, most of whom were volunteers from the army. Christened the C.S.S. *Virginia* (but often called *Merrimack*), her venture into Hampton Roads on March 8 was her first sea trial.

Work on the Confederate ironclad was common knowledge throughout the North and caused demand among Federal authorities for an armored ship to counter the enemy threat. John Ericsson, a Swedish-born marine engineer and inventor, completed construction of a Union ironclad in less than four months.

The sleek iron ship of revolutionary design, with two heavy cannons in a revolving gun turret, was christened the U.S.S. *Monitor.* She was commissioned in the U.S. Navy on February 25, 1862, one day after the *Virginia* was launched. Under the command of Navy Lieutenant John L. Worden, the *Monitor* put to sea on March 6 with a crew of 59 volunteers. Her orders were to proceed to the blockade fleet outside Hampton Roads, Virginia. Everyone knew a confrontation between the two iron monsters was only a matter of time.

Located between the York and James rivers at the tip of the Virginia Peninsula, Hampton Roads was the doorway to the eastern approaches to the Confederate capital at Richmond, 100 miles upriver. Planning for spring 1862, Federal strategists hoped to outflank the main Southern force blocking the overland route to Richmond by moving Union

Major General George McClellan's army aboard transports down Chesapeake Bay to Fort Monroe, off Hampton Roads. Marching up the Virginia Peninsula, McClellan hoped to strike Richmond from behind Confederate defenses. Before attempting the move, however, the Federal general informed his superiors in Washington that the *Virginia* must be neutralized because of the threat she would pose to the landing and supply of his army.

As the *Monitor* steamed from New York, the *Virginia* struck the unsuspecting Union warships at Hampton Roads at about 2:00 P.M. on March 8. The first ship attacked was the *Cumberland.* The *Virginia*'s shells wreaked havoc on the deck of the Federal vessel. "The dead, as they fell," recalled an officer aboard the *Cumberland,* "were thrown to the port side of the deck, out of the way." Throughout the attack, the *Virginia* moved through a hail of projectiles fired from Union vessels and shore batteries at Newport News. The balls, however, bounced and ricocheted from her sides harmlessly into the waters of Hampton Roads.

The *Virginia* plowed straight for the *Cumberland* "like a huge, half submerged crocodile," her iron-tipped prow pointing like a giant arrowhead at the ship's wooden hull. The crash was "terrific in its results," wrote a Confederate sailor. Striking the *Cumberland*'s starboard side below the water line, the *Virginia*'s prow opened a hole large enough to drive a "horse and cart" through. The *Virginia*'s prow broke away as it backed out, and the *Cumberland* sank in minutes.

The *Virginia* attacked the *Congress* next, flailed her with shot, and drove the Yankee vessel aground. Federal battery fire from the shore failed to save the *Congress,* and Confederate Flag Officer Buchanan, wounded in the exchange of shots, set the Union ship ablaze.

The 47-gun steam frigate U.S.S. *Minnesota* sailed against the *Virginia* from her station two miles away but ran aground in mud shoals en route. Only darkness and the ebb tide saved the *Minnesota* from destruction.

Later that night, as news of the disaster to U.S. naval arms caused panic across the North, the *Monitor* quietly dropped anchor beside the *Minnesota.* At sunrise, the *Virginia,* now under the command of Lieutenant Commander Catesby ap R. Jones, started for the *Minnesota;* suddenly, the *Monitor,* nicknamed "cheese box on a raft," loomed into view. To a startled Confederate officer, it was "the strangest looking craft we had ever seen." The *Monitor* opened fire, beginning the first duel between the ironclads.

For four hours the two vessels pounded shot after shot against impenetrable iron walls. Each tried to ram the other but without effect. While the smaller, fleet *Monitor* could outmaneuver the ponderous, unwieldy *Virginia,* neither vessel inflicted any more than superficial damage to the other. With both crews shell-racked and exhausted by the ordeal, the engagement ended when a Confederate shell blasted against the vulnerable pilothouse in the *Monitor*'s bow quarter, temporarily blinding Lieutenant Worden. The *Monitor* drew away during the exchange of command on board. Interpreting the move as a retreat and satisfied with its own performance, the *Virginia* also steered away from the scene of the action.

Within nine months of the historic sea battle that made wooden warships obsolete, both ironclads suffered tragic ends. The *Virginia* was destroyed by her crew in May 1862 to prevent her capture by McClellan's Union troops as the Federals marched up the Virginia Peninsula. The *Monitor* sank in a gale off Cape Hatteras, North Carolina, in December 1862, killing four officers and 12 men.

BATTLE OF SHILOH
(PITTSBURG LANDING)
April 6–7, 1862

Major General
Ulysses Grant, USA

General
Albert Johnston, CSA

Criticized for allowing the Federals into Tennessee after losing Fort Donelson, Confederate General Albert Johnston launched a surprise attack April 6, 1862, against Major General Ulysses Grant at Pittsburg Landing, Tennessee. For two days, 62,000 Federals fought 40,000 Confederates in the first major battle in the west. When the smoke cleared, the Confederates had retreated to Corinth, Mississippi. The Federals suffered 13,000 casualties, the Confederates lost 10,600, including Johnston. The battle served as a rude awakening for both sides.

In early April 1862, war was still a grand adventure for many of the young Union soldiers camped among the wild flowers and blossoming peach orchards on the bluffs south of the Tennessee River near Pittsburg Landing. The days were warm and the nights, observed one private, "just cool enough to sleep well."

Over several weeks, the heavily forested countryside of ravines and ridges surrounding nearby Shiloh Church had been transformed into a vast bivouac. Sounds of drums and trumpets filled the air from morning to night, and, as one soldier noted, one might stroll for miles and "see nothing but the white tents of infantry, cavalry, and artillery."

Poised just two miles south of this Yankee tent city in the early hours of April 6, 1862, 40,000 Rebel soldiers anxiously awaited the signal to attack. The Confederates were arrayed in three orderly battle lines with 9000 men in the front line. The young infantrymen, dressed in homespun gray- and butternut-colored uniforms, prepared for battle.

After Major General Ulysses S. Grant's Federal ground and naval forces breached the Confederate defenses in western Tennessee at Forts Henry and Donelson in February 1862, they penetrated Confederate territory along the Mississippi, Tennessee, and Cumberland rivers. Confederate forces evacuated strategic Nashville at the end of February. In March, Union amphibious forces took the Mississippi River bastion at New Madrid, and by early April they were attacking the strong river fort at Island No. 10.

As spring approached, Grant led a combined expedition up the Tennessee River, capturing Confederate strong points and railroads along the way. Torrential rains, however, forced one of Grant's commanders, Union Brigadier General William T. Sherman, to cancel a raid into

northern Mississippi. Sherman withdrew his force to Pittsburg Landing, 10 miles inside the Tennessee state line. The site, he thought, "admits of easy defense by a small command."

Grant also chose the site to concentrate the rest of his army. All but one of his divisions had gathered there by the last week in March. More than 42,000 Federal troops occupied the sprawling tent city while another 36,000 Union soldiers under Major General Don Carlos Buell were stationed at Nashville.

The Southern press and many civil and military leaders blamed General Albert Sidney Johnston, the Western Department commander, for losing territory in Kentucky and Tennessee. Johnston decided upon a bold scheme to regain the lost territory. By the end of March, he had collected an army of 40,000 men at Corinth, Mississippi, 25 miles south of Pittsburg Landing.

Alarmed by reports that Buell was moving to reinforce Grant, Johnston determined to strike at Grant before the two Union armies joined forces. By mid-afternoon on April 3, Johnston's force was clear of Corinth and marching on the narrow, rutted roads leading north. The distance a veteran force would have covered in a day and a half, however, took Johnston's raw troops three days to cover. Slowed by snarls of wagons and artillery on dirt trails turned into muck by heavy rainfall, the Confederate Army of the Mississippi finally deployed at jump-off points two miles from Grant's camp late on April 5.

Fearing that the element of surprise had been lost by their slow, clumsy approach, some Confederate officers urged Johnston to cancel the assault. "Gentlemen," replied Johnston, "we shall attack at daylight tomorrow. I would fight them if they were a million."

Federal outposts had skirmished with advance elements of Johnston's army on April 5. Sherman, in command at Pittsburg Landing

since Grant was quartered a few miles upriver at Savannah, Tennessee, while awaiting Buell's arrival, discounted the reports. He thought the reports were the exaggerations of amateur soldiers with "as much idea of war as children." Sherman told a staff officer, "There is no enemy nearer than Corinth." When heavy firefights erupted along the Union perimeter before dawn on April 6, it was already too late for any warning. About 8:00 A.M., a massive Confederate battle line burst from the trees upon Sherman's tent city.

Routed from their quarters, the Federals raced wildly between their tents. Trails of uniform coats, knapsacks, bedding, rifles, and equipment of all kinds littered the ground in the wake of the Union fugitives. Thousands did not stop running until they reached cover beneath steep bluffs near the landing. Federal officers, however, were able to rally several thousand soldiers to form ragged firing lines. The most successful defense was organized by Brigadier General Benjamin Prentiss.

Although Confederate General Johnston was mortally wounded during six hours of savage fighting around the "Hornet's Nest," Prentiss was compelled to surrender. By then Grant had already established a solid, last-ditch defense on a ridge overlooking Pittsburg Landing. A line of artillery and two gunboats at the river's edge supported Grant's new line. Under the cover of this new line, the Federal commander disengaged his remaining forces from around Shiloh Church to bolster this new position. With darkness approaching, Confederate General Pierre G.T. Beauregard, having replaced Johnston as commander of the Confederate force, suspended the attack for the day.

After nightfall, most of Buell's army, as well as Major General Lew Wallace's division, reinforced Grant's spent command. Ferried over

the Tennessee River, Buell's men disembarked at Pittsburg Landing amid taunts and warnings from thousands of Union fugitives huddled on the river bank.

At 10-minute intervals throughout the rain-swept night, the Federal gunboats *Lexington* and *Tyler* bombarded the Confederate troops gathered opposite Grant's line. Beauregard regrouped his command and prepared to drive Grant into the Tennessee River the next morning. The aggressive Federal general, however, was not about to give the Confederates the opportunity to gain the upper hand two days in a row; the Federals struck first.

Starting at 7:30 A.M., Grant launched his fresh troops across the shallow valley separating the two lines. The weary, hard-pressed, and outnumbered Confederate troops retreated beyond the range of Federal guns and tried to form a solid front to stop Grant's advance. With an eye to the south, where he vainly hoped to glimpse 20,000 reinforcements reportedly en route from Mississippi under Confederate Major General Earl Van Dorn, Beauregard battled on throughout the morning. Van Dorn never appeared, however, and a massive Union assault was launched that swept the Confederates from the field. Past Shiloh Church and through the Union campsites they had triumphantly captured the previous morning, Confederate survivors crowded the muddy roads back to Corinth. "I wanted to pursue," wrote Grant, "but had not the heart to order the men who had fought desperately for two days, lying in the mud and rain when they were not fighting."

Overnight, this first major battle of the war in the west transformed the Union and Confederate troops into veteran soldiers. More than 10,000 men on each side had become casualties in the process, a grim reminder that war was not the grand adventure it had so recently seemed to be.

BATTLE OF WILLIAMSBURG
May 5, 1862

Major General
George McClellan, USA

Major General
James Longstreet, CSA

In spring 1862, Federal Major General George McClellan began his Virginia Peninsula Campaign with more than 100,000 men. Confederate General Joseph Johnston, outnumbered more than two to one, began a long retreat toward Richmond. In a sharp rearguard action fought near Williamsburg, Virginia, McClellan suffered more than 2000 casualties. Although Johnston's army lost more than 1700 men, the battle protected vital Confederate supply wagons and ensured the continuation of a strong defense of Richmond.

From atop a rain-swept, wooded ridge two miles east of Williamsburg, Virginia, Federal Colonel Amasa Cobb, commanding the 5th Wisconsin Volunteer Infantry, watched the Confederate battle line approach. Behind Cobb's regiment rode Brigadier General Winfield Scott Hancock cautioning the riflemen, "Aim low, men. Aim low. Do not be in a hurry to fire until they come nearer."

As the distance steadily closed between the opposing lines, Cobb's soldiers could hear the Confederates raise shouts of "Ball's Bluff" and "Bull Run," taunting the Union troops about defeats they had suffered the previous year. Sniping erupted between the skirmishers, and soon rolling volleys of musket fire blazed from the blue and gray battle lines. The Confederate troops were fighting a rearguard action to keep the Federals from capturing the wagons of General Joseph Johnston's army during its withdrawal toward Richmond.

On May 5, 1862, Williamsburg sat squarely in the path of two great armies. As Johnston directed his retreating army through its cobblestone streets, the leading cavalry and infantry formations of Major General George McClellan's ponderous Union army pressed on his heels. Outnumbering the Confederates almost two to one, more than 100,000 Union troops and everything needed to sustain them marched up the Virginia Peninsula.

The Virginia Peninsula extends northwest from Hampton Roads up to Richmond, bordered on the north by the York River and on the south by the James River. It became the focus of Union military planners in early March 1862. Overestimating the number of Confederates blocking the overland approach from Washington, D.C., to the Confederate capital at Richmond, McClellan proposed to outflank the Confederate defenses in northern Virginia. McClellan proposed an ambitious waterborne sweep down Chesapeake Bay to Federal Fort Monroe off Hampton Roads, the gateway to the Peninsula. From there McClellan could strike at the Confederate capital's weaker southern approaches.

The Federals started to land at Fort Monroe in late March 1862, and McClellan himself arrived on April 1. With 50,000 troops on hand and thousands more steadily arriving, McClellan began his advance up the Peninsula two days later.

A cautious, meticulous officer, McClellan moved slowly along unimproved roads mired by torrential rains that began to fall on April 5. His advance, however, was abruptly halted that same day when his army confronted enemy earthworks that stretched from around Yorktown, Virginia, to the northern banks of the James River, over five miles away. Enhancing the Confederate line was the flooded Warwick River, which ran parallel to the front of Johnston's entrenchments. "[N]o part of the line," wrote a Union officer, "could be taken by assault without an enormous waste of human life." McClellan began siege operations to capture Yorktown and thus outflank the Confederate barrier. For the next month McClellan constructed picture-perfect entrenchments.

President Lincoln and his cabinet grew extremely impatient with the lack of activity on the Peninsula and prodded their general to advance. These requests went unheeded by the egotistical McClellan; he was determined to strike only when satisfied an attack would succeed. "No one but McClellan could have hesitated to attack," wrote Confederate General Johnston, who knew McClellan's reputation for extreme caution from their Mexican service together. The Confederate army commander knew full well that his numerically inferior army could never withstand a concentrated Union attack. His Warwick River line was predominantly a facade to trick McClellan into believing the Confederate force was larger than it really was.

As the Federals were finally about to strike, Johnston quietly evacuated Yorktown on the night of May 3 and began his retreat toward Richmond. Confederate columns, however, could average only less than one mile an hour under persistent showers, and the first leg of the trek carried Johnston's army a mere 12 miles west, to Williamsburg.

Once McClellan realized the Confederates had withdrawn, he sent horsemen to harass the retreating columns, particularly their cumbersome supply wagons. To counter Union pursuit and put distance between his own army and McClellan's, Johnston occupied a chain of fieldworks at a key intersection two miles east of Williamsburg. This rear guard was ordered to hold off the enemy as long as possible. The fieldworks, occupied by Confederate Major General James Longstreet's division, consisted of an impressive fort flanked by a chain of smaller garrisons.

What began as a simple holding action quickly blossomed into a bitter battle. It opened when Union Brigadier General Joseph Hooker's infantry division stormed the Confederate left flank under cover of an artillery barrage. After trading fire for two hours, Longstreet counterattacked, slowly pushing Hooker away until Federal Brigadier General Phil Kearny's division arrived to stabilize the Union position.

Kearny's hard-nosed command drove Longstreet back into his works. There, Longstreet was joined by Confederate Major General D.H. Hill's division. A few moments after arriving, Hill noticed a flurry of activity atop a low wooded ridge behind the Confederate left flank. While he was inquiring as to the identity of these troops, the Union Stars and Stripes unfurled on the crest. Federal General Hancock's brigade had worked itself around the Confederate left flank and occupied several abandoned redoubts.

In a desperate effort to drive the Federals from this critical position, Hill launched four regiments, 2700 men, up the slope. A firefight erupted during which Hancock ordered his brigade to withdraw behind the crest of the ridge. Cobb obeyed, falling back slowly and fighting as he withdrew. Sensing a Federal retreat, the jubilant Confederates surged ahead to within 30 paces of Hancock's command. At that moment the fearless Union general cried out, "Gentlemen, charge with the bayonet." With that, "the whole line moved forward with a short and well directed fire," wrote Colonel Cobb, "driving the enemy before them like chaff, they fleeing in wild confusion, leaving the field strewn with their dead and wounded." Hill's assault force was completely routed and dispersed.

With his left flank turned and in danger of being cut off from the rest of Johnston's army, Longstreet retreated through Williamsburg after nightfall. Longstreet, sustaining over 1700 casualties, had paid in bloodshed for the time Johnston needed to save his army. Federal losses exceeded 2000.

The Battle of Williamsburg marked the beginning of fighting in earnest on the Virginia Peninsula. There would be much more during the next two months. Before the battle smoke cleared and the campaign ended with McClellan bottled up along the James River, more than 23,000 Federals and 28,000 Confederates would fall victim to the conflict.

BATTLE OF ANTIETAM
(SHARPSBURG)
September 17, 1862

Major General
George McClellan, USA

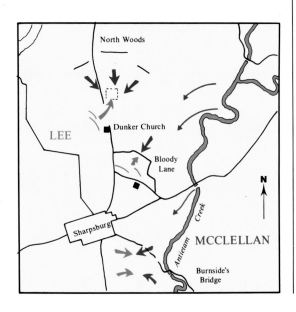

On September 17, 1862, Robert E. Lee's 40,000-strong Army of Northern Virginia collided with George McClellan's Federal Army of the Potomac, numbering 75,000, along an obscure Maryland creek. In the bloodiest day of the war, Federal forces lost more than 12,500 men, while the Confederates suffered 13,700 casualties. The result was a virtual stalemate, and McClellan would claim victory when the Confederates fell back across the Potomac, ending Lee's first invasion of the North.

General
Robert E. Lee, CSA

"The first thing we saw appear was the gilt eagle that surmounted the pole, then the top of the flag, next the flutter of the Stars and Stripes; then their hats came in sight; still rising, the faces emerged; next a range of curious eyes appeared, then such a hurrah as only the Yankee troops could give broke the stillness, and they surged towards us." A Confederate private described this attack of the 9th New York Zouaves on Confederate General Robert E. Lee's right flank just southeast of the town of Sharpsburg, Maryland, on the afternoon of September 17, 1862.

Following a delay of several hours, Federal Major General Ambrose E. Burnside's corps, to which the 9th New York was assigned, stormed over the Lower Bridge of Antietam Creek a little after noon. The battle had been raging north of Burnside's position since dawn and, after the long delay, the Federal corps

commander was about to deliver the crowning blow to the fortunes of the Confederate Army of Northern Virginia.

The Federals easily overpowered the Confederate defenders. "Oh, how I ran!" wrote another Confederate soldier. "I was afraid of being struck in the *back,* and I frequently turned around in running, so as to avoid if possible so disgraceful a wound."

Lee's right flank had been shattered, and he had no fresh troops to send against the advancing Federals. The fate of his army hung in the balance, and there was very little he could do to save it. This was a unique situation for the Confederate commander. Since assuming command of the Army of Northern Virginia, there had been very few situations outside of Lee's control.

Command of this Confederate army had been handed to Lee three and a half months earlier, after Confederate General Joseph E. Johnston was severely wounded during the Battle of Seven Pines, Virginia, on May 31, 1862. At that time, McClellan's Federal troops were within six miles of Richmond and upon Lee's shoulders fell the unenviable burden of repelling a Federal force that far outnumbered his own.

During a series of battles from June 25 to July 1 (later called the Seven Days Campaign), Lee took the offensive and drove McClellan's Union army from the doorstep of the Confederate capital back to the James River. Lee then turned his attention to the short-lived Federal Army of Virginia, commanded by Major General John Pope, approaching Richmond from the north.

Following successive Confederate victories at Cedar Mountain and Manassas (the Second Battle of Bull Run), Lee presented Confederate President Jefferson Davis with a bold proposal. "The present," Lee wrote, "seems to be the most

propitious time since the commencement of the war for the Confederate Army to enter Maryland." Lee offered Davis several reasons for carrying the war north of the Potomac River, each based more on economic and political grounds than military necessity. The Confederate general wished to free Virginia of the Federal invaders long enough for Southern farmers to harvest their crops while at the same time replenishing his own army's stocks with Northern goods. Lee also hoped that a Confederate victory on Northern territory would affect the Northern fall elections as well as influence European powers to recognize and support the Confederacy.

On September 4, as Lee's Army of Northern Virginia crossed the Potomac with about 50,000 men and 292 guns, regimental bands played *Maryland, My Maryland.* When his force reached Frederick, the Confederate commander issued Special Order No. 191, which detailed a bold, aggressive plan based on the assumption that it would take McClellan at least two weeks to catch the Confederate army.

Lee's plan called for Confederate Major General James Longstreet to take two divisions toward the Pennsylvania border to prepare for a possible invasion of that state and to guard the Army of Northern Virginia's left flank. Major General Thomas J. "Stonewall" Jackson, with six divisions, was to encircle and capture the Federal garrison at Harpers Ferry. Finally, Major General Daniel H. Hill's division moved to guard the northern gaps through South Mountain. Lee's experience in dealing with McClellan during the summer on the Virginia Peninsula led the Confederate commander to believe that each of these three commands could accomplish their mission and reunite with the main Confederate army in plenty of time to meet any Federal resistance.

It did not take McClellan as long to react to the invasion of Maryland as Lee had expected, however. The day the Confederates entered Frederick, the Federals left Washington in pursuit. McClellan's army entered Frederick on September 12, on the heels of the Confederate rear guard. Two Federal infantrymen made a chance discovery the next day that would decide the course of the campaign. If acted on aggressively, it would also present McClellan with the opportunity to destroy the Confederate army.

Two members of the 27th Indiana Volunteer Infantry discovered a piece of paper wrapped around three expensive cigars. The heading on the paper read, "Headquarters, Army of Northern Virginia, Special Orders No. 191." It was signed, "By command of General R.E. Lee: R.H. Chilton, Assistant Adjutant-General."

The soldiers immediately turned the paper over to their regimental commander. It was quickly passed up through channels until it was in McClellan's hands. Upon reading the order and discovering the division of the Confederate army, McClellan exclaimed, "Here is a paper with which, if I cannot whip Bobbie Lee, I will be willing to go home." The next morning, McClellan marched his army out of Frederick, aiming to drive a wedge between Lee's divided force.

Lee discovered that the order had fallen into Federal hands on the 14th of September. He immediately rushed a directive to Longstreet instructing him to fall back in support of Hill's division at South Mountain. With almost 90,000 Federal troops poised to attack his divided command, Lee realized the survival of his army depended on holding off the enemy long enough to unite the divided Confederates. Since Jackson had not yet captured the 12,000-man garrison at Harpers Ferry, Lee decided to fall

SEVEN DAYS' CAMPAIGN/SECOND BATTLE OF BULL RUN

When Robert E. Lee assumed command of the Confederate army in Virginia in 1862, he withdrew to the defenses of Richmond and devised a plan to drive the Federal army of George McClellan from the threshold of the Confederate capital. From June 25 to July 1, Lee's troops battled the enemy at such little-known Virginia locales as Mechanicsville, Gaines' Mill, White Oak Swamp, and Malvern Hill.

When the Seven Days' Campaign ended, McClellan's Army of the Potomac had been driven back to its supply base on the James River. The fighting had been costly for both sides, the Federals losing almost 16,000 men and the Confederates over 20,000. Lee had achieved the first of his many successes as the commander of the Army of Northern Virginia.

As McClellan's army sat helplessly along the banks of the James River, the Federal War Department reassigned some of his troops to Major General John Pope's newly formed Army of Virginia. Pope had been brought to Washington fresh from a series of victories in the western theater. Pope's orders were to protect Washington and the Shenandoah Valley while advancing toward Charlottesville, Virginia, to draw off some of the enemy from McClellan's front.

Upon learning of Pope's advance, Lee sent Thomas "Stonewall" Jackson with more than 16,000 men to intercept the Federals. Jackson's troops met a portion of Pope's force at Cedar Mountain on August 9, 1862, and though the action was mismanaged on both sides, Jackson's men drove Pope's troops from the field.

When Lee learned that McClellan's force was being withdrawn from the Virginia Peninsula to join Pope's command, Lee took the remainder of his army and joined Jackson at Cedar Mountain. Outnumbered 75,000 to 49,000, Lee, in the type of bold move that would become his trademark, sent Jackson around Pope's right flank to cut Pope's lines of communication with Washington.

The armies of Lee and Pope clashed in the vicinity of Manassas Junction on August 29–30 in the Second Battle of Bull Run, resulting in the Federals being driven back to Washington. Pope lost more than 16,000 men while Lee suffered more than 9000 casualties.

Following Pope's defeat at Second Bull Run, McClellan was once again called upon to restore order from chaos, a repeat of the aftermath of First Bull Run. His command back, McClellan set out to drive Lee from Maryland.

The Lower Bridge over Antietam Creek, later renamed Burnside's Bridge. Federal General Ambrose Burnside did not cross this bridge for several hours, costing the Federals complete victory over Lee's outnumbered army.

back toward the Potomac. This maneuver gave Lee the option to abandon the campaign and return to Virginia if necessary.

Throughout the 14th, General Daniel H. Hill's division stubbornly fought the Federals along South Mountain, buying valuable time for Lee to secure his supply wagons. After dark, Lee ordered the South Mountain line abandoned and began his withdrawal toward the Potomac. He stopped for the night at the small Maryland town of Sharpsburg.

On the morning of the 15th, Lee learned that Harpers Ferry had finally been taken. Bolstered by Jackson's promise that his six divisions could reach Sharpsburg before the Federals, Lee decided to make a stand along the banks of Antietam Creek. He positioned his infantry, cavalry, and artillery batteries, about 18,000 men in all, in a thin line along a ridge running between Sharpsburg and Antietam Creek, both flanks resting just short of the Potomac. The terrain between the ridge and the creek was dotted with farmland, limestone outcroppings, and patches of woods. The terrain was adequate for defense, but it certainly would not help Lee stop 90,000 Union soldiers. The Confederate general's decision to stay and fight might seem to have been a dangerous gamble, particularly since his small force was heavily outnumbered. But judging from McClellan's past performance, Lee was confident that Jackson would arrive long before the Federals ventured across Antietam Creek.

The Federals arrived east of the creek much sooner than Lee had anticipated. Two Federal

divisions reached the vicinity on the 15th. The bulk of the Federal Army of the Potomac, however, did not reach the creek until after dark.

Throughout the 15th, McClellan and his command celebrated their victory at South Mountain. "Our troops, old and new regiments," McClellan wrote retired General Winfield Scott, "behaved most valiantly and gained a signal victory." The occasion even prompted Lincoln to wire the Federal commander, "God bless you and all with you. Destroy the rebel army if possible."

As the Federals deployed east of the creek, there was more an air of celebration than intensity to carry the fight to the enemy less than two miles away. "Nobody seemed to be in a hurry," one of McClellan's aides observed. "Corps and divisions moved as languidly to the places assigned them as if they were getting ready for a grand review instead of a decisive battle."

McClellan had the opportunity to make good on his vow to "whip Bobbie Lee" if he attacked promptly. But true to his reputation for caution and deliberateness, McClellan spent the afternoon of the 15th and the morning of the 16th studying the enemy position before committing his men to battle. Finally, early on the afternoon of the 16th, McClellan put the finishing touches on his battle plan. He planned a dawn attack to strike the Confederate left flank with three corps and the enemy right flank with Major General Ambrose Burnside's corps. Two corps would be held in reserve either to

strike the Confederate center or support the flank attacks.

Lee was not idle while McClellan studied his lines and planned his attack. On the evening of the 16th, Jackson arrived at Sharpsburg with a total of 9000 men in three divisions. He informed Lee that two more divisions totaling close to 10,000 men would arrive before daybreak. Jackson's largest division, Major General Ambrose P. Hill's Light Division, would remain behind at Harpers Ferry to parole the 12,000 Federal prisoners.

Lee's army now numbered 27,000 men, about a third of the enemy's strength. Lee remained composed and optimistic, however. When one of his division commanders, John Walker, reported to him, Walker found Lee to be "calm, dignified, and even cheerful. If he had had a well-equipped army of a hundred thousand veterans at his back, he could not have appeared more composed and confident."

The Confederate commander deployed Jackson's divisions along his left flank, placed Daniel H. Hill's division in the center in a weathered wagon path called the Sunken Road, and assigned the center and right flank to the divisions of James Longstreet. His dispositions made, Lee waited for McClellan to make the first move.

Lee did not have long to wait. At about 6:00 P.M. Federal Major General Joseph Hooker's corps crossed the Antietam and engaged Jackson's picket line. A brief firefight ensued, accompanied by artillery fire, before both armies settled down for the night, anticipating what the morning would bring.

Hooker launched his attack at about 5:30 A.M. on the 17th of September. The center of his line advanced through a cornfield heading for the Confederate left flank. Intense fighting erupted among the stalks of corn. In his official report, Hooker described the effects of an artillery barrage on Confederates deployed in the cornfield: "In the time I am writing," he recorded, "every stalk of corn in the northern and greater part of the field was cut as closely as could have been done with a knife, and the slain lay in rows precisely as they had stood in their ranks a few moments before."

The fighting along the Confederate left flank throughout the morning was not the series of coordinated thrusts planned by McClellan. Instead, it was a series of fragmented actions with little order, providing Lee with the opportunity to shift his reserves to various positions along the left flank to meet each Federal threat. Various local landmarks, including the Dunker Church, Miller's cornfield, the East Woods, the West Woods, and the Sunken Road, became either rallying points or objectives for both sides during the many charges and countercharges of the morning. Federal bodies piled up on the grassy

SOUTH MOUNTAIN/ HARPERS FERRY

Once Confederate General Robert E. Lee's Lost Special Order No. 191 fell into the hands of Federal Major General George B. McClellan, the Union general realized that the key to driving a wedge between Lee's dispersed army lay in a quick passage over South Mountain, Maryland. McClellan divided a portion of his command into two wings, sending one corps southwest toward Crampton's Gap and two other corps to strike at Turner's and Fox's gaps several miles to the north. The only Confederate commands standing in the way of the possible destruction of the Confederate Army of Northern Virginia were the divisions of Major Generals Daniel H. Hill at Turner's and Fox's gaps and Lafayette McLaws's at Crampton's.

The Federals struck Hill at Turner's Gap at about 9:00 A.M. on September 14 and Fox's Gap at about noon. The Confederates were able to hold off the Federals long enough for reinforcements to arrive from Major General James Longstreet's command. This combined force held the gaps until 10:00 P.M., but at a heavy cost of 2600 Confederate and 1800 Federal casualties. McLaws's division fought the Federals at Crampton's Gap until nightfall, suffering nearly 1000 casualties while inflicting about 500 losses on the Federals. Once through the gap, the Federals fell short of their objective to reinforce the Federal garrison at Harpers Ferry, which the Confederates had placed under siege.

Harpers Ferry, in western Virginia, was situated on low ground at the confluence of the Potomac and Shenandoah rivers. As a garrison, it was indefensible. On September 13, 1862, six Confederate divisions under the command of Major General Thomas "Stonewall" Jackson surrounded the town by occupying the three heights that loomed over it. The defense of the 12,000-man garrison was terribly mismanaged by Brigadier General Julius White and Colonel Dixon Miles. Although killed during the latter stages of the siege, Miles was subsequently charged with treason, drunkenness, and ineptitude. Flags of surrender were raised in the town following a Confederate artillery barrage on the morning of September 15.

Before the morning of September 17, Jackson and five of his divisions joined the main Confederate line at Sharpsburg, Maryland, just in time to meet McClellan's attack. Confederate Major General Ambrose P. Hill's division had remained at Harpers Ferry to parole the Federal prisoners. Hill's timely arrival at Sharpsburg turned back Federal Major General Ambrose Burnside's assault on the shattered left flank of the Confederate Army of Northern Virginia.

slope leading to the Sunken Road, while bodies of Confederate defenders filled the ditch, earning it the nickname "Bloody Lane."

Throughout the morning, McClellan urged Burnside to cross the Antietam and attack the Confederate right flank to relieve some of the pressure on the other side of the Federal line. One attempt was made by a Federal brigade to storm the Lower Bridge (later called Burnside's Bridge), but it suffered extensive casualties without establishing a bridgehead across the creek.

The lack of activity along his right flank enabled Lee to draw troops from there to support his left. By noon, only three Georgia regiments, amounting to 500 men, and a handful of South Carolina troops made up Lee's right flank. They were successful in holding Burnside's entire corps east of the creek until two Yankee regiments finally pushed across the bridge, sending the Confederate defenders falling back in the direction of Sharpsburg.

Once across the bridge, Burnside needed more than two hours to organize his troops for the final thrust toward the town. With the 9th New York Zouaves in the lead, Burnside's men finally advanced, meeting little resistance. "We were now left to oppose the numerous masses before us with a mere picket line of musketry," a Confederate private recalled as he watched the approaching Federals. "There may have been other troops to our left and right but I did not see any. The Yankees, finding no batteries opposing them, approach closer and closer, cowering down as near to the ground as possible…[then] they rise up and make a charge for our fence. Hastily emptying our muskets into their lines, we fled back through the cornfield."

Lee had been carefully watching the situation along his right flank, but there was little he could do. He had no reserves to throw against the fresh Federal force, having committed every available man to his left. His only hope was the arrival of General Ambrose P. Hill's Light Division from Harpers Ferry.

At about 4:00 P.M., Lee and his staff observed a column approaching from the west. A nearby battery officer was asked to identify the troops, and Lee was informed that the column carried the Union flag. Lee then asked the battery officer to focus on another line approaching from the west. This time he was told, "They are flying the Virginia and Confederate flags." Lee responded, "It is A.P. Hill from Harpers Ferry." The reinforcements needed to save his army had arrived.

Hill had rushed 3000 men 17 miles from Harpers Ferry to join the fight. His exhausted troops had a resurgence of energy when they discovered the exposed left flank of Burnside's corps. They slammed into the Federal line,

sending the Federals reeling back toward the Antietam. Hill's men relentlessly hammered away at the Federal line until the Confederate right was once again whole. Hill's attack marked the end of the day's fighting. McClellan was unwilling to commit fresh reserves in the later stages of the fighting for fear they would be needed should Lee counterattack across the creek.

The cost of the battle was high for both sides. The Federals lost more than 12,000 men, while almost 13,800 Confederates were listed as casualties.

Both commanders met with their lieutenants that night to discuss the feasibility of attacking the enemy the next morning. Lee surprised his officers by advocating a counterattack against the Federal right flank. After much discussion, the Confederate commander agreed not to renew the fighting, but he refused to leave the field. If McClellan should attack the next morning, Lee's army would be ready. Across the battle line, McClellan's lieutenants argued against renewing the fight the next morning, fearful that Lee had uncommitted reserves. In reality, the number of fresh troops available to McClellan outnumbered Lee's total command.

Both armies sat and waited throughout the 18th, the wounded from the day before left unattended in the no-man's-land between the two enemy lines. After a day of relative inactivity, Lee's army quietly recrossed the Potomac that evening, putting an end to the Maryland Campaign.

It would be almost two weeks before McClellan followed the Confederates across the Potomac. Impatient with his commander's lack of aggressiveness and poor record against Lee, Lincoln relieved McClellan of command on November 5, 1862, replacing McClellan with Burnside. The fortunes of the Army of the Potomac, however, would not change under Burnside, the man who would forever be identified with the bridge that stood in the way of a Federal victory at Antietam.

After the Battle of Antietam, President Lincoln personally visited General McClellan to urge him to follow Lee, but McClellan waited nearly two weeks before doing so.

MAJOR GENERAL GEORGE B. McCLELLAN

"The effect of this man's presence, upon the Army of the Potomac—in sunshine or rain, in darkness or in daylight, in victory or defeat—was electrical," recalled a Federal officer after the war, "and too wonderful to make it worthwhile attempting to give a reason for it." This man was George B. McClellan, who created the Federal Army of the Potomac in July 1861, after the devastating Federal defeat at First Bull Run. Within months he had molded it into a fighting unit capable of standing up to the Confederate armies of Joseph Johnston and Robert E. Lee.

"Little Mac," as he was affectionately nicknamed by the men of his command, was born December 3, 1826, in Philadelphia, Pennsylvania. He graduated from West Point in 1846 second in his class and served as an engineer on Winfield Scott's staff during the Mexican War. Following a military career that included a term as instructor at West Point, a surveyor, and a military observer during the Crimean War, McClellan resigned his commission in 1857 to pursue a career in the railroad industry.

In April 1861, McClellan was commissioned a major general and placed in command of all Ohio

volunteers. Within three weeks, Lincoln appointed him a major general in the Regular Army and placed him in command of the Department of Ohio. Minor victories in western Virginia placed McClellan in the public eye just before the Federal defeat at Bull Run. Lincoln brought him to Washington to reestablish order from the chaos of defeat.

Although McClellan fought Lee to a stalemate along Antietam Creek, his failure to aggressively pursue the Confederates back to Virginia caused him to be permanently relieved from command. He unsuccessfully ran for President in 1864 on a platform that called for peace at almost any price. After the war, Confederate Colonel William Allen offered an explanation for McClellan's failure in battle. "[He] was not conspicuous for his energy and skill in handling large bodies of troops," Allan wrote. "He directed…strategy,…but left…tactics…almost entirely to his subordinates."

Although McClellan failed to achieve success on the battlefield, his imprint on the army he created and the love his men felt for him lasted to the end of the war. In his farewell address to his troops, he correctly stated, "As an army you have grown up under my care."

BATTLE OF CORINTH
October 3–4, 1862

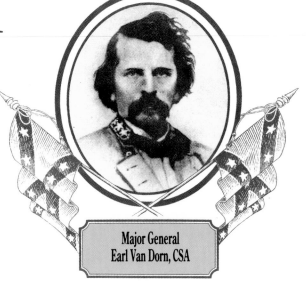

With temperatures reaching close to 100 degrees, 22,000 Confederates under Major General Earl Van Dorn and 23,000 Federals under Major General William S. Rosecrans fought for control of the town of Corinth, Mississippi, on October 3–4, 1862. When they failed to capture the Union earthworks, the Confederates withdrew, leaving behind 4200 casualties. Although the Union defenders lost some 2500 soldiers, the Federals remained in control of vital western Tennessee.

The heat was so intense by mid-afternoon on October 3, 1862, that rifles were too hot to handle. Weapons were beginning to misfire, and a few officers warned Colonel Tom Sweeny that cartridges had actually exploded prematurely in some gun barrels. The Yankee colonel had little recourse. The open fields before him were crowded with Rebel troops attacking his defensive position around Corinth. "Continue to fire," barked Sweeney, "if necessary until the guns burst."

The Battle of Corinth, Mississippi, on October 3–4, 1862, was as much a contest against the elements as it was a fight between enemy armies. Temperatures in the 90s had dried local wells and caked roads with several inches of dust. "You load a man down with a sixty pound knapsack, his gun and forty rounds of ammunition, a haversack full of hardtack and a sow belly, and a three pint canteen full of water," moaned a Federal infantryman, "then start him along this narrow roadway with the mercury up to 100 and the dust so thick you could taste it, and you have done the next thing to killing this

Winter quarters at Corinth: some of the Federal troops— typical American Yankees as well as German, Irish, Swedish, and French immigrants—who fought against Van Dorn's Confederates.

man outright." Heavily laden soldiers of both armies did march that autumn of 1862, however, and the dusty roads they passed over in northeast Mississippi led them to Corinth.

Located at a junction of the Memphis & Charleston and Mobile & Ohio railroads, Corinth controlled the movement of men and supplies in the entire region. Corinth had been occupied by the Federals since the Union victory in Spring 1862 at Shiloh, less than 20 miles north. Corinth had remained peaceful for four months, during which Union troops gradually departed for combat zones in Kentucky and Tennessee. By late September 1862, only 15,000 Union soldiers, commanded by Major General William S. Rosecrans, were at Corinth. Another 8000 Federals were posted in neighboring communities.

Seizing the initiative, Major General Earl Van Dorn, commander of Confederate forces in Mississippi, determined to strike Corinth with his army of 22,000 men. "[T]he taking of Corinth," Van Dorn reasoned, "was a condition…to the accomplishment of anything of importance in west Tennessee." With his army in fine spirits, Van Dorn marched toward the rail junction from his camp southwest of Corinth, hoping to surprise Rosecrans and defeat the divided Union forces. Van Dorn wrote, "[T]his blow should be sudden and decisive."

This would not be the first meeting between the opposing commanders. They had both graduated from West Point in 1842. Rosecrans ranked 5th and Van Dorn 52nd in the class of 56 cadets.

Union cavalry patrols disputed the Confederate advance. But with several routes available to the Confederates, Rosecrans was unsure of Van Dorn's objective. When the brash Confederate leader finally showed his hand, descending on Corinth on October 2, it was too

late for help to reach Rosecrans, or so it seemed to Van Dorn. Rosecrans had actually drawn in support at the first sign of the Confederate approach. By October 1, about 23,000 Union soldiers defended the old Confederate earthworks outside Corinth.

After a 10-mile march over the parched countryside early on the morning of October 3, Van Dorn massed three divisions of assault troops in the sweltering, thick woods north and west of Corinth. After the Federal picket line had been driven in by Van Dorn's troops, a no-man's-land of stumps and fallen timber 400 yards wide separated the two battle lines. Van Dorn launched his veterans from left to right against the outer line of entrenchments, including Federal Colonel Tom Sweeny's riflemen. The Federals battled with "stubborn ferocity," according to Rosecrans, but slowly fell back in stages. By 1:30 P.M., the whole line of outer works was carried by the Confederates.

The battle lulled in the rising early afternoon heat while both sides consolidated their forces. A Union counterattack against the Confederate left flank at about 3:00 P.M. went awry when a Federal officer misread his orders. The fighting petered out at nightfall. "I had been in hopes that one day's operations would end the contest," lamented Van Dorn, who blamed the Confederate failure on the fatigue of the troops after the long morning trek, without water, over the drought-stricken countryside. He also praised the courage of his opponents but remained confident of victory.

That night, illness sidelined the officer Van Dorn had assigned to lead his assault on October 4, and the sick man's replacement bungled his assignment in preparation for the attack. Despite this miscue, and over the advice of several of his subordinates, Van Dorn drove his assault force forward early that morning. Waiting behind breastworks at the center of the

Union perimeter, an Ohio officer described the scene: "All the firing ceased and everything was as silent as a grave. The enemy formed one column of perhaps 2000 men in plain view, then another, and crowding out of the woods, another, and so on. I thought they would never stop coming out of the timber.…[T]hey started at us with a firm, slow, steady step."

Opposite the Ohioans, a Confederate lieutenant recalled the charge after his men advanced to the crest of a hill: "The whole of Corinth with its enormous fortifications burst upon our view.… We were met by a perfect storm of grape, canister, cannon balls and minie balls.… The men fell like grass." The Confederate attack swept against a dirt fort called Battery Robinett, which contained four cannons supported on right and left by infantry. Repulsed at first, the Confederates reformed and charged again, battling the Union defenders hand to hand. Battling into the fort, Van Dorn's men held it for a short time until they, in turn, were driven out by a Federal counterattack.

Assaults at other points along the Union entrenchments north and west of Corinth verged on success. The Confederates even managed to penetrate the streets of Corinth, fighting near Rosecrans's headquarters. But superior Federal numbers began to tell. Spirited, relentless Union counterpunches finally forced Van Dorn back. Badly mauled, suffering 4200 killed, wounded, and captured, the Confederate commander pulled his army away from Corinth leaving the vital rail and supply hub in Union hands.

General Rosecrans rode out to Battery Robinett that evening, where many of the 2500 Union casualties were suffered, and saluted the survivors. With his sentiments echoing throughout the army, he bared his head and told the soldiers: "I stand in the presence of brave men and I take my hat off to you."

BATTLE OF FREDERICKSBURG
December 13, 1862

Major General
Ambrose Burnside, USA

General
Robert E. Lee, CSA

Federal Major General Ambrose Burnside's 130,000 Army of the Potomac had caught the Confederates napping. Burnside was poised to take Fredericksburg, Virginia, but foul weather and administrative bungling stalled his advance. The delay gave Robert E. Lee's 78,000 Army of Northern Virginia time to regain their footing. When the armies clashed on December 13, the Confederates lost 5300. All Burnside could show for his series of unimaginative assaults was 12,600 casualties and another defeat that capped a disheartening year for Union forces.

From his camp on the rain- and snow-swept bluffs along the Rappahannock River opposite Fredericksburg, Virginia, Union Colonel Robert McAllister had grimly watched as Federal and Confederate armies prepared for combat. Almost daily for two weeks, his letters to his wife, Ellen, noted the buildup of men and matériel on both sides of the river. "[W]e are right in front of the Rebel army," he wrote on November 29, 1862. Then, on December 11, while the skies over Fredericksburg flashed and thundered during a shattering artillery duel between Union and Confederate cannons, McAllister wrote, "The ball is opened....We are soon to cross on the pontoon bridge that we are building....It is going to be a big fight."

Located between Washington and Richmond on the direct land route connecting the opposing capitals, Fredericksburg was a focus of military actions throughout the war. In the fall of 1862, Union Major General Ambrose Burnside, newly appointed commander of the Army of the Potomac, planned to make Fredericksburg the doorway for his campaign to capture Richmond.

Burnside proposed a flank maneuver eastward toward Fredericksburg to outflank General Robert E. Lee's Confederate army. This would place Burnside's 130,000-man army between Lee's 78,000 men and Richmond. Key to the plan was to have pontoon bridging equipment available when he arrived opposite Fredericksburg. With bridges in place, Burnside could cross the Rappahannock River and be marching to Richmond before Lee knew what was happening. President Lincoln approved Burnside's plan on November 14. "It will succeed if you move very rapidly," the President informed Burnside, "otherwise not."

Divided into three "Grand Divisions" commanded by Major Generals Edwin Sumner,

Joseph Hooker, and William Franklin and trailing 374 artillery pieces, the Union army began a rapid advance on November 15. By November 17, Sumner had about 40,000 men at Falmouth, Virginia, just a mile upstream from Fredericksburg, with the rest of the Union army within supporting distance. Burnside had accomplished a feat few commanders could boast of after the war: He had the jump on Lee.

But when Burnside reached the Rappahannock, he made a discovery that would affect the course of the campaign. The pontoon bridges he had ordered were not there.

Administrative bungling and dismal weather that had ruined dirt roads prevented timely delivery of the vital equipment. Union troops could have waded the Rappahannock at several fords, as some officers suggested. But Burnside, irate over the absence of the pontoons, refused to order an advance, fearing that rising water might trap part of his force across the river. Burnside's entire army was opposite Fredericksburg by November 19, but the pontoon equipment, only enough for one bridge, didn't appear until November 25.

Lee, while surprised by the uncharacteristically rapid Union movement, quickly dispatched Lieutenant General James Longstreet's corps, located 30 miles away, to Fredericksburg. By November 19, Longstreet's 30,000 men were digging into the heights about a mile east of town and placing the first of Lee's 255 cannons along the slopes. Lee also recalled Lieutenant General Thomas "Stonewall" Jackson's 30,000 men from their post at Winchester, Virginia, on November 26. Jackson arrived at Fredericksburg on December 1. Lee deployed Jackson's men and guns on a series of wooded ridges to the right of Longstreet's position, pushing his line to the south of town.

When General Burnside realized he had lost the element of surprise, he tried to modify his plan. But when it became apparent that no viable alternatives existed, he finally began bridging the Rappahannock before dawn on December 11. "The enemy opened a galling fire on us," wrote a Union engineer officer who supervised the bridge construction from the riverbank opposite Fredericksburg. "My men were working without arms, had no means of returning the enemy's fire, and were driven from the work." In reply, Burnside directed 100 artillery pieces at the Confederate sharpshooters who had sheltered themselves in evacuated buildings along the river.

The Federal artillery bombardment blasted the town to ruins but failed to dislodge the 1600 Confederate gunmen, who maintained their deadly fire. Finally, four Federal infantry regiments volunteered to row across the river in the pontoon boats to clear out the pesky sharpshooters.

Below town, where there was less opposition, bridges were thrown across the river. However, indecision by Union Major General William Franklin stalled his Grand Division until evening, several hours after the bridges had been finished. Confederate General Lee made good use of the delayed crossing by strengthening his already formidable defenses.

When Burnside announced his plan for a frontal attack against the nearly impregnable Confederate line, many of his subordinates protested. One disgruntled officer told Burnside, "The carrying out of your plan will be murder, not warfare."

The battle began on the morning of December 13 on the Federal left flank. Advancing under the cover of thick fog, General Franklin's Grand Division attacked "Stonewall"

Jackson's position. "Suddenly at 10 o'clock, as if the elements were taking a hand in the drama," wrote General Longstreet from his vantage point near the town, "the warmth of the sun brushed the mist away and revealed the mighty panorama in the valley below." Advancing in stages against furious cannon fire, Union Major General George G. Meade's division plunged into the wooded slopes held by Jackson's Confederate infantry. Spearheading Franklin's attack, Meade struck a weak point in the enemy line and charged into the gap. Franklin, however, failed to support the breakthrough, and a Confederate counterattack drove Meade from the woods and back onto the open plain. There the opposing battle lines blazed away at each other all afternoon.

On the open fields between Fredericksburg and Marye's Heights, Burnside hustled more than a dozen separate charges against the Confederate line. Poised in a sunken road behind a stone wall so their rifle barrels were at ground level, Longstreet's Confederate veterans slaughtered Edwin Sumner's troops. The bodies of the Union dead were piled so high that they impeded the progress of the living. By 4:30 P.M. even the Federal generals could stand no more. "Finding that I had lost as many men as my orders required," wrote General Hooker, "I suspended the attack." On the slopes before the stone wall alone, 6000 Union casualties were heaped, almost half Burnside's 12,500 losses. Confederate casualties for the entire battle came to 5300 men.

Two nights after the battle, in the midst of a heavy rainstorm, Ambrose Burnside returned his Federal army to the eastern bank of the Rappahannock River and destroyed the bridges behind him. This concluded active campaigning in the east for 1862.

BATTLE OF STONES RIVER
(MURFREESBORO)
December 31, 1862–January 2, 1863

Major General
William Rosecrans, USA

General
Braxton Bragg, CSA

On December 26, 1862, Union Major General William Rosecrans and 44,000 soldiers of the Army of the Cumberland marched out of Nashville to strike at Confederate General Braxton Bragg's 35,000-man Army of Tennessee, encamped in Murfreesboro, Tennessee. Heavy fighting raged on December 31 and continued on January 2. The 12,900 Federal casualties were a high price to pay, but Bragg's Confederate army, suffering 11,700 casualties, was forced to evacuate Murfreesboro, securing central Tennessee for the Federals.

In some spots, opposing enemy lines around the town of Murfreesboro, Tennessee, were only 100 yards apart on the night of December 30, 1862. Somewhere in the darkness, chords of "Yankee Doodle" and other popular Northern tunes came from a regimental band. When the music faded among the cedar thickets bordering Stones River, a Confederate band answered with "Dixie" and many other Southern favorites. The musical volleys continued until the Federal band played "Home Sweet Home." "[I]mmediately a Confederate band caught up the strain," recalled a soldier, "then one after another until all the bands of both armies were playing 'Home Sweet Home.' When the music died away, both sides rested fitfully on their arms, anticipating the bloodshed that winter morning would bring."

Earlier that winter, the main Union and Confederate armies in the west had been urged by their respective War Departments to take action. The Confederates wished to revive their fortunes after defeats at Corinth, Mississippi, and Perryville, Kentucky. The Federals hoped for a victory in Tennessee to relieve the frustrations of the defeat at Fredericksburg and the stalled advance against Vicksburg. Bragg was stationed at Murfreesboro on the east bank of Stones River; Rosecrans was at Nashville.

Miserable winter weather had turned dirt roads into quagmires that limited both armies to cavalry raids and skirmishing. On Christmas night, Rosecrans told his generals, "We move tomorrow, gentlemen.... Press them hard! Drive them out of their nests.... Fight them! Fight, I say!" Early the next morning, Rosecrans led 44,000 Union soldiers out of Nashville.

With three corps led by Major Generals George H. Thomas, Alexander McCook, and Thomas Crittenden, Rosecrans converged on Murfreesboro from the northwest. Crittenden held the Federal left flank, which rested on Stones River, Thomas held the center, and McCook anchored the right of the Federal position.

Facing Rosecrans across cedar thickets and meadows were Bragg's 35,000 men, divided into two corps commanded by Lieutenant Generals William Hardee and Leonidas Polk. Bragg had started to reposition his troops as soon as the Federals began to move, and the Confederates were now posted west of Stones River. Hardee's men held the left flank while Polk defended Bragg's center. East of the river, Major General John C. Breckinridge's division of 8000 men, detached from Hardee's corps, covered the northern approaches to Murfreesboro.

With maneuvers and positioning completed, Bragg and Rosecrans completed their attack plans. Each commander decided to strike his enemy's right flank in an attempt to get behind his opponent and cut his line of retreat. The advantage lay with the army that moved first. On the night of December 30, while the men listened to the serenade of military bands, Bragg ordered Hardee to attack Rosecrans's right flank at about 6:00 A.M.—one hour earlier than Rosecrans had planned to hit Bragg's right.

"We could see the enemy advancing over the open country for about half a mile in front of our lines," observed a Union officer. "They moved in heavy masses, apparently six lines deep." The surprise and strength of Bragg's flank attack crushed the Federal right flank in less than 30 minutes. In little more than an hour, the entire right half of Rosecrans's army had been sent reeling back to the Federal center.

Before Bragg's assault had begun, Rosecrans had busied himself with preparations for his own attack on the Confederate right flank. Headquartered almost two miles north from where his right flank was on the brink of destruction, Rosecrans seemed indifferent to the distant rumble of artillery and small arms fire. He assumed McCook could handle matters on the right. The Federal commander grew anxious, however, at the sight of riderless horses and the increasing flow of wounded coming from his right. Staff officers finally confirmed the extent of the disaster. Rosecrans suspended his flank attack, then in progress, and shifted reinforcements to his threatened right flank. Staunch defense by Federal Brigadier General Philip Sheridan's division of McCook's corps and the troops of Thomas's command eventually stabilized the Union right flank.

Bragg's success had come at a frightful toll. "The crest occupied by the Yankees," wrote a Confederate private in Polk's corps, "was belching loud with fire and smoke, and the Rebels was falling like leaves of autumn in a hurricane." Despite losses he could ill afford, Bragg pressed the attack. Forced into a U-shaped perimeter with its back to Stones River, Rosecrans's army stopped each assault until darkness ended the bloodbath.

Closeted in a log cabin that night, Rosecrans polled his army commanders for a decision. Should the Federals retreat or face Bragg for another day, at the end of which Federal ammunition would probably be exhausted? "This army does not retreat," answered General Thomas, and so the majority ruled.

Bragg, confident that he had beaten the Federals, had already telegraphed Richmond: "The enemy has yielded his strong position and is falling back. God has granted us a happy New Year."

With dawn's light, Bragg was shocked to see that Rosecrans not only remained in his front but had even extended his line to occupy a commanding hill east of the river. Neither commander was willing to seize the initiative, however, so New Year's Day was spent in scattered skirmishing and recovering from the previous day's fighting.

The fighting was renewed on January 2, 1863, when Bragg probed Rosecrans's front. The Confederate commander then gave an ill-advised order to Breckinridge to attack Crittenden's hilltop post east of Stones River. With the hilltop in his possession, Bragg reasoned, the Confederates could place artillery behind Rosecrans's line and blast the Federal army into submission.

Breckinridge attacked at dusk, driving Crittenden's brigades from the hill and pursuing them to the river bank. Between Breckinridge and the retreating Federal soldiers was a wide expanse of open ground covered with briars and scrub brush. The entire space was in full view of 45 Union cannons aligned wheel to wheel on the opposite river bank. "On we moved,..." wrote one of Breckinridge's survivors, "[c]onfronted in front by their infantry...swept by their artillery from the left...now attacked by both infantry and artillery...from the right." Breckinridge's attack, and Bragg's hope of victory, disintegrated in the face of this blast of enemy fire.

During the struggle along Stones River, more than 12,900 Federals and 11,700 Confederates became casualties, almost one quarter of the men in the battle. Bragg's retreat on the afternoon of January 3 signaled yet another setback for Confederate fortunes in the west.

BATTLE OF CHANCELLORSVILLE
May 1–4, 1863

Major General
Joseph Hooker, USA

General
Robert E. Lee, CSA

Through a slick maneuver, Federal General Joseph Hooker and his 134,000-man Army of the Potomac had gained a rare but short-lived advantage over Confederate General Robert E. Lee. Although outnumbered more than two to one, Lee seized the initiative near Chancellorsville, Virginia, when Hooker made several errors. Lee then drove the Federals back across the Rappahannock River, inflicting Federal losses of 17,200 men. But the cost of the Confederate victory was high: Among the 12,700 Confederate casualties was General "Stonewall" Jackson.

On the afternoon of May 2, 1863, Confederate forces had shattered the Union right flank at Chancellorsville, Virginia, sending the Federals reeling back in confusion. In the resulting melee, the Confederates also became disorganized in pursuit of the fleeing Federals. That evening, while riding toward the battle front to organize the Confederate line and launch a night assault to further demoralize the ranks of the Federal Army of the Potomac, the architect of this stunning maneuver, Lieutenant General Thomas J. "Stonewall" Jackson, was accidentally shot by his own men.

A staff officer helped Jackson off his horse and sent an aide to find a surgeon. Realizing the significance of what had happened and the effect the information could have on the men of the 2nd Corps, the officer admonished the aide to keep Jackson's wounds secret from everyone else. In a matter of a few short minutes, the course of the battle and, many believe, the ultimate fate of the war had been decided.

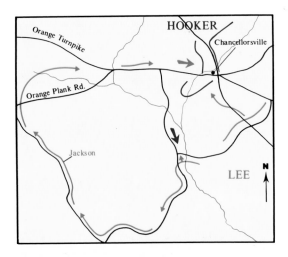

When Jackson's successor, Major General Ambrose P. Hill, was also wounded a short time later, command of the 2nd Corps passed to the popular cavalry leader, Major General J.E.B. Stuart. By the time Stuart arrived to assume command, the opportunity to attack had long since passed.

It would be several hours before Confederate General Robert E. Lee learned of the turn of events on his left flank. Shaken by news of Jackson's wounds, Lee uttered, "Any victory is a dear one that deprives us of the services of Jackson, even for a short time."

With Jackson's able assistance that day, Lee had achieved his greatest success yet in his short career as the commander of the Army of Northern Virginia. He had seized the initiative from his opponent, Federal Major General Joseph Hooker, and ended the day with the Army of the Potomac fighting for its survival around Chancellorsville.

The campaign had begun with every sign of success for the Federal commander. Hooker replaced Major General Ambrose Burnside as commander of the Army of the Potomac in January 1863. The morale of the men and officers of the army had plummeted following its devastating defeat at the Battle of Fredericksburg on December 13, 1862, and the failure of an ill-advised attempt to maneuver around the Confederate right flank in mid-January, which Yankees and Rebels alike dubbed the "Mud March."

Confidence in Burnside's ability to command had diminished. In assessing the state of the army, one Union corporal wrote, "It has strong limbs to march and meet the foe, stout arms to strike heavy blows, brave hearts to dare. But the brains, the brains—have we no brains to use the arms and limbs and eager hearts with cunning?"

Lincoln relieved Burnside from command. As his replacement, Lincoln chose "Fighting Joe" Hooker. Although he had a newspaper story's missing punctuation to thank for his nickname, Hooker had earned a reputation for aggressive command of troops in the campaigns of the Army of the Potomac. In a letter to his new commander, Lincoln wrote, "Beware of rashness, but with energy and sleepless vigilance, go forward, and give us victories."

Hooker's first order of business was to improve the living conditions and morale of his army. He introduced dietary and sanitary reforms, instituted a corps/division badge identification system, and formed his cavalry into a separate corps. It did not take long for these and other changes to instill a new confidence in the members of his army. "General Hooker has now a fine army," a private wrote on March 27, "and he has overhauled all the departments and made many useful and efficient changes. Our camps were never so clean and the food better, the introduction of soft bread was a beneficial and humane act and he has our thanks for that, if nothing else. He is energetic, crafty and a fighting general." With his 134,000-man army now ready to renew the conflict, Hooker turned his attention to the Confederate forces camped across the Rappahannock River at Fredericksburg.

Conditions in the Confederate camp during the winter respite from campaigning provided a marked contrast to the situation of the Federals across the river. "Symptoms of scurvy are appearing," Lee wrote, "and, to supply the place of vegetables, each regiment is directed to send a daily detail to gather sassafras buds, wild onions, lamb's quarter, and poke sprouts; but for so large an army the supply obtained is very small." One Louisiana staff officer wrote, "Overcoats, from their rarity, are objects of curiosity."

In February 1863, Confederate Lieutenant General James Longstreet was sent with 13,000 troops to southern Virginia to protect railroads and vital crops and provisions. This left Lee with about 60,000 troops, less than half the strength of Hooker's army. While anxious to carry the fight across the Rappahannock to the Federals, the lack of manpower forced Lee to wait for Hooker to make the first move.

The Confederate general did not have long to wait. Ruling out a repeat of Burnside's futile direct attack against the heights just west of Fredericksburg, Hooker decided on a more imaginative plan that would split his army into two attack groups, threatening the front and rear of the Confederate line. Hooker's plan called for sending three corps, with about a third of his men, on a wide swing around Lee's left flank. They would cross the Rappahannock about 20 miles upriver from Fredericksburg, ford the Rapidan River, and approach the Confederate line from behind. To mask this move, two Federal corps would cross the Rappahannock south of Fredericksburg. The remaining two corps would remain in Falmouth, ready to support either column.

Hooker presented this plan personally to Lincoln during the President's visit to Falmouth in early April. Throughout his presentation, Hooker frequently used the phrase, "when I get to Richmond." Lincoln, tired of such unfulfilled promises, corrected his general at one point, stating, "If you get to Richmond, General." Hooker quickly responded, "Excuse me, Mr. President, but there is no if in this case. I am going straight to Richmond if I live."

Lincoln later offered this analogy to a companion, "The hen is wisest of all the animal creation because she never cackles until after the egg is laid."

Although the President was not a schooled military strategist, he had learned one valuable lesson during two years of war and offered it as advice to his new commander. Before leaving Falmouth, Lincoln cautioned Hooker, "in your next fight, put in all your men." Had Hooker listened, the campaign may have had a much different outcome.

With the President's approval, Hooker initiated his plan. Preceding any move by his infantry, Hooker directed his cavalry corps to begin a swing around the Confederate army, camped along the Rappahannock River, creating confusion, cutting its line of communication with Richmond, and blocking any route of retreat. Heavy rains, however, had swollen the river, delaying the cavalry move and decreasing its effectiveness during the campaign.

On April 27, Hooker sent three corps, about 40,000 men, marching northwest to make a wide swing around the Confederate left flank. By April 30, the Federals had forded the Rapidan River and were passing through the Wilderness, an impenetrable forest of bogs, briars, and dense foliage. Hooker halted his command at the tiny crossroads hamlet of Chancellorsville—primarily the white-columned Chancellor mansion with outbuildings—and waited throughout the rest of the day for the arrival of his two reserve corps. While some of his subordinates were anxious to take advantage of their highly successful maneuver and proceed immediately to the attack, Hooker seemed to believe that an attack might not be necessary. "The operations of the last three days," he stated in an order to his men camped around Chancellorsville, "have determined that the enemy must either ingloriously fly or come out from behind his entrenchments and give us battle on our own ground, where certain destruction awaits him."

As Federal troops arrived at Chancellorsville, Lee had no idea of the extent of the danger to his command several miles behind him. On April 28th, Lee had received word that a large enemy force was moving up the river, but the Confederate commander had no idea of its destination. It was not until the next day that Lee began to realize Hooker's true intentions, three days after the Federals had begun their maneuver around his flank.

Early on the 29th, Lee was informed that Federal troops were crossing the Rappahannock downstream of Fredericksburg. Lee bolstered his line in front of these Federals and awaited Hooker's next move. Throughout the day, however, Lee received disturbing news from his cavalry commander, General Stuart. He learned that other Federal troops were crossing the Rappahannock upstream of Fredericksburg and, later in the day, that Union infantry and cavalry were crossing the Rapidan River. That night, Lee sent a division of infantry, under

This picture of the stone wall on Marye's Heights was taken by Federal Captain A.J. Russell about 20 minutes after the position was carried by the 6th Maine Infantry. The Confederate dead still lying behind the wall give an indication of the brutality of the fighting around Marye's Heights.

Major General Richard Anderson, to cover the western approaches to Fredericksburg. Advancing close to Chancellorsville, Anderson confirmed that Federal troops were massing there. Withdrawing from the Wilderness, Anderson established a position on a ridge in open ground.

Throughout the 30th, Lee closely reviewed his intelligence reports, trying to determine Hooker's intention. The most significant piece of information for Lee was that the Federal force south of Fredericksburg remained inactive. If Hooker's main thrust was to come from the south, these troops surely would have advanced. Lee decided, therefore, that the main Federal advance would come from the west. Leaving little more than a division to hold the Federals along the Rappahannock in check, Lee ordered most of his command west to block the Federal advance.

Hooker began his advance from the Wilderness early on the morning of May 1. The Confederates struck Hooker's lead division as it left the dense forest, but the Federals were quickly supported. Following several hours of fighting along the edge of the Wilderness, and with his army poised to advance against an enemy half its size, Hooker issued a remarkable order to his corps commanders. He directed them to break off the fight and fall back into the Wilderness to their defenses around Chancellorsville.

Major General Darius Couch, commanding the Federal 2nd Corps, met with Hooker to discuss the order to fall back. "It is alright, Couch," Hooker said, "I have gotten Lee just where I want him, he must fight me on my own ground." Couch wrote later, "to hear from his own lips that the advantages gained by the successful marches of his lieutenants were to

culminate in fighting a defensive battle in that nest of thickets, was too much, and I retired from his presence with the belief that my commanding general was a whipped man."

Hooker later offered his own explanation for turning the offensive over to Lee. "For once," Hooker said, "I lost confidence in Hooker."

Never one to pass up the opportunity to seize the initiative, Lee began to plan his attack after learning that the Federals were retreating into the Wilderness. He met with Jackson that evening to discuss the situation. Confederate scouts had discovered that the Federal right flank, since it faced away from the Confederate army, was lightly defended. Lee's engineers reported that the rest of the Federal line was solidly defended by earthworks and artillery. The two generals realized that their attack must be against the Federal right flank. Jackson proposed a brash plan that would send his corps of 25,000 men on a 14-mile march along the Federal front the next day to strike the exposed enemy flank. This would leave Lee with only about 20,000 men to face Hooker's army of about 70,000. The success of the plan depended on the Confederate army's ability to mask the movement from Hooker's scouts. If discovered, Lee's army could be destroyed; but with few alternatives available, Lee instructed his lieutenant, "Well, go on."

Jackson's corps set out on their long march early the next morning. While Lee hoped the movement would be effectively concealed by the dense undergrowth of the Wilderness, the Federal commander received reports throughout the day that a Confederate column was marching along his front. Hooker knew this meant the Confederates were either retreating or attempting to flank him. In case it was the latter, Hooker sent a dispatch to Major General Oliver Howard, whose 11th Corps guarded the Federal right flank, to shore up his line. "I am taking measures," Howard responded, "to resist an attack from the west." Unfortunately for the Federal army, Howard's preparation consisted of realigning only two infantry regiments and reserve artillery to the west.

Hooker sent one corps forward to strike the Confederate line, but the Federals attacked the rear of the column and did little to impede Jackson's advance. Hooker received information from his attacking soldiers that led the Federal commander to decide Lee was in full retreat. Within a few hours Hooker would discover he had sorely misjudged his opponent.

Jackson launched his attack on the Federal right at about 5:00 P.M. Jackson's corps struck the unprepared Federal 11th Corps. It took only 15 minutes for the right flank of the Army of the Potomac to collapse.

Since the dense undergrowth muffled the sounds of battle, it was more than an hour before Hooker learned of the collapse of his right flank. He immediately began sending reserves to check the Confederate attack.

The fighting along the Federal right continued into the night. Hooker drew his army back into a more concentrated line, while Confederate officers, under Jackson's direction, tried to reorganize their scattered command to renew the attack. It was during this period of confusion that Jackson was wounded while reconnoitering between the two armies.

Throughout the night of May 2, Hooker concentrated on ensuring that his command was thoroughly entrenched in the expectation of a renewed Confederate attack the next morning. He rejected the possibility of a Federal attack, although circumstances were definitely in his favor. Jackson's corps had failed to link up with the rest of Lee's command, leaving a large gap in the Confederate line. The arrival of fresh troops from Fredericksburg increased Hooker's

strength to more than 90,000. However, Hooker failed to seize the initiative.

Having assumed command of Jackson's corps, Confederate General J.E.B. Stuart resumed the attack at dawn on May 3, pushing the Federals back even further. During the ensuing struggle, a shell from a Confederate battery struck a pillar next to which Hooker was standing, knocking him senseless. Hooker refused to give up command, however, until about 9:30 A.M., when he summoned his 2nd Corps commander and said, "Couch, I turn the command of the army over to you." Hooker expressly directed his aggressive corps commander to continue the retreat.

By 10:00 A.M., Lee's broken line was finally united, and he prepared to press the attack along the whole Federal line. Lee was informed, however, that Federal troops had stormed Fredericksburg and were rapidly advancing toward Chancellorsville, behind Lee's line. Undaunted, the Confederate commander detached all but Stuart's command to attack the advancing Federal column near Salem Church, Virginia. The Federals valiantly tried to break through the Confederate line to reunite with their comrades at Chancellorsville, but their advance was effectively checked by the Confederates.

Scattered fighting resumed near Salem Church on May 4, lasting throughout the day

with neither side gaining the advantage. In the meantime, Stuart, with less than 25,000 men, effectively kept Hooker's command of more than 90,000 in check. After night fell, the Federal command at Salem Church retraced its steps and recrossed the Rappahannock. When Lee discovered the Federal withdrawal, he decided to strike Hooker on May 6. But he would find the enemy lines abandoned.

Following a council of war on the evening of May 4, Hooker decided, against the desire of the majority of his corps commanders, to retreat across the Rappahannock. By the morning of May 6, all of Hooker's shaken, disheartened troops had safely recrossed the river and were headed for Falmouth.

Little had been gained for either side after four costly days of fighting: The Federals lost almost 17,200 men, the Confederates, 12,700. The battle was an empty victory for Lee, who could not afford to lose men without achieving some significant strategic advantage.

Across the river, Hooker attempted to bolster the spirits of his defeated command by issuing a general order congratulating his army "on its achievements of the last seven days." Although shaken by their defeat, the men of the Army of the Potomac realized that they were victims of Hooker's inept leadership more than Confederate guns.

The ruins of George E. Chancellor's house on Orange Plank Road testify to the furious fighting of the battle.

THE DEATH OF "STONEWALL" JACKSON

"Let us cross over the river, and rest under the shade of the trees." These were the last words of Thomas J. "Stonewall" Jackson, uttered on the afternoon of May 10, 1863.

With the news of his death, "a great sob swept over the Army of Northern Virginia," wrote a Confederate officer. "It was the heart-break of the Southern Confederacy." Jackson's death came as a shock to many supporters throughout the South who had thought he had been on the road to recovery.

Eight days earlier, at about 9:00 P.M. on May 2, "Stonewall" Jackson and a small detachment of staff officers, couriers, and signalmen had ridden east along Orange Plank Road toward the battle front, less than one mile from the Federal headquarters in the tiny hamlet of Chancellorsville, Virginia. Artillery and musket fire swept Orange Plank Road, forcing Jackson and his aides to rein into the woods to the left. Passing beyond the Confederate picket line, an aide advised Jackson, "General, don't you think this is the wrong place for you?"

"The danger," Jackson responded, "is all over—the enemy is routed!—Go back and tell A.P. [Confederate General Hill] to press right on!"

Riding close enough to hear Federal officers hastily barking orders to establish a defensive line, Jackson turned and started back toward his line. Hearing sounds in their front, Confederate pickets fired a volley into the darkness. "Cease firing," a member of Jackson's staff yelled, "You are firing into your own men!"

"Who gave that order?" someone responded. "It's a lie! Pour it into them, boys!"

A second volley rang through the trees, this time striking Jackson in the right hand and twice in the left arm. Jackson's horse dashed toward the enemy line; Jackson struck several tree boughs, almost being knocked off, before a staff officer finally caught up with him.

Within hours of his wounding, his left arm was amputated in a field hospital at the rear of his corps. He informed his doctors that he felt better when he awoke a few hours later, leading them to believe that his recovery would be successful and rapid.

On May 4 he was transferred to Guiney's Station, Virginia, where he seemed to be recovering ahead of schedule throughout the next two days. On the morning of May 7, however, he complained of nausea and abdominal pain, which his doctor diagnosed as pneumonia of the right lung.

When informed of the change in Jackson's condition, Lee offered words of encouragement. "Tell him to make haste and get well, and come back to me as soon as he can. He has lost his left arm, but I have lost my right."

Jackson died from pneumonia three days later. Although words of regret were expressed throughout the South, his loss was most deeply felt in the ranks of the Army of Northern Virginia. The sentiments of the men he had led on many battlefields during the previous two years were perhaps best expressed by an officer Jackson had recommended for court-martial for prematurely withdrawing the "Stonewall Brigade" from the Battle of Kernstown, Virginia, in 1862. While tearfully viewing Jackson's body in the Governor's Mansion in Richmond, Brigadier General Richard Garnett told two of the deceased general's aides, "You know of the unfortunate breach between General Jackson and myself; I can never forget it, nor cease to regret it. But I wish here to assure you that no man can lament his death more sincerely than I do.... He is dead. Who can fill his place!"

Less than two months later, outside the small Pennsylvania town of Gettysburg, Garnett would join his fallen commander in death.

BATTLE OF CHAMPION HILL
May 16, 1863

Major General
Ulysses Grant, USA

Lieutenant General
John Pemberton, CSA

Sidney Champion's plantation near Vicksburg, Mississippi, was the site of a spirited clash between the 29,000 troops of the Federal Army of the Tennessee, commanded by Major General Ulysses Grant, and the 22,000-man Confederate army of Lieutenant General John Pemberton. The Confederates, striving to block Grant's advance on Vicksburg, were driven from the field with a loss of more than 3800 men. The Federals suffered 2400 casualties but took an important step toward capturing Vicksburg.

"I cannot think about this bloody hill without sadness and pride," said Union Brigadier General Alvin P. Hovey after the May 16, 1863 Battle of Champion Hill. The 42-year-old Hovey had good reason for his sentiment. His division, credited by Major General Ulysses Grant for the Federal army's decisive victory that day, had borne the brunt of the fighting. One out of every three men in Hovey's division had become a casualty in the bloodiest battle of the entire Vicksburg Campaign. This was a heavy price to pay, but by May 1863, Grant's force desperately needed a victory.

Since the spring of that year, General Grant's Union Army of the Tennessee had made several unsuccessful attempts to take the strategic Confederate stronghold on the Mississippi River at Vicksburg, Mississippi. Located on steep bluffs on the east bank of the river, this heavily fortified city remained, along with Port Hudson, Louisiana, the only Southern bastion preventing the North from securing control of the entire length of the Mississippi River. If these fell to the Federals, the flow of vital supplies from the west to the Confederacy would be cut off.

Grant had opened his Vicksburg Campaign in November 1862 by setting up a huge supply depot at Holly Springs, Mississippi, before advancing down the Yazoo River on Vicksburg. But Grant's efforts to strike at Vicksburg from the north never got off the ground. Confederate raiders, led by Major General Earl Van Dorn and Brigadier General Nathan Bedford Forrest, sacked Holly Springs and broke Grant's railroad lines in late December, forcing the Union commander to abandon his offensive. Meanwhile, Grant had sent Major General William T. Sherman with 32,000 men down the Mississippi by boat to the mouth of the Yazoo River. Sherman then proceeded up the south

bank of the Yazoo to Chickasaw Bluffs, clashing there on December 27–29 with Confederate forces led by Brigadier General Stephen D. Lee. "I reached Vicksburg at the time appointed," said Sherman of the results, "landed, assaulted and failed."

Determined to maintain the offensive, Grant tried to construct canals at various sites designed to bypass Vicksburg's formidable artillery defenses. A combination of natural setbacks and human error, however, stifled each project. Eventually, Grant ferried his troops to the west bank of the Mississippi, moved south along a series of rivers and bayous, and aimed to recross downstream to attack Vicksburg from the south. His first attempt to recross was at Grand Gulf, 50 miles below town, and failed before stiff Confederate opposition. Finally, on April 30, 1863, Grant successfully ferried his troops across the Mississippi at Bruinsburg, about 10 miles below Grand Gulf, his 44,000 troops struck inland. It was a bold, unprecedented move, made against the advice of his subordinates, and destined to catapult Grant into the ranks of history's great generals.

With Confederate forces concentrated at Vicksburg and at Jackson, Mississippi, 45 miles due east, Grant planned to get between the separate wings and defeat his enemy piecemeal. First, the Federals defeated a Confederate roadblock at Raymond, Mississippi. Grant then unleashed the corps of Sherman and Major General James McPherson in a driving rainstorm against Confederate entrenchments around Jackson on May 14. Federal forces entered Jackson about 4:00 P.M. The roads leading west to Vicksburg were wide open, and Grant lost no time setting in readiness his three corps for an advance.

Grant's passage was disputed by Confederate Lieutenant General John C. Pemberton.

Between Jackson and Vicksburg, Pemberton set up his 22,000 men in hastily prepared defenses along a hill on the plantation belonging to one Sidney Champion. Champion's Hill rose 75 feet above the surrounding countryside, and soldiers there could dominate and block the main Vicksburg–Jackson road. From left to right, facing east, Pemberton placed the divisions of Major General Carter Stevenson, Brigadier General James Bowen, and Major General William Loring to meet Grant.

With Sherman's corps still en route from Jackson, Grant opposed Pemberton with the 29,000 men of McPherson's and Major General John McClernand's corps. Grant planned for McClernand to strike the center and right of Pemberton's line while McPherson assailed the Confederate left flank. McClernand, a former congressman and an officer by virtue of political connections, was a timid fighter and delayed stirring to action his more aggressive subordinate, General Alvin Hovey, until about 10 A.M. on May 16. By design, Hovey's troops engaged in a long-range firefight with Stevenson's Confederate soldiers while awaiting McPherson's advance. Hovey's cue came at about 10:30 A.M. With little support from McClernand's other three divisions, Hovey's Federal troops raised a cheer and charged headlong up the slope of Champion's Hill. Putting the startled Confederate defenders to flight, Hovey captured 11 cannons on the crest of the hill. As Hovey's men gathered up their prizes, they were hit in turn by Confederate General Bowen's powerful counterattack. Hovey lost his artillery trophies, but retreated, in his words, "slowly and stubbornly, contesting with death every inch of the field [we] had won." Grant rushed two of McPherson's brigades to Hovey's aid, and the Federals managed to hold the foot of the hill. For half an hour, a witness

recalled, "each side took their turn in driving and being driven." He called the fight there "unequal, terrible and most sanguinary."

Meanwhile, McClernand's halfhearted offensive allowed Pemberton to reinforce his left against McPherson's attack, which was led by Federal Major General John A. Logan's division. Logan, also a political appointee but more militarily competent than McClernand, displayed a zeal for combat that prompted a Northern journalist to write, "If you ever hear that Logan was defeated, make up your mind that he and most of his men have been sacrificed."

Logan arrived on the field with "the speed of a cyclone," a Federal soldier recounted, and rallied the faltering 34th Indiana Infantry Regiment. Under relentless pressure from both Logan's and Hovey's commands, the Confederate left flank began to crumble.

Pemberton made another plea for reinforcements from Confederate General Loring, who faced the lethargic McClernand. Loring refused, pointing to the serried blue ranks to his front. Without Loring's men to bolster his left flank, Pemberton's defense there collapsed. The battle was already decided when Loring and McClernand bestirred themselves. By then, as one of Loring's officers observed, Confederate soldiers were "rushing pell-mell from the scene of action." Pemberton ordered a general retreat.

While Grant prepared his pursuit, his army took stock of its victory at Champion's Hill. Grant had suffered 2441 casualties; Pemberton, 3851. As General Hovey inspected his ranks, he asked some soldiers of his old regiment, the 24th Indiana Infantry, "Where are the rest of my boys?" Pointing to the corpse-strewn slopes of Champion's Hill, one veteran replied, "They are lying over there." Hovey rode off with tears in his eyes.

SIEGE OF VICKSBURG
May 18–July 4, 1863

Major General
Ulysses Grant, USA

Lieutenant General
John Pemberton, CSA

Federal Major General Ulysses Grant had seven months of frustrating and tough campaigning before his 75,000-man Army of the Tennessee was close enough to place Vicksburg, Mississippi, under siege. He met stiff resistance from the citizens of Vicksburg and the Confederate army of Lieutenant General John Pemberton, numbering 30,000. For 48 days the Confederates held out, fighting hunger, disease, and mounting Federal pressure. Surrender of the city ultimately signaled Union control of the Mississippi.

The folks in the streets of Vicksburg on Sunday morning, May 17, 1863, could not tell if the church bells were signaling victory or defeat. The anxious citizens were well aware of the battles that had been raging for weeks east of Vicksburg, and many gathered on street corners to discuss the latest rumors. The blue sky and bright sunshine over the Confederacy's Mississippi River stronghold contrasted starkly with the gloom and fear etched on the resident's faces.

Soldiers began to appear on the streets, individually and in small groups. Many were without weapons, and their uniforms were tattered and dusty. The stream of weary Confederate veterans that shuffled into Vicksburg increased as the day progressed. "About three o'clock the rush began," recalled a young lady watching from the curb. "I shall never forget that woeful sight of a beaten, demoralized army....Wan, hollow-eyed, ragged, footsore, bloody—the men limped along... followed by siege-guns, ambulances, gun carriages, and wagons in aimless confusion."

The arrival in Vicksburg of Confederate General John Pemberton's beaten army ended the long campaign of maneuvering to control the approaches to the city. Earlier that morning, Pemberton's force had battled Major General Ulysses Grant's Union army along the banks of the Big Black River, 10 miles east of Vicksburg. After their decisive and costly defeat at the Battle of Champion Hill on May 16, the Confederates had made a stand at the crossing of the Big Black in a last desperate effort to stall Grant's relentless advance on Vicksburg.

Some 30,000 of Grant's men attacked the 5000 Confederates defending the bridges over the Big Black. Overwhelmed, Pemberton ordered the bridges burned. The Confederate survivors were among the dejected soldiers who later thronged the streets of Vicksburg.

That night, Pemberton received an urgent telegram from Confederate General Joseph E. Johnston, overall commander of Confederate troops in the west. Evacuate Vicksburg if possible, ordered Johnston. "Instead of losing both troops and place, we must save the troops." But at a council of war, Pemberton received unanimous support from his immediate subordinates to stay and fight. Pemberton replied to Johnston, "I have decided to hold Vicksburg as long as possible." The message signaled the start of a grim siege.

Grant was eager to take advantage of Pemberton's defeated, disorganized army, hoping to prevent a protracted siege. The Federal commander attacked Vicksburg's defenses on the afternoon of May 19. Unfortunately for Grant, however, he had struck a part of the Confederate line held by troops that were far from demoralized, as they had not been engaged in any of the recent devastating engagements. The Union attack was soundly defeated.

Undaunted, the stubborn Grant determined to try again. Grant planned his attack for the morning of May 22 and preceded it with a nightlong artillery barrage delivered from land batteries and the river gunboats of Union Admiral David Porter. At 10:00 A.M. on the 22nd, Confederate soldiers watched as masses of Federal troops emerged with a yell from tree cover 400 yards away.

"The artillery opened upon the lines as they approached," recalled a Confederate soldier in the trenches, "and the infantry joined in as soon as they were within range....[T]he destruction among the Federal ranks was fearful."

Grant launched three army corps against the enemy works. The blue masses rolled up to the parapets but failed to penetrate the Confederate position. Union corps commander Major General John McClernand called to Grant for reinforcements, claiming his troops had

penetrated the Confederate works. Grant weakened his other two corps to provide McClernand with the extra men, but McClernand had exaggerated his own success. When his attack ultimately faltered like the others, McClernand publicly blamed the other corps commanders, Major Generals William T. Sherman and James McPherson. Relieved of duty several weeks later, McClernand was officially blamed for at least half of the 3200 casualties Grant's army sustained on May 22.

While Grant methodically started siege operations, the dead and wounded Union soldiers from the May 22 assault lay between the lines unattended for three days. As the corpses putrefied in the torrid heat, one Confederate cracked that Grant was trying to "stink them out." A short armistice was finally agreed to for the burial of the dead and care of the wounded. During the lull, a Union sergeant recalled that the combatants "mingled together in various spots, apparently with much enjoyment....Here a group of four played cards....There, others were jumping...everywhere blue and gray mingled in conversation."

The playful distractions were brief. Confederate hopes that their May 22 victory might encourage relief from the outside soon faded. Instead, they suffered the brutal reality of constant artillery bombardment, rapidly dwindling food supplies, and limited manpower stretched to the breaking point. Clean water was scarce. The entire military and civilian population was reduced to living in caves. The filthy hovels were carved into the sides of the steep gullies and ravines that abounded in Vicksburg.

Food for the Confederates became scarce in quantity and poor in quality. "I am so tired of corn bread," wrote one young housewife, "that I eat it with tears in my eyes....I can't eat the mule meat." Confederate soldiers suffered much worse from lack of food than this young lady.

As the siege dragged on week after week, even simple corn bread became a luxury. The same young housewife would later write of rats "hanging dressed in the market" and of a friend who had eaten one to find its flavor "fully equal to that of squirrels." Dogs and cats also were noticeably absent from city streets.

While Grant slowly starved Vicksburg into submission, he sped the process along with endless skirmishing and short forays. Union siege works inched closer and closer to Pemberton's line. At some places mere yards separated opponents, and vicious hand-to-hand struggles were common. "Hand grenades and loaded shells are lighted and thrown over the parapet as you would play ball," recalled a Union private.

On June 25, Union troops detonated 2200 pounds of black powder beneath Confederate trenches northeast of the city. The blast tore a hole in the Confederate works, but the follow-up attack failed miserably. "My God!" gasped a Federal officer, "They are killing my bravest men in that hole." Another Union powder charge ripped a hole in the same line on July 1. A heavy artillery barrage followed this blast, but no infantry troops were sent against the works.

Two days later Grant's war of attrition finally succeeded. With no prospects of reinforcements and his own army too weak to attempt a break out, Pemberton requested terms of surrender. Grant demanded unconditional surrender, which the Confederate commander refused. Finally, more liberal terms, which included the parole of 30,000 Confederate troops, were agreed to. On July 4, 1863, the 48th day of the siege, Vicksburg surrendered.

Five days later, upon learning of Vicksburg's fall, the Confederate garrison at Port Hudson, Louisiana, surrendered. The entire Mississippi River was now open to Union shipping, effectively splitting the Confederacy in two.

BATTLE OF GETTYSBURG
July 1–3, 1863

Major General
George Meade, USA

General
Robert E. Lee, CSA

The bloodiest battle of the Civil War, the clash at Gettysburg, Pennsylvania, pitted the 65,000 Confederate troops of Robert E. Lee's Army of Northern Virginia against George Gordon Meade's 85,000-strong Army of the Potomac. More than 23,000 of Meade's men were killed, wounded, or captured during the furious fighting. Lee and the Confederacy sustained casualties in excess of 20,000, a staggering loss that ended Lee's second invasion of the North and marked the end of the Confederates' two-year domination of the Army of the Potomac.

Along Cemetery Ridge, south of the Pennsylvania town of Gettysburg, the Federal troops watched in awe as the long Confederate line advanced toward them on the afternoon of July 3, 1863. One spectator, Federal Lieutenant Frank Haskell, later recorded his impression of the charge. "More than half a mile their front extends, more than a thousand yards the dull gray masses deploy, man touching man, rank pressing rank, and line supporting line. The red flags wave, their horsemen gallop up and down; the arms of eighteen thousand men, barrel and bayonet, gleam in the sun, a sloping forest of flashing steel. Right on the move as with one soul, in perfect order...magnificent, grim, irresistible."

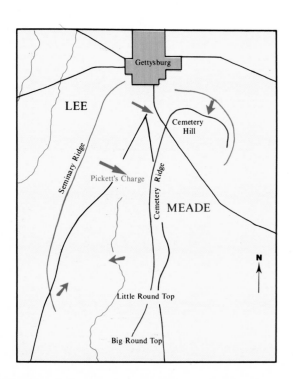

Haskell and his comrades watched as almost 15,000 Confederate troops, half belonging to Major General George Pickett's division, advanced in silence on the center of the Union line. With encouraging words, Federal artillery and infantry officers prepared their men to meet the Confederate thrust. "Let your work this day," one officer cried out to his men, "be for victory or death."

"Pickett's Charge" was Confederate General Robert E. Lee's last-ditch effort to drive the Federal Army of the Potomac from its strong position along Cemetery Ridge. Attacks on the enemy flanks the day before and earlier that morning had failed. Faced with dwindling supplies and mounting casualties, Lee realized that the success of his invasion of the North rested with the ability of these men to drive the Federals from the heights south of Gettysburg. Failure would cut short a campaign vital to the survival of the Confederacy. It would take almost half an hour before his men would reach the Federal line, and the eyes and hearts of the Confederacy were on them as they smartly marched forward.

From the beginning, this campaign had been a daring gamble for Lee and his army. Lee first considered invading Pennsylvania during his ill-fated invasion of Maryland the year before. Following his victory at Chancellorsville, Virginia, in May 1863, the Confederate commander traveled to Richmond to propose to Confederate President Jefferson Davis and his cabinet a plan for invading the North. Lee felt his army must carry the fighting north of the Potomac for two reasons. First, if left unchecked, the Federal Army of the Potomac would become so strong that it could virtually brush Lee's undermanned force aside as it descended on Richmond. Second, and more pressing, supplies available to Lee's troops were

running short. "The question of food," Lee told one of his officers, "gives me more trouble and uneasiness than anything else." Pennsylvania loomed as a promised land for troops who barely had enough to eat in their camps along the Rappahannock.

Some cabinet members argued that Lee's army should withdraw to the defenses of Richmond and send reinforcements to lift the Federal siege of Vicksburg, Mississippi. But Lee finally convinced his superiors to approve the plan. Before launching his invasion, however, Lee had to find a replacement for his 2nd Corps commander, Lieutenant General Thomas "Stonewall" Jackson, who had died on May 10, 1863. Instead of the original two corps, Lee divided his army into three corps and placed Lieutenant Generals James Longstreet, Richard Ewell, and Ambrose P. Hill in command of the 1st, 2nd, and 3rd Corps, respectively. With his army reorganized, Lee began his advance on June 3.

When Federal Major General Joseph Hooker, commander of the Army of the Potomac, learned that several Confederate units had broken camp and crossed the Rappahannock River, he wired Federal President Abraham Lincoln requesting permission to cross the river and "pitch into" Lee's rear. Having little confidence in his commander after his poor performance during the Chancellorsville Campaign, Lincoln denied Hooker's request. The President feared the Federal army would be "entangled upon the river, like an ox jumped half over a fence and liable to be torn by dogs front and rear, without a fair chance to gore one way or kick the other."

From information gained during the cavalry battle of Brandy Station on June 9, Hooker's suspicions that Lee was headed north were confirmed. The Federal commander again

proposed crossing the Rappahannock, this time to quickly capture Richmond. Hooker assured Lincoln that he would then send reinforcements north to protect Washington and stop Lee. Again Lincoln informed his general that the plan could not be approved. The President reminded Hooker that Lee's army, not Richmond, was Hooker's primary objective. All other options thus closed to him, Hooker turned his 85,000-man army northward in pursuit of the Confederates.

Ewell's corps was Lee's vanguard, and it rapidly marched north, entering Chambersburg, Pennsylvania, on June 24. By the 27th, most of Lee's 65,000-man command had reached the Pennsylvania town.

The Federal army did not cross the Potomac River until June 26. A series of disagreements with the Federal War Department finally prompted Hooker to offer his resignation on June 27. Having little confidence in his ability to command the army, the War Department quickly accepted Hooker's resignation and appointed 5th Corps commander, Major General George G. Meade, as his replacement. Meade reluctantly accepted the position. "I've been tried and condemned without a hearing," he later wrote, "and I suppose I shall have to go to execution."

After assuming command, Meade met with Hooker to discuss the change of commands. "[Hooker] was ready to turn over to me the Army of the Potomac," Meade wrote his wife, "that he had enough of it, and almost wished he had never been born." Meade gained little information in this final meeting with Hooker. The new commander was left with no plan of action, incomplete information on the disposition of the scattered units of his army, and little idea of where he could find the enemy.

LINCOLN'S GETTYSBURG ADDRESS

In early November 1863, Federal President Abraham Lincoln received an invitation to "make a few remarks" at the dedication of the national cemetery at Gettysburg, Pennsylvania, on November 19. Lincoln accepted the invitation and arrived at the town by train the night before the dedication.

After a long, slow procession to the cemetery south of town, Edward Everett, a famous orator of the time, delivered an eloquent two-hour speech describing the battle and drawing lessons from European military history. After thundering applause from the thousands in attendance, President Lincoln rose, stepped to the front of the platform, and delivered his 20-line tribute to the men who fought and died during those first three days of July 1863.

"Four score and seven years ago our fathers brought forth on this continent a new nation, conceived in Liberty, and dedicated to the proposition that all men are created equal.

"Now we are engaged in a great civil war, testing whether that nation or any nation so conceived and so dedicated, can long endure. We are met on a great battle-field of that war. We have come to dedicate a portion of that field, as a final resting place for those who here gave their lives that that nation might live. It is altogether fitting and proper that we should do this.

"But, in a larger sense, we can not dedicate—we can not consecrate—we can not hallow—this ground. The brave men, living and dead, who struggled here, have consecrated it, far above our poor power to add or detract. The world will little note, nor long remember what we say here, but it can never forget what they did here. It is for us the living, rather, to be dedicated here to the unfinished work which they who fought here have thus far so nobly advanced. It is rather for us to be here dedicated to the great task remaining before us—that from these honored dead we take increased devotion to that cause for which they gave the last full measure of devotion—that we here highly resolve that these dead shall not have died in vain—that this nation, under God, shall have a new birth of freedom—and that government of the people, by the people, for the people, shall not perish from the earth."

Applause interrupted the speech five times, and a tremendous ovation and three cheers followed its completion. While Lincoln confided later that he felt the speech a "flat failure," Everett summed up the impact of the President's "few remarks" when he told him, "[t]here was more in your twenty lines than in my twenty pages."

Photographer Timothy H. O'Sullivan captured this graphic scene of Union and Confederate dead at Gettysburg battlefield. The epic three-day battle ended General Lee's second invasion of the North and marked the peak of the war's fighting.

Meade spent most of the 28th studying intelligence reports and locating the position of his widespread command. By the evening of the next day, Meade's army was aligned along the northern Maryland border east of Emmitsburg, ready to push into Pennsylvania once the Confederate army had been located.

With Lee's cavalry off on a futile excursion around the Federal army, the Confederate commander did not learn until the night of June 28 that the enemy had crossed the Potomac two days earlier. Scouts also informed Lee that Meade had replaced Hooker. Once Lee learned that the Army of the Potomac was close at hand, he worked quickly to consolidate his army. By June 30, Lee's line consisted of Ewell's corps at Heidlersburg, Hill's corps near Cashtown, and Longstreet's corps at Chambersburg.

When Meade learned of the general location of Lee's command, he chose Gettysburg as the place to concentrate his army. The Federal cavalry division of Brigadier General John Buford was already stationed in the town.

That evening, Confederate Major General Henry Heth received Hill's permission to take his division to Gettysburg the next morning to drive away Buford's cavalry force and secure much-needed shoes for his troops. Although Hill had received orders from Lee not to bring on an engagement with the enemy until all three corps were in supporting distance, the Confederate 3rd Corps commander did not believe Heth's venture into Gettysburg would violate those orders.

Heth's division moved toward Gettysburg at dawn on July 1. A Federal cavalry officer on picket duty along the Chambersburg Pike spotted gray-clad figures approaching through the mist at about 5:30 A.M. and fired the opening shot of the battle. The Federal officer then ordered his men to fall back to Buford's main line along McPherson's Ridge. Although outnumbered almost three to one, Buford's command held the Confederates in check until about 10:00 A.M., when Federal Major General John Reynolds's 1st Corps arrived from the south. As Reynolds directed his men into line, a shot from a Confederate sharpshooter struck him behind the right ear, killing him almost immediately. The fighting continued west of Gettysburg throughout the morning, with the Federals able to hold off repeated Confederate thrusts.

Shortly after 11:00 A.M., the Federal 12th Corps, commanded by Major General Oliver Howard, began to arrive south of town. When Howard learned that Ewell's Confederate troops were approaching Gettysburg from the north, he deployed his troops along a line north of the town.

Ewell attacked Howard's Federal troops at about 4:00 P.M., just as Hill sent fresh troops against the Federal 1st Corps. The combined Confederate attack was too much for the two Union corps, and the Federals were driven back through the town to a new defensive position along Cemetery Hill.

When fresh Confederate troops arrived on the field, some of Ewell's subordinates thought that he should pursue the Federals all the way up the slopes of Cemetery Hill. Ewell's orders from Lee did not require him to attack, however, so the 2nd Corps commander decided against it.

Both armies strengthened their positions throughout the night. When Meade arrived on the field, he deployed his army in a fishhook shape beginning southeast of town on Culp's Hill, curving around Cemetery Hill, and then stretching south along Cemetery Ridge. Lee shaped his own line to conform to the Federal position, curving through the town and extending south along Seminary Ridge.

Lee was determined to strike the first blow the next morning. He planned to attack the Federal left and right flanks with his 1st Corps and 3rd Corps. But Longstreet's troops did not begin to reach their stations along Seminary Ridge until after midnight. They had been camped near Chambersburg when the fighting began on July 1 and endured a forced march to reach Gettysburg as soon as possible. By dawn, two of Longstreet's divisions had finally arrived. The third, commanded by George Pickett, would arrive too late to join in the day's fighting.

Throughout the morning of July 2, Lee impatiently waited for Longstreet's assault to begin, but the attack was delayed while Longstreet deployed his exhausted troops around the Federal left flank. It was not until 4:00 P.M. that his corps was finally in position to attack.

The Federal unit anchoring Meade's left flank was the Federal 3rd Corps, commanded by Major General Daniel Sickles. A political appointee with no prior military service before the war, Sickles's main claim to fame had been the killing of Francis Scott Key's son, who had been having an affair with Sickles's wife. Before the end of the day, Sickles would be better known for his destruction of his 3rd Corps.

Dissatisfied with the position assigned to his men along the lower edge of Cemetery Ridge, Sickles advanced his corps, without orders, to higher ground to his front. This left a large gap between the Federal 2nd Corps and 3rd Corps. When he inspected Sickles's position shortly before 4:00 P.M., Meade informed the 3rd Corps commander that the alignment of his troops had disrupted Meade's defensive plans. Sickles offered to withdraw his troops back to their

This photograph of Little Round Top (left) and Big Round Top (right) was taken by an assistant to Mathew Brady. Little Round Top, held by Federal Brigadier General Gouverneur Warren, was the key to the Federal position.

original position, but the booming of Confederate guns warned both Federal generals that an attack was imminent. "I wish to God you could [withdraw]," Meade exclaimed, "but the enemy won't let you!"

For the next three hours, Confederate and Federal troops fought desperately. The key to the Federal position, Little Round Top, would have fallen into Confederate hands if not for the astute observation of the chief of Federal engineers, Brigadier General Gouverneur K. Warren. Noticing Confederate troops advancing toward the unoccupied hill, Warren immediately sent for reinforcements. Several regiments of the Federal 5th Corps arrived just as the gray-clad troops charged up the hill. The left flank of the Federal line, which curved around Little Round Top, was guarded by Colonel Joshua Chamberlain's 20th Maine Infantry Regiment. Chamberlain's men valiantly fought off repeated Confederate attacks and finally drove the enemy away with an attack of their own, preserving the Federal position.

Some of the bloodiest fighting of the war took place along the Federal left flank. One veteran vividly described the scene many years later. "The hoarse and indistinguishable orders of commanding officers, the screaming and bursting of shells, canister and shrapnel as they tore through the struggling masses of humanity, the death screams of wounded animals, the groans of their human companions, wounded and dying and trampled under foot by hurrying batteries, riderless horses and the moving lines of battle, all combined an indescribable roar of discordant elements—in fact a perfect hell on earth, never, perhaps to be equaled, certainly not to be surpassed, nor ever to be forgotten in a man's lifetime. It has never been effaced from my memory, day or night, for fifty years."

Longstreet's two divisions and a division from Hill's corps held their own against six Federal divisions, at times even temporarily piercing the Federal line. But Federal countercharges closed the gaps as quickly as they were opened. When the fighting ended, the wounded and dead littered the fields. General Sickles suffered a wound that cost him his right leg and his corps had been so badly mauled that it would cease to exist in a few short months. The only documented civilian casualty also fell on the second day. Jennie Wade, 20 years old and engaged, was killed when a bullet from Confederate snipers firing at Federal soldiers pierced the front door of her home on the slope of Cemetery Hill.

Except for occupying a position that Meade had never intended to hold, Longstreet's troops had accomplished little. Ewell's attack on the Federal right flank that evening also failed to dislodge the enemy. It had been a costly day for the Confederate army, but Lee was not willing to turn the offensive over to Meade. That night Lee met with his corps commanders and proposed the plan of attack for the next day. The Federal center would be shelled with as many guns as could be brought to bear on it. Then 15,000 men, the majority being from Pickett's fresh division, would cross the open field between Seminary and Cemetery ridges, about three-fourths of a mile wide, and crush the Federal center.

Longstreet barely concealed his rage as Lee explained his plan. "General," Longstreet began after Lee had finished, "I have been a soldier all my life. I have been with soldiers engaged in fights by couples, by squads, companies, regiments, divisions and armies, and should know as well as anyone what soldiers can do. It is my opinion that no 15,000 men ever arrayed for battle can take that position." Unfazed, the

Confederate commander ordered preparations to begin for the attack.

Ewell's corps made one last attempt to drive the Federals from Culp's Hill on the morning of July 3. The fight lasted until 11:00 A.M., when the Confederates abandoned the attack.

Throughout the morning, Confederate artillery officers lined almost 140 guns along Seminary Ridge, all trained on the center of the Federal line. At 1:00 P.M. Longstreet, who was given overall command of the attack, ordered the artillery to open fire. The bombardment lasted almost two hours—the thunder of 300 Federal and Confederate guns echoing for miles.

As the Confederate guns subsided, Confederate officers quickly aligned their men and began advancing toward the Federal line. As the soldiers smartly marched off, they were told to use a clump of trees along Cemetery Ridge as their guide. Several hundred yards from the Federal position the Confederate units began to pack together to form a mass that Lee hoped would be able to punch through the enemy's line. While the Confederates continued their deliberate advance, Federal artillery and infantry poured fire into the Confederate flanks and along its front. As each man fell, however, another moved up into his place. As they neared the Federal position, the Confederate ranks let out the Rebel Yell and rushed forward. Few who began that marvelous charge actually reached the Federal line; those that did were killed or captured within minutes. The charge itself lasted less than an hour. What began as one of the most remarkable spectacles of the war ended with disorganized gray-clad groups of soldiers streaming to the rear. Almost 7000 Confederates lay dead or wounded between the two ridges.

Meade was urged by several subordinates to launch a counterattack against the broken Confederate ranks, but the Federal commander declined. His army had been sorely tested over the past three days, and Meade believed his troops were in no condition to launch a counterattack.

Both armies faced each other throughout July 4, but neither side was willing to renew the fight. The cost of the previous three days had been extremely high. Since the beginning of the conflict on July 1, the Federals had suffered more than 23,000 casualties and the Confederates, 20,000.

That night, Lee's Army of Northern Virginia began its long retreat to Virginia. Although they had been defeated, Lee's men had not given up. A Confederate soldier was overheard to say, "We'll fight them, sir, till hell freezes over, and then we'll fight them on ice!" But the fight would never be the same; the Federal army had finally stood up to Lee's men and shown that they were up to the task of preserving the Union.

GEORGE GORDON MEADE

With the Confederate army roaming freely through Pennsylvania in late June 1863, Lincoln needed to quickly replace Major General Joseph Hooker, who had resigned as commander of the Federal Army of the Potomac on June 27. Although initially reluctant to assume the responsibilities of army command, Lincoln left Major General George G. Meade little choice in the matter. Meade was a deliberate, competent fighter who followed orders—all qualities Lincoln felt had been missing in Hooker and were essential to succeed against Confederate General Robert E. Lee.

The Confederate commander acknowledged that Meade would be a far better opponent than Hooker. "General Meade will commit no blunder on my front," Lee stated upon learning of Meade's appointment to command, "and if I make one, he will make haste to take advantage of it."

Born in Cadiz, Spain, on December 31, 1815, while his father was overseas as a naval agent for the United States, Meade graduated from West Point in 1835. Most of his military service before the start of the war was as an engineer.

Meade was appointed a brigadier general of Pennsylvania volunteer troops in August 1861. His command joined George McClellan's Army of the Potomac in June 1862 and participated in the later stages of the Peninsula Campaign, during which Meade was wounded in the hip and arm.

During the next year, Meade rose to commander of the 5th Corps, primarily because of his administrative ability and his performance in such battles as Second Bull Run, Antietam, Fredericksburg, and Chancellorsville. He had no aspirations to command the Army of the Potomac, but his strong dedication to duty made it impossible for him to decline the appointment when Lincoln offered it to him.

After his great victory at Gettysburg, Meade was criticized by Lincoln for allowing Lee's army to escape back to Virginia. "My dear general," Lincoln wrote his general, "I do not believe you appreciate the magnitude of the misfortune involved in Lee's escape....Your golden opportunity is gone, and I am distressed immeasurably because of it."

It was no coincidence that when Lieutenant General Ulysses Grant assumed command of all Federal armies, he established his headquarters with Meade's army. While Meade's superiors had confidence in his ability to fight, they lacked faith in his capacity to wage a successful campaign. Indeed, by the end of the war, Meade was little more than a figurehead, eclipsed by Grant's other lieutenants, Major Generals William Sherman and Philip Sheridan.

THE STORMING OF FORT WAGNER
July 18, 1863

Major General
Quincy Gillmore, USA

Brigadier General
William Taliaferro, CSA

Brigadier General Truman Seymour sent almost 6000 Federal troops against a mere 1785 soldiers commanded by Confederate Brigadier General William Taliaferro at Fort Wagner, one of the key works guarding Charleston Harbor. The assault was spearheaded by the 54th Massachusetts Volunteer Infantry, made up entirely of blacks. Repulsed by the Confederate defenders, the Federals left behind over 1500 casualties. The Confederates lost less than 200. Unfortunately, this loss of Federal troops was unnecessary as the Confederates would abandon the fort less than two months later.

It was an awesome spectacle in the skies above Charleston Harbor, South Carolina. For more than seven hours during the afternoon and early evening of July 18, 1863, the flash and roar of a massive artillery barrage descended on Confederate-held Fort Wagner. The storm of shot and shell prompted a witness to quip that enough ammunition had been exhausted to establish "several first class iron foundries." If there was any humor in the scene, however, it died on the lips of that observer. Certainly none of the 6000 or so Union soldiers who waited in silence to attack the Confederate strongpoint once the cannon fire lifted found anything to laugh about.

Just a week earlier, a similar attack on the fort had failed. This failure did not discourage Federal Major General Quincy A. Gillmore, commanding the Department of the South; he made preparations for another attack on the fort at dusk of July 18.

Since June 1862, when Federal Major General David Hunter landed on James Island just south of Charleston, the capture of this key port city had been a major goal of the Federal authorities. The harbor's complex of channels, shoals, and tricky currents was a boon to daring blockade runners. The military command in Washington realized that the most direct way to close this breach in their blockade was to take the city itself. Emotional considerations also played a significant part in singling out Charleston as a primary target for capture, since Fort Sumter was the site where hostilities began in April 1861.

Several attempts prior to July 1863 had been made on the port city, but all had failed. By the time General Gillmore assumed command of Federal land forces in June 1863, Federal strategists had determined that it would be

necessary to expand the army's role in the attempt to subdue Charleston; Fort Sumter, they reasoned, was the key.

Military planners deduced that the fall of Fort Sumter would deprive Charleston of its main fortress, thus opening the city to capture by the Union fleet, commanded by Rear Admiral John A. Dahlgren. The army's role would include an amphibious assault on Morris Island, a slender piece of sand that brushed the coast immediately south of the harbor entrance. Gillmore planned to place heavy rifled guns at Cummings Point on the northern tip of the island and less than a mile from Fort Sumter. These guns, supported by naval fire, would pound the fort into submission. First, however, Gillmore's troops had to overwhelm the Confederate strongpoints of Fort Wagner and Battery Gregg, then occupying Cummings Point. "If this assault failed," Gillmore wrote, "the promise to demolish Fort Sumter failed also."

The first assault on Fort Wagner came on July 11, 1863. The Confederate defenders concentrated a heavy fire on the attacking Federals, forcing them back with heavy casualties.

The massive artillery barrage over Fort Wagner on July 18 heralded Gillmore's second attempt to carry the works. It was hoped that the Federal guns would silence the heavy pieces in the fort and demoralize the defenders.

From where the 6000 assault troops, commanded by Brigadier General Truman Seymour, crouched in readiness, Fort Wagner appeared to be little more than a succession of low, irregular, harmless sandhills about 800 feet wide rising amid scrub growth and brittle grass. The sand wall stretched from coastal waters on the right to marshy inland waters on the left. At one point, the approaches narrowed to a width of only 80 feet.

Fort Wagner's vulnerable appearance was deceptive, however. Beneath the sandhills was a solid core of palmetto logs and sandbags that protected the Confederate defenders commanded by Brigadier General William Taliaferro. Within the fort was a massive bombproof shelter capable of housing half the garrison at one time. Well armed with powerful artillery pieces that were double-shotted with canister and sited to sweep the approaches to the fort, the Confederate defenders waited confidently throughout the relatively ineffective Federal bombardment for whatever the enemy had in store for them. Only eight of the 1700 defenders were killed or wounded during the sustained barrage, and none of their guns were silenced.

The Union attack commenced at 7:30 that evening, when twilight shrouded the storming parties from the view of Fort Wagner's defenders as well as from the other Confederate forts. Spearheading the assault was the 54th Massachusetts Volunteer Infantry of Brigadier General George Strong's brigade, a black regiment led by white officers and commanded by 25-year-old Colonel Robert Gould Shaw. Shaw had volunteered his men for this post of honor, hoping to prove the mettle of one of the U.S. Army's first black combat units. "The eyes of thousands will look on what you do tonight," Shaw told the regiment just before he brandished his sword and led them forward. In solid regimental column, the 54th slowly led the advance. They were followed, in tight formation, by 15 regiments in three assault waves.

Before the signal was given to double their pace, the assault force was hit with a tremendous burst of artillery and small arms fire. A torrent of shot and shell rained down from Fort Wagner, Fort Sumter, Battery Gregg,

and other Confederate works. Shaw and others pressed on, struggling through a wide moat and clawing their way over shifting sands up the steep parapets of the fort. They were met there by defenders who engaged them in a fierce hand-to-hand struggle. The blacks wielded their bayonets and the Confederates swung their handspikes and gun rammers. The fight did not last long, and those outnumbered Federals who were not killed, wounded, or captured were driven from the works.

Union casualties were heavy. Of its 650 men engaged, the 54th Massachusetts lost 272. The casualties of this first wave were not limited to enlisted men, however. Colonel Shaw fell dead with a bullet through his heart, Brigadier General George Strong was mortally wounded, and General Seymour was seriously wounded. Succeeding waves were also slaughtered, reaching a toll of 1500 before the attack was mercifully suspended. The Confederate defenders lost less than 200 men.

No one would question the bravery of the 54th Massachusetts or any of the regiments that charged across that narrow, shell-swept corridor of sand into the guns of Fort Wagner. In fact, Sergeant William Carney of the 54th Massachusetts earned a Medal of Honor for his bravery in saving the national colors from capture that day.

Perhaps, however, the real story of the attack told on the faces of the men who lived through the hell on Morris Island that evening. The "deathly glare from sunken eyes," recorded a Northern newspaper correspondent, "tells that their kind services are all in vain." If those same eyes had the power to see the future, they would have looked ahead to 19 months of grim siege warfare before Charleston finally fell into Union hands.

BATTLE OF CHICKAMAUGA
September 19–20, 1863

Major General
William Rosecrans, USA

General
Braxton Bragg, CSA

More than 16,000 Federal and 18,000 Confederate soldiers fell at Chickamauga Creek, Georgia, during a great battle pitting Federal Major General William Rosecrans's army of 58,000 against Confederate General Braxton Bragg and his 66,000-man army. The Confederates failed to break through Federal lines on the first day of fighting, but a monumental blunder by Rosecrans the next day led to a Federal defeat. The Confederate victory stalled the Federal advance and boosted the morale of the Southern civilian population.

Throughout the morning of September 20, 1863, the second day of the Battle of Chickamauga, Federal Major General William Rosecrans had been shifting troops from the center and right of his line to support his hard-pressed left flank. At about 10:30 A.M., Rosecrans received startling news: An aide thought there was a gap in the center of the Federal line. His chief of staff, Brigadier General James A. Garfield, being occupied, Rosecrans dictated an order to another aide that would prove disastrous for his Army of the Cumberland.

Federal Brigadier General Thomas J. Wood's command was well-entrenched behind breastworks, awaiting an enemy attack, when Rosecrans's order arrived. "The general commanding directs you to close up on [Major General Joseph J. Reynold's division] as fast as possible, and support him." Wood read the order incredulously. He knew Rosecrans's aide

had been wrong in assuming a gap existed in the Federal line. Wood also knew that if he withdrew his two brigades, a large gap would indeed be created. But Wood had been stung that morning by a severe rebuke from Rosecrans for not moving his men fast enough in response to an order. He would not subject himself to such abuse again. Within 10 minutes Wood's division was abandoning its well-fortified position, creating a gaping hole in the Federal line. Unknown to either Rosecrans or Wood, the gap would shortly be struck by 11,000 Confederate infantrymen.

In the course of a few minutes, the fruits of a campaign that, since June 1863, had successfully maneuvered the Confederate Army of Tennessee out of two strong positions would seem lost. Union soldiers along the right flank of Rosecrans's line fled from their position along Chickamauga Creek, Georgia. The tables had been turned on the Union Army of the Cumberland.

After the Battle of Stones River, Tennessee, in January 1863, Rosecrans's 75,000-man Army of the Cumberland had settled at Murfreesboro, Tennessee, for a short winter respite. In the springtime, armies of both sides usually break winter camp and renew active campaigning, but Rosecrans's troops remained at their base in Murfreesboro. The Federal commander answered all appeals to move from the War Department in Washington with requests for more supplies, horses, and mules. Without these, Rosecrans reasoned, he could not wage a successful campaign against the enemy.

While Rosecrans bided his time in Murfreesboro, Confederate General Braxton Bragg's 40,000-man Army of Tennessee closely watched the Federals from a base at Tullahoma, Tennessee. Throughout the early months of

1863, Bragg was content to launch his excellent cavalry, 15,000 troopers led by Major General Joseph "Fighting Joe" Wheeler, against Rosecrans's lines of communication. The threat posed by the Confederate cavalry was the primary reason Rosecrans felt he could not launch a campaign without a sufficient number of troopers to meet the threat.

Finally in mid-June 1863, Rosecrans felt his army was ready to fight. Rosecrans deceived Bragg into thinking that the main Federal thrust would be against the Confederate left flank. In the meantime, three Federal corps passed far enough to the east to turn Bragg's right flank and cut the Confederates off from their base in Chattanooga. Rosecrans used the mountainous terrain and his rejuvenated cavalry command to his advantage and completely deceived his Confederate opponent. Bragg was forced to abandon Tullahoma on June 30. The Union army lost less than 600 soldiers; Confederate losses were never fully reported.

Rosecrans entered Tullahoma on July 3, 1863. At any other time, his success would have been hailed by the Northern press as a great victory. But it was eclipsed by the Federal victory at Gettysburg, Pennsylvania, on July 3, and the surrender of Vicksburg, Mississippi, on July 4. The proud Federal commander was sensitive to the neglect his success received by the authorities in Washington. On July 7, he received a remarkable dispatch from Secretary of War Edwin Stanton. "Lee's army overthrown; Grant victorious," Stanton wrote. "You and your noble army now have the chance to give the finishing blow to the rebellion. Will you neglect the chance?"

Rosecrans did not hesitate to express his dissatisfaction over this slight. "You do not appear to observe the fact that this noble army

has driven the rebels from Middle Tennessee. I beg in behalf of this army that the War Department may not overlook so great an event because it is not written in letters of blood."

While Rosecrans bickered with Washington over the extent of his success, Bragg's troops retreated to their base in Chattanooga and received reinforcements of more than 20,000 men. Strategically located and considered the gateway to the Deep South, Chattanooga was the most important junction for a series of railroads that linked the eastern Confederate states to the western. "If we can hold Chattanooga and Eastern Tennessee," President Abraham Lincoln wrote, "I think the rebellion must dwindle and die."

Rosecrans's advance stalled following the Tullahoma Campaign. The Federal commander responded to the War Department's orders to move by stating that before he could safely advance, he would need the repair of the Nashville & Chattanooga Railroad to the Tennessee River, corn that would not be ripe until August, and support for his flanks due to rumors that Confederate troops were coming to support Bragg.

Rosecrans began his advance August 16 when he learned that Major General Ambrose Burnside's Army of the Ohio—24,000 men—was poised to enter eastern Tennessee to capture Knoxville and protect the Army of the Cumberland's left flank. Rosecrans's plan was to cross the Tennessee River below Chattanooga, turn the Confederate left flank, and cut Bragg's lines of communication with Atlanta. Rosecrans sent a small force of infantry and cavalry to draw Bragg's attention to the north of Chattanooga while the main Federal force moved to the south. Because of the rugged, mountainous terrain around Chattanooga, Rosecrans thought

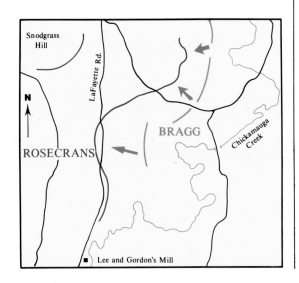

WILLIAM S. ROSECRANS

"With Rosecrans to lead, we think we can go anywhere in the Confederacy." The subordinate who wrote this comment was echoing the sentiments of most of the men in William S. Rosecrans's command. Another stated, "[I]f I was about to fight a battle for the dominion of the universe, I would give Rosecrans the command of as many men as he could see and who could see him."

"Old Rosy," as Rosecrans was affectionately nicknamed by his men, was born in Delaware County, Ohio, on September 6, 1819. Graduating in 1842 and ranking fifth in his West Point Class, Rosecrans entered the Corps of Engineers. Unlike many other Federal and Confederate general officers who gained valuable fighting experience in the Mexican War and various Indian wars before 1860, Rosecrans spent the years following his graduation from West Point stationed in the eastern United States. In 1854, he resigned from the Regular Army as a first lieutenant.

At the beginning of the Civil War, Rosecrans served as an aide to Federal Major General George B. McClellan. By the end of June 1861, he was appointed a brigadier general of the Regular Army. Rosecrans's first experience at independent command pitted him against Confederate General Robert E. Lee in the mountains of western Virginia. After driving the Confederates from that portion of Virginia, Rosecrans was transferred to the western theater in early 1862.

Rosecrans was appointed a major general on October 25, 1862, and given command of the Army of the Cumberland two days later. When the Confederates withdrew from Murfreesboro, Tennessee, after the Battle of Stones River, the stage was set for Rosecrans's successful Tullahoma and Chattanooga campaigns. But then came Chickamauga. While a master of strategy, Rosecrans's inability to seize the initiative on his greatest field of battle ultimately led to this devastating defeat.

Despite his previous successes, the Federal War Department's confidence in Rosecrans's ability to carry the war into the Deep South plummeted after his defeat at Chickamauga, Georgia, and the subsequent siege of his army at Chattanooga. Relieved of command by Major General Ulysses S. Grant on October 19, 1863, Rosecrans spent the remainder of the war in relative inactivity, commanding the Department of Missouri.

Lee and Gordon's Mill on Chickamauga Creek, where Federal General Thomas Crittenden was stationed. The failed Confederate attack there on September 12 was an indication of the general disagreement between Bragg and his subordinates.

he could successfully mask his move from the Confederates.

Rosecrans was correct in his assumption, for Bragg was easily deceived. Turning his attention north of town, Bragg left the river crossings to the south virtually undefended. By September 4, the majority of the Federal army had crossed the Tennessee and, unknown to Bragg, threatened the Confederate position from the rear. Once he discovered the Federal deception, Bragg realized his only recourse was to abandon Chattanooga. Although discouraged by their second major setback in little more than two months, Bragg's 60,000-man army executed an orderly withdrawal.

On September 9, thinking the Confederates were in disorganized retreat, Rosecrans sent three corps in pursuit. Major General Alexander McCook's corps was dispatched toward Alpine, Georgia. Major General Thomas Crittenden was to garrison Chattanooga with one brigade and pursue the Confederates with the rest of his corps. Major General George Thomas's corps was sent toward Trenton, Georgia. The flanks of these three columns were more than 40 miles apart across mountainous terrain; each column was separated from the others by a march of several days. Rosecrans was not concerned about the separation of his command, however, for Confederate deserters had brought in constant reports of Confederate disorganization and demoralization. But these deserters had been purposely sent by Bragg, who withdrew his army to LaFayette, Georgia, only about 25 miles south of Chattanooga. It would have been particularly distressful to Rosecrans had he known that Bragg's 60,000-man army was closer to each of the three Federal corps south of the Tennessee River than they were to each other.

When Bragg learned of Rosecrans's blunder, he decided to take advantage of it. Bragg planned to strike a portion of Thomas's corps on September 10, but Confederate Lieutenant General Daniel H. Hill and Major General Thomas C. Hindman failed to carry out Bragg's orders before the Federals withdrew back to the main column.

A second attempt by Bragg to attack an exposed Federal corps, this time Crittenden's on September 12, also failed because Confederate General Leonidas Polk failed to strike the outnumbered bluecoats near Lee and Gordon's Mill on Chickamauga Creek. Bragg blamed the failure of his subordinate commanders to carry out orders for these aborted attempts. But his junior officers blamed ambiguous orders from Bragg. They were "impossible orders," contended Hill, "and therefore those entrusted with their execution got in the way of disregarding them."

This disagreement between Bragg and his subordinates concerning the failed attacks of September 10 and 12 was certainly not the first occurrence of its type and would ultimately be a major contribution to Bragg's resignation from the command of the Army of Tennessee. "Bragg and his generals do not agree," noted Southern diarist Mary Chesnut. "I think a general worthless whose subalterns quarrel with him. Something is wrong about the man. Good generals are adored by their soldiers."

On September 11 Bragg learned that Confederate Lieutenant General James Longstreet, with about 12,000 men, was on his way to Georgia. These reinforcements had left Virginia on September 9. The distance Longstreet's force would have to travel was about 900 miles by railroad lines through Virginia, North Carolina, South Carolina, and Georgia. Even in the days before the war, the maze of short rail lines throughout the South was ill-equipped. By 1863, however, haphazard management, severe equipment shortages, and rolling stock taxed to the breaking point created a logistics problem that had to be overcome before Longstreet's men could reach Bragg. Miraculously, it took only nine days for the first group of Longstreet's troops, about 7000 men, to reach the Army of Tennessee. They arrived in time to take part in the opening stages of the Battle of Chickamauga on September 19.

By the evening of September 12, Rosecrans began to realize that he had been wrong about the condition of the Confederate command. Rather than disorganized and in a state of chaos, it was poised to destroy his divided command. The Federal commander issued orders to reunite his army. He brought the reserve corps of Major General Gordon Granger from Bridgeport, Alabama, to Chattanooga; he ordered Crittenden to remain near Lee and Gordon's Mill along Chickamauga Creek; and he instructed McCook's corps to move northward to join Thomas and these two corps were then to proceed north to unite with Crittenden. McCook chose to retrace his march over rugged terrain instead of taking a more direct route to Thomas. Thomas and McCook were not within supporting distance of Crittenden until the night of September 17, but that was soon enough to counter the strike Bragg aimed at Crittenden's isolated corps.

On September 14 Bragg devised a plan to cross Chickamauga Creek north of Lee and Gordon's Mill, pass around Crittenden's left flank, cutting off his lines of communication with Chattanooga, and then either smash the Federals along the creek or drive them back into the mountains of northern Georgia. He planned to launch his attack on the morning of September 18.

Although three brigades of Longstreet's corps arrived to reinforce Bragg's command, stiff opposition by Federal cavalry prevented the Confederates from crossing Chickamauga Creek until late afternoon on September 18. Throughout the night, Bragg's 66,000-man army crossed the meandering creek and maneuvered into position along the west bank. His right flank was anchored by Brigadier General Nathan B. Forrest's cavalry corps.

Realizing Bragg's force was close at hand, Rosecrans strengthened his line by deploying Thomas's corps to the left of Crittenden's and placing McCook's corps along the Federal right, a total of almost 58,000 men. Although the Confederate and Federal lines were only a few hundred yards apart at some points, the densely wooded terrain prevented the opposing commanders from discovering the other's position during the night of the 18th.

Federal General Thomas initiated the battle on the morning of the 19th. He sent a division forward to strike an enemy infantry brigade that the corps commander thought was isolated from the main Confederate line. Instead, the Federals struck Forrest's dismounted troopers. Throughout the morning, the fighting was primarily limited to the Federal left flank but by about 3:00 P.M. had spread the length of the Federal line. Bragg's troops repeatedly struck Rosecrans, hoping to capture the LaFayette Road, the main route to Chattanooga. At one point, the Confederates pierced the Federal center and thrust forward almost to Rosecrans's headquarters. But Union troops hit both Confederate flanks and drove the enemy back.

One Federal soldier described the fighting along the Union left flank: "The line in front of

Federal General George Thomas, the "Rock of Chickamauga," led a staunch defense on Snodgrass Hill.

These soldiers of Company A of the 9th Indiana Infantry fought with General Thomas on Snodgrass Hill. The brave stand of these and other troops under Thomas's command saved Rosecrans's army from complete destruction.

us stalks grimly into the smoke. Men cheer, but in that awful roar the voice of a man cannot be heard 10 feet away. Men fall to the right and left. The line stumbles over corpses as it hurries on. There are flashes in the smoke cloud, terrible explosions in the air, and men are stepped on or leaped over as they throw up their arms and fall upon the grass and scream in the agony of mortal wounds."

Bragg launched one more assault against the Federal left flank before dark, but the attack was beaten back. Neither side had gained an advantage by the fighting on the 19th. The sporadic manner in which Federal and Confederate units were sent into the battle showed that neither Rosecrans nor Bragg entered the fighting with an organized plan of battle. Both commanders were determined to correct that mistake before fighting resumed the next morning.

Rosecrans held a council of war on the evening of the 19th. He decided to tightly compress his six-mile-long line and ordered his subordinates to fortify the line throughout the night with breastworks.

Across the battle line, Bragg briefed Longstreet, who had finally arrived on the field that evening. Bragg decided that Longstreet's presence enabled him to divide his command into two wings. He placed Polk in command of the right and gave Longstreet the left. Bragg was determined to renew the fighting at dawn the next morning by opening the attack on the Federal left flank and then launching right to left each successive division against the Union line.

Contrary to Bragg's orders, however, the attack did not begin until after 9:30 A.M., another indication of the communication problems that existed throughout Bragg's command structure. Thomas's Federal soldiers

stood firm in the face of savage Confederate charges. Throughout the morning, Rosecrans shifted troops from his center and right to support his heavily engaged left flank. It was during the confusion of shifting troops along the Federal front that Rosecrans issued his fateful order to Brigadier General Thomas Wood, creating the large hole on the Federal right flank. At 11:00 A.M., 11,000 Confederates in Longstreet's line struck the gap, smashing the right portion of the Federal line. In the confusion McCook, Crittenden, and most of their two corps were driven from the field, leaving Thomas in command of the remnants of the Union army.

Bragg failed to take advantage of Longstreet's success, however, which gave Thomas time to compact his line by wrapping it around Snodgrass Hill. Throughout the afternoon, Thomas beat back Confederate attacks with infantry and artillery fire. His staunch defense during this stage of the battle led to his nickname: "Rock of Chickamauga." Finally, at about 6:00 P.M., Thomas began an orderly, fighting withdrawal from the field. By 8:00 P.M., Thomas's men were on their way to join Rosecrans in Chattanooga. More than 16,000 Federal and 18,000 Confederate casualties were left on the field after the two days of fighting.

Despite the heated objections of Longstreet and other subordinates, Bragg did not order a pursuit, a mistake that many later compared with the Confederate failure to follow up their success after the first Battle of Bull Run in 1861. Instead, Bragg chose to entrench around the Federal army at Chattanooga, Tennessee, placing Rosecrans's army under siege. This decision would prove fatal to the fortunes of Confederate efforts in the west.

BRAXTON BRAGG

"Bragg was a remarkably intelligent and well-informed man," Ulysses S. Grant once wrote of Braxton Bragg, "professionally and otherwise. He was also thoroughly upright. But he was possessed of an irascible temper and was naturally disputatious. A man of the highest moral character and the most correct habits, yet in the old army he was in frequent trouble. As a subordinate he was always on the lookout to catch his commanding officer infringing his prerogatives; as a post commander he was equally vigilant to detect the slightest neglect, even of the most trivial order."

Grant captured those peculiarities of Bragg's character that made it extremely difficult for the Confederate commander to form constructive relationships with peers and subordinates. Junior officers attempted to have him removed from command of the Confederate Army of Tennessee on more than one occasion. But if Bragg had one friend in the world, that person was Confederate President Jefferson Davis. Their friendship dated back to the Mexican War; Davis supported Bragg until it was absolutely impossible for the general to function any longer as an effective army commander.

A native of Warrenton, North Carolina, born on March 22, 1817, Bragg graduated from West Point in 1837. Serving as an artillery officer under the command of Zachary Taylor during the Mexican War, Bragg, along with Jefferson Davis, then a colonel of Mississippi militia, was recognized for his gallantry at the Battle of Buena Vista. He and Davis, although possessing similar temperaments that made it difficult for them to form close relationships with others, established a friendship that would last until Bragg's death in 1876.

At the start of the Civil War, Bragg was made a brigadier general in the Confederate Army. In September 1861, he was made a major general and served in General Albert S. Johnston's command in the western theater. Bragg replaced General Pierre G.T. Beauregard in June 1862 as the head of the Army of Tennessee.

Bragg resigned from the command of the Army of Tennessee following his devastating defeat at Chattanooga in November 1863. He transferred to Richmond, where he became the military adviser to Davis. Bragg held that post until General Robert E. Lee was appointed General in Chief of all Confederate armies in January 1865.

While Bragg demonstrated flashes of strategic brilliance as commander of the Army of Tennessee, particularly at Chickamauga, his terrible temper and incompetence as a leader ultimately led to his fall from command.

BATTLE OF CHATTANOOGA
November 23, 1863

Major General
Ulysses Grant, USA

General
Braxton Bragg, CSA

After his victory at Chickamauga, Confederate commander Braxton Bragg and 60,000 soldiers besieged Federal General William Rosecrans's 35,000 troops at Chattanooga, Tennessee. Rosecrans was prepared to abandon this vital town when Federal General Ulysses Grant replaced him with Major General George Thomas. Grant and Thomas then took steps to lift the siege. A light battle for Orchard Knob was a prelude to heavier fighting.

On the evening of October 19, 1863, Federal Major General Ulysses S. Grant found Secretary of War Edwin M. Stanton dressed in night clothes and anxiously pacing the floor of a Louisville, Kentucky hotel. Sniffling from a cold and mumbling something about no retreat, Stanton handed Grant a dispatch he had just received from an agent in Chattanooga. The message stated that unless someone stopped him, Union Major General William Rosecrans would withdraw his beleaguered army from that strategic southern Tennessee city. "A retreat must be prevented," barked Stanton.

Recently given command of the newly formed Military Division of the Mississippi, which included Chattanooga, Grant reacted immediately to the crisis. He relieved Rosecrans of command of the Army of the Cumberland and chose Major General George H. Thomas as Rosecrans's replacement. That same night Grant wired Thomas, "Hold Chattanooga at all hazards. I will be there as soon as possible."

The situation had become critical for the 35,000 Federal soldiers garrisoned in Chattanooga. Fleeing pell-mell from Chickamauga, Georgia, after the Union defeat there on September 19–20, 1863, Rosecrans's army found itself locked in the southern Tennessee city. With the rain-swollen Tennessee River to the north and west of Chattanooga and the 60,000-man Confederate Army of Tennessee under General Braxton Bragg strung out along the dominating heights south and east of the city, Rosecrans's army was effectively besieged. To the southwest, Lookout Mountain rose 1500 feet above the city. East and south of Chattanooga stood rugged Missionary Ridge, a long, 200- to 500-foot-high roadblock bristling with three tiers of Confederate infantry and artillery entrenchments.

By October 19, 1863, Rosecrans's army faced starvation. In the month since the fateful battle near Chickamauga Creek, the combination of

Confederate defenses and foul, rainy weather that made the few mountain roads nearly impassable had almost choked off supplies to the Federals at Chattanooga. Although the situation bordered on the critical, Thomas's reply to Grant's order to "hold Chattanooga at all hazards" was that he had seven days' worth of rations on hand and "I will hold the town till we starve."

While Stanton headed for Washington, D.C., Grant took a train to Stevenson, Alabama. From Stevenson, Grant took the rails northeast to Bridgeport, Alabama, where the tracks ended at the rubble of a Tennessee River bridge. At sunrise the next morning, Grant and a small escort set off cross-country on the final leg of his journey to Chattanooga. After a rugged two-day ride, Grant reached Thomas's headquarters in Chattanooga after dark on October 23, "wet, dirty and well," wrote Grant years later.

Efforts to restore the numerical strength and morale of the besieged army were already in progress when Grant arrived. By the last week in September 1863, 37,000 reinforcements were already en route to Chattanooga. These consisted of 17,000 troops led by Major General William Sherman and 20,000 men under Major General Joseph Hooker. All reinforcements were detained, however, at the railhead near Bridgeport, Alabama. "It would have been folly to send them to Chattanooga," Grant observed, "to help eat up the few rations left there."

A plan to open a new supply line to increase the flow of food, clothing, medical supplies, and ammunition to the besieged army had also been prepared upon Grant's arrival. Brainchild of Brigadier General William F. Smith, chief engineer of the Army of the Cumberland, the plan entailed opening a shorter, more direct trail to Chattanooga. Since the siege had started, Confederate cannons and sharpshooters had controlled all rails and roads leading into the city. The Confederates also commanded traffic

on the Tennessee River where it made a hairpin turn at the base of Lookout Mountain. Federal wagons, therefore, were forced to travel over a grueling 60- to 75-mile mountain path along steep, narrow roads north of the Tennessee River. Army supply wagons needed from eight to 20 days to cover the hazardous course—if they were lucky enough to survive the trip at all.

Smith's plan called for one Federal force to move eastward from Hooker's camp at Bridgeport while part of Thomas's army made an amphibious move westward from Chattanooga. Under cover of fog at dawn on October 22, the two Union forces struck and overwhelmed a weak Confederate force guarding the finger of land formed by the river's hairpin turn. The Federals then constructed a pontoon bridge over the river at Brown's Ferry, creating a land and water route between Bridgeport and Chattanooga well beyond the range of Confederate guns. The "Cracker Line"—so called for the army's staple food (hardtack) carried over it—was more than 40 miles shorter than the tortuous old route. Soon supplies and reinforcements began to accumulate in Chattanooga.

As the Union Army of the Cumberland recovered its strength and morale, Grant made plans to break the remaining Confederate hold on Chattanooga. Almost 60,000 Confederate troops on the heights around the city blocked a Union advance to the south or east. While awaiting the arrival of Sherman's 17,000 men— at that time still a two-weeks' march away— Grant made a careful reconnaissance of the entire front line, at times coming into personal contact with Confederate pickets. He soon issued attack orders to his generals but left out the specific hours and dates, pending weather conditions upon Sherman's appearance. "I have never felt such restlessness before," Grant confided, "as I have at the fixed and immovable condition of the Army of the Cumberland."

Confident that his mountaintop position at Chattanooga was impregnable, Bragg unwittingly aided Grant by detaching 20,000 Confederate troops under Lieutenant General James Longstreet to defeat Major General Ambrose Burnside's Union army at Knoxville in an attempt to reclaim east Tennessee. But Bragg's strategy backfired when Sherman arrived near Chattanooga on November 15. Grant now outnumbered Bragg by 20,000 men and went ahead with his plan of attack. Rains delayed assaults scheduled for November 21 and 22. Finally, spurred by reports that Bragg was retreating, Grant struck on the afternoon of November 23.

With Hooker securing his right flank west of Lookout Mountain and Sherman anchoring his left flank east of Chattanooga, Grant unleashed Thomas's "Cumberlanders" from the center of his line. "It was an inspiring sight," a witness noted. "Flags were flying...the bright sun lighting up ten thousand bayonets till they glistened and flashed." To the beat of drums, the blue-clad battle line advanced "with the steadiness of a machine." The objective of the attack was Orchard Knob, a low, wooded hill halfway between the town and Missionary Ridge. The fight was brief since a weak skirmish line was the only Confederate force on Orchard Knob. The Confederate main line just beyond was carried by the Federals with equal ease, and the whole fight ended after 45 minutes.

At the expense of only a few hundred casualties, Grant had expanded his perimeter a mile beyond his old line. In addition to this extra breathing room, Grant had also provided himself a convenient jump-off point for future attacks, which he began to plan the next day. The easy Union victory at Orchard Knob, however, was not likely to be repeated. Still ahead of the Federal army at Chattanooga loomed the forbidding peaks of Lookout Mountain and Missionary Ridge.

BATTLE OF LOOKOUT MOUNTAIN
November 24, 1863

Major General
Ulysses Grant, USA

General
Braxton Bragg, CSA

In a fight that took place literally above the clouds, Federal Major General Joseph Hooker led 10,000 men against 7000 of General Braxton Bragg's Confederate soldiers perched atop Lookout Mountain. Hooker's attack was part of a larger Federal plan to lift the siege of Chattanooga. Despite the misfire of several elements of the plan, Hooker succeeded in taking Lookout Mountain, losing about 500 men. The Confederates lost about 1200.

Confederate soldiers on the heights outside Chattanooga, Tennessee, had not seen anything like it for months. Some of the fellows even climbed from their trenches to get a better look. In full view, on the sun-splashed meadows below them, thousands of Union soldiers marched out of the city to the sound of drums and bugles. The bluecoats must be holding a grand review, guessed the curious Southerners who looked on at high noon, on November 23, 1863.

For almost two hours, the Federal soldiers continued to march and countermarch over the fields until they were arrayed in long, neat lines. At a given signal, the lines stepped forward with the precision of veterans on parade. The long blue lines steadily advanced. At another signal, the soldiers broke into a run; suddenly, the "grand review" had become a grand charge. The startled Confederate "spectators" tumbled back into their trenches and prepared to defend themselves. Soon, the blue wave engulfed the Confederate outpost on Orchard Knob Hill. Just 45 minutes later, Orchard Knob was in Union hands.

Confederate General Braxton Bragg's gray-coated soldiers manning the entrenchments on Lookout Mountain and Missionary Ridge watched their comrades on Orchard Knob in the valley below. After Orchard Knob fell, these soldiers knew it was only a matter of time before the blue waves rolled toward them.

After two months of relative inactivity, Major General Ulysses Grant, overall Union commander at Chattanooga, had seized the initiative. He wasn't about to let it go. Within hours of capturing Orchard Knob at the center of his line, Grant ordered an advance from his left flank. This movement was against Confederate forces on Missionary Ridge, east of Chattanooga. Grant also ordered an assault on Lookout Mountain, which towered over the city to the west.

Action on the Union left flank began at midnight on November 23–24. From staging areas on the north bank of the Tennessee River, Federal Major General William T. Sherman embarked his soldiers aboard pontoon boats. Sherman's troops had orders to establish a bridgehead across the river. "These orders were skillfully executed," Sherman wrote, "and by daylight of November 24, two divisions of about 8000 men were on the east [south] bank of the Tennessee."

Once over the river, the men immediately set about digging rifle pits. In the chilly darkness behind them, the first planks of a pontoon bridge were being laid. The bridge-building progressed under the personal direction of Brigadier General William F. Smith, the ingenious architect of Grant's "Cracker Line" that fed and clothed the army. "I doubt if the history of war can show a bridge of that extent [viz., 1350 feet]," praised Sherman, "laid down so noiselessly and well in so short a time." Using the pontoon bridge and a captured steamboat, the rest of Sherman's three divisions were across the river by noon of November 24.

By 3:30 P.M., Sherman had taken the crest of the hill without serious opposition. But, as he peered through the mist, Sherman was shocked to discover he was on the wrong slope. When he had studied maps of the area, Sherman had thought Missionary Ridge was a continuous rise, "but we found ourselves," Sherman later wrote, "on two high points, with a deep depression between us." The next hill over was his actual target. Deciding there was not enough daylight left to attack the adjacent hill, Sherman fortified this position.

On Grant's far right flank, west of Lookout Mountain, action had commenced about 8:00 A.M. on November 24. Packing rations for one day and 60 rounds of rifle ammunition per man, the first of Major General Joseph Hooker's

three divisions advanced toward the base of the 1500-foot height. "[I]ts high palisaded crest; and its steep, rugged, rocky, and deeply-furrowed slopes," Hooker wrote of the mountain, "presented an imposing barrier to our advance."

Approaching from the west, Lookout Mountain was accessible by only three narrow paths that required single-file passage. To avoid these three suicidal trails, Hooker was ordered to skirt the northern tip of the mountain via the lesser slopes along the Tennessee River. Hooker's goal was to outflank Confederate earthworks defending the valley between Lookout Mountain and Missionary Ridge. The maneuver would force the 7000 Confederates off Lookout's crest to prevent being cut off from the rest of Bragg's army.

Hooker's 10,000 men advanced in two wings. One reinforced division on Hooker's right flank advanced halfway up the western slope of Lookout Mountain and then swung to the north. Harassed by Confederate skirmishers in front and peppered by riflemen sheltered by the natural rock parapets above, the Union soldiers pressed ahead. "The men were full of animation and enthusiasm," a Federal officer wrote, "regardless of the active work of the sharpshooters."

Hooker's other two divisions struck directly at the river-bank passage from the west. Battling Confederate skirmishers every step of the way, these two wings formed a juncture on the northern slope of Lookout Mountain around noon. This new line covered about a half mile, from the river's edge up to a fortified plateau of land on the middle of the north slope. Here, around a frame dwelling called the Craven House, Hooker's men battled furiously with Confederate infantry who blocked the pass. "A dense cloud had settled on the side of the mountain," recalled a Confederate defender, "so dense a man could not be seen twenty paces away." With the fog came a lull in the action.

But artillery, revealed by powder-flash and the noise of explosions, dueled on despite the fog cover. Confederate cannons posted on the summit of Lookout Mountain, however, could not lower their muzzles enough to provide direct artillery support to Confederate troops below. Instead, the gray gunners contented themselves with long-distance counter battery fire. On the other hand, Union gunners siting from heights west and north of Lookout Mountain, punished Confederate lines. One Confederate soldier recalled a Union airburst above his regiment's campsite at mealtime. The blast plunged shell fragments into his camp chest, "sending our dishes and dinner hell-west-and-winding." Shots like this wreaked havoc on and behind Confederate lines all afternoon.

Infantry action resumed when the fog diminished. Hooker launched charge after charge against Confederate breastworks. By 1:30 P.M., Union troops had forced the Confederates back to their second line, 400 yards east of Craven House. Here, the graycoats were reinforced by units that had made their way downhill from atop Lookout Mountain. But these support troops were too little too late. With their ammunition dwindling and the odds heavily against them, the Confederate soldiers prepared to evacuate Lookout Mountain. "The mountain was held until 2 o'clock the next morning [November 25]," recalled a Confederate officer, "and the troops, artillery and trains were withdrawn."

The Battle of Lookout Mountain—or "The Battle Above the Clouds" as it was styled by Northern newspapers—was over. Federal losses numbered close to 500 men while the Confederates lost more than 1200, including about 1000 captured. Making their way across the dark valley, the Confederate troops joined their comrades on Missionary Ridge.

BATTLE OF MISSIONARY RIDGE

November 25, 1863

Major General
Ulysses Grant, USA

General
Braxton Bragg, CSA

Confederate General Braxton Bragg rallied his troops along Missionary Ridge before dawn on November 25, preparing for the attack to come. The Federal assault, conducted by Federal General Ulysses Grant, eventually hit Bragg's center and flanks. Bragg was driven from the ridge, and Chattanooga, an important transportation center and the doorway to the heart of the Confederacy, was securely in Union hands.

After sundown on November 24, the clouds above Chattanooga, Tennessee, rolled away and temperatures dropped sharply. The orderly outside a Federal staff officer's tent, however, tapped so insistently that the officer finally left his warm shelter to see what was the matter. What the officer saw upon the distant, darkened mountain was worth the intrusion. "[T]here on the side of 'Lookout' like a thousand fire flies," he later wrote to a friend, "the skirmishers were at it—cr-r-ack—cr-r-ack—flash after flash.... All hands enjoyed this work of death until midnight.... By daylight the brave old flag was once more floating from the top peak of Lookout Mountain." This midnight skirmish was the Confederacy's last gasp on the mountain. By morning, only Missionary Ridge remained in Confederate hands.

At his headquarters on Orchard Knob, located about a mile northwest of Missionary Ridge, Major General Ulysses Grant rose early on November 25 to direct the final battle for Chattanooga. Unlike the previous day, the morning dawned clear and bright.

Four miles north of Grant, Union Major General William T. Sherman prepared his three divisions to renew the attack on the north end of Missionary Ridge. Five miles south of Grant, Major General Joseph Hooker reorganized his veterans after capturing Lookout Mountain. Hooker's assignment on November 25 was to advance from the mountain across the valley leading to the south end of Missionary Ridge. While Sherman pounded Bragg's right flank, Hooker was to strike the Confederate left flank. Poised near Orchard Knob, at the middle of Grant's line, Union Major General George H. Thomas's Army of the Cumberland was directed to wait for orders from Grant to attack.

Sherman moved first, sending out a strong skirmish line at dawn. The main attack began about 10:00 A.M. In two long battle lines, Sherman's troops marched down the hill they occupied, crossed a shallow valley, and began to climb the steep, timbered slope to the Confederate position. Sherman later recalled, "the hill was held by the enemy with a breastwork of logs and fresh earth, filled with men and two guns." But this was only the enemy's first line of defense. A still higher hill, just behind the first, was also heavily defended by Confederate infantry and artillery.

Long-range Confederate cannon fire hit Sherman's men as they tramped over the rough no-mans-land between the opposing hilltops. As the Federals closed in, Confederate cannoneers opened fire with canister—artillery ammunition having the effect of a giant shotgun blast—"but still the enemy advanced," wrote 35-year-old Irish-born Confederate Major General Patrick Cleburne. An aggressive division commander, Cleburne—whom Confederate General Robert E. Lee likened to "a meteor shooting from a clouded sky"—then waited until the Federals reached within 50 steps of his line. At that distance, Cleburne poured on a heavy volley of artillery and rifle fire before leading a savage counterattack. Fighting raged hand-to-hand over the rugged slope until Sherman's men fled to cover. Sherman renewed his assault time and again throughout the morning and afternoon but with the same bloody result.

Frustrated by Sherman's repeated failures to crush the Confederate right, Grant pinned his hopes on Hooker's blue-clad ranks advancing on the Confederate left flank. "The appearance of Hooker's column," Grant wrote, "was at this time anxiously looked for and momentarily expected." Hooker left two regiments to hold Lookout Mountain and marched toward Missionary Ridge at 10:00 A.M. on November 25. A two-mile journey brought the bluecoats to the banks of Chattanooga Creek, where they halted. "[I]t was discovered," Hooker wrote, "that the enemy had destroyed the bridge, and, in consequence, our pursuit was delayed nearly three hours." Grant claimed Hooker was delayed closer to four hours by the missing bridge.

Without Hooker's support, the commanding general began to fear for Sherman's safety. Grant had intended Hooker's attack on the Confederate left flank to tie down Confederate troops, preventing Bragg from sending reinforcements to oppose Sherman. Grant had also intended Hooker's arrival at Missionary Ridge "as the signal for storming the ridge in the center with strong columns." Thomas, standing with Grant on Orchard Knob, merely awaited Grant's signal to unleash his army at the core of the Confederate defenses.

Realizing that Sherman's condition was getting more critical as the day wore on, Grant decided at about 2:00 P.M. to send in Thomas before Hooker appeared. Grant's order to attack, however, failed to reach the division commanders responsible for leading the assault. Grant had to repeat the order an hour later before anyone budged. Finally, at about 4:00 P.M., six Union cannons were fired in rapid succession to signal the advance.

Before the smoke from the signal guns had cleared, the Federal assault troops were moving forward. "Fifteen to twenty thousand men," recalled a Union lieutenant in the charge, "in well-aligned formation, with colors waving in the breeze, almost shaking the earth with their cadenced tread... move to battle."

The Federal troops were barely away from their start line when Confederate cannon fire erupted along the length of the ridge. Confederate rifle fire added to the din as the Federal soldiers neared the first line of defense at the base of Missionary Ridge. "A terrific cheer rolls along the line," wrote the Union lieutenant. "The quick step has been changed to the 'double quick.' Another cheer, and the enemy's first line of works...is ours."

Still under intense Confederate fire from higher up the slopes, the massive Union battle lines quickly regrouped at the foot of the ridge and surged upward. In his memoirs, Grant recorded how, "our troops went to the second line of works; over that and on for the crest." Confederate fire was fierce but generally inaccurate. Afraid of hitting their own men who were retreating from the first two Confederate lines, Bragg's troops on the crest fired too high. Many Confederate soldiers, caught in the cross fire between the lines, surrendered.

The trim Federal battle lines lost any semblance of order as the onslaught continued uphill. "Officers caught the enthusiasm of the men," Federal General Gordon Granger wrote, "and the men in turn were cheered by the officers. Each regiment tried to surpass the other in fighting its way up....[E]ach tried first to plant its flag on the summit."

Hooker, finally free of the water barrier, hit Bragg's left flank just as Thomas's men began to plant their banners on the crest of Missionary Ridge. Bragg, pressured by Sherman on his right flank and Hooker on his left, watched helplessly as the center of his line crumbled. "Having secured much of our artillery," Bragg wrote, "they soon availed themselves of our panic, and turning our guns upon...the lines, both right and left, rendered them entirely untenable."

Bragg himself barely escaped capture as his army fled Missionary Ridge. Almost 6700 Confederate casualties lay on the slopes of Missionary Ridge after this last battle. Federal losses amounted to nearly 6000. Later, Bragg regrouped his shattered units and led them into northern Georgia for the winter.

ASSAULT ON FORT SANDERS
(FORT LOUDON)
November 29, 1863

Major General
Ambrose Burnside, USA

Lieutenant General
James Longstreet, CSA

Fort Sanders was held by 500 men of Major General Ambrose Burnside's Federal Army of the Ohio. Confederate Lieutenant General James Longstreet launched a 3000-man assault to regain this vital link in the defenses of Knoxville, Tennessee. Meeting only temporary success in piercing the defenses of the fort, the Confederates were repulsed, losing about 800 men. The Federals suffered only 12 casualties. Knoxville and most of eastern Tennessee remained firmly in Union hands.

The powder flash of artillery bursts illuminated the sky over Fort Sanders, and the roar of cannon fire echoed through the hills surrounding the east Tennessee city of Knoxville. It was just after 6:00 A.M. on November 29, 1863. The sudden gunfire signaled the start of a ferocious Confederate barrage aimed at the fort, one link in the chain of defenses located northeast of the besieged city. Crouching in the bitter chill darkness a mere 150 yards away from the 500-man Union garrison, 3000 Confederate infantrymen awaited the order to attack. Federals had been holding Knoxville for almost three months, and these Confederates were determined to drive them away.

A vital Southern railroad and supply hub, Knoxville was Federal Major General Ambrose Burnside's primary target when he had led his 12,000-man Army of the Ohio into east Tennessee in early fall 1863. Union sentiment ran high in that mountainous section of the state, and Burnside's campaign was designed to wrest control of the loyal region from Confederate hands. Another objective of the operation was to cut the direct railroad connection between Virginia and Tennessee. This would force the flow of Confederate supplies and reinforcements to shift to more circuitous routes, along frail rail lines already pushed to the breaking point.

Thus, the Union celebrated Burnside's relatively bloodless occupation of Knoxville on September 2, 1863. From this base, Burnside's army helped support Union Major General William Rosecrans's campaign in middle Tennessee and posed a potential threat to Confederate General Robert E. Lee's Army of Northern Virginia.

To counter Burnside's success, Confederate Lieutenant General Braxton Bragg looked to Lieutenant General James Longstreet, on loan from Lee to Bragg's Army of Tennessee. Bragg dispatched Longstreet and 20,000 men to reinforce a small Confederate force under Major General Simon Buckner, who was already sparring with Burnside outside Knoxville. When the larger Confederate force approached in early November, Burnside withdrew into the fortifications around the city.

Located on the north bank of the Holston River, Knoxville was protected by a line of works constructed by the Confederates early in the war. Burnside improved and expanded these fortifications. The linchpin in the defensive perimeter was Fort Loudon, a three-sided structure of earth and timber that faced roughly southwest, anchoring the right flank of the defenses. In addition to its 500-man garrison of New York, Massachusetts, and Michigan soldiers, 12 cannons were positioned at embrasures cut into the fort's thick, earthen walls.

Positioned on a hill overlooking Knoxville, Fort Loudon's walls sloped down sharply for 15 feet to a ditch surrounding the fort. The ditch was 12 feet wide with vertical walls cut to an average depth of eight feet. Beyond it, the open ground sloped gently to the west, where only stumps remained of the trees that had once stood there. To take advantage of the landscape, telegraph wire had been stretched between the stumps and stakes, creating web-like entanglements to hamper assaults. Various spiked wooden obstructions also dotted the terrain around Fort Loudon to vex attackers.

The fort was renamed Fort Sanders in honor of Federal Brigadier General William P.

Sanders, who was mortally wounded on November 18 while his cavalry command fought a desperate delaying action against Longstreet's approaching Confederates. Under wet and foggy skies 10 days later, a sharp but limited attack drove Federal pickets back to their main line, and Confederate troops took up positions within 150 yards of Fort Sanders.

The main blow fell on Fort Sanders early on the morning of November 29, after a brief but fearsome artillery barrage. In darkness, over frozen ground, three Confederate brigades of Mississippi and Georgia troops raised the Rebel Yell and attacked the fort, advancing with fixed bayonets. The Confederates were only slightly slowed by the obstacles across the landscape, but a hail of minnie balls and canister from inside the fort felled many. The real slaughter, however, began when the Confederates reached the outer ditch. Facing nearly vertical walls and without ladders, the Confederates resorted to lifting one another onto the steep parapets and clawing their way up the slippery walls. Soon the battle flags of the 13th and 17th Mississippi Infantry and the 16th Georgia Infantry dotted the crest. Some fearless Confederate soldiers, singly and in small groups, actually penetrated the fort.

Private Joe Manning of the 29th Massachusetts Volunteer Infantry was in the fort when the Confederates struck. "The rebel infantry poured in upon us," recalled Manning, "scaling the parapet and climbing through the embrasures, but as fast as they did so, we shot them down, and they rolled back into the ditch." As the Confederates rallied to their flags, they were either killed or captured. Their flags were also taken, including the banner of the

16th Georgia, seized by Private Manning, an act for which he earned the Medal of Honor.

Meanwhile, the growing mass of Confederates huddled in the ditch was subjected to a deadly flank fire from triple-shotted guns trained to sweep the defile. One Federal lieutenant even transformed cannon shells into hand grenades by lighting the fuses and tossing them from the crest of the parapet into the crowded ditch. "It stilled them down there," he said.

An attempt to reinforce the attackers with another brigade proved futile, and a general withdrawal commenced among the troops outside the ditch. But the orderly retreat soon degenerated into an ugly rout as Federal troops mercilessly raked the fleeing Confederates.

For the ill-fated soldiers stuck in the ditch, the war ended abruptly in bloodshed or surrender. About 200 unwounded men emerged from the ditch, bound for Union prisoner of war camps. Longstreet's brigades suffered 813 casualties—129 killed, 458 wounded, and 226 captured. In stark contrast, of the 440 Federals in Fort Sanders actively engaged in the fight, only eight were killed and four wounded.

The end of Longstreet's assault on Fort Sanders also marked the close of his campaign to retake Knoxville, preserving east Tennessee for the Union. While casualties were still being removed from the battleground, the Confederate commander received orders to withdraw from Knoxville in the wake of Confederate General Braxton Bragg's decisive defeat at Chattanooga several days earlier. Accordingly, on the chill winter night of December 3, Longstreet's bloodied columns headed northeast toward Virginia along muddy roads to rejoin Robert E. Lee's command and prepare for the spring campaign.

BATTLE OF OLUSTEE
(OCEAN POND)
February 20, 1864

Brigadier General
Truman Seymour, USA

Brigadier General
Joseph Finegan, CSA

Federal Brigadier General Truman Seymour was advancing with 5500 soldiers across the Florida Peninsula, hoping to cut Florida from the Confederacy. Confederate Brigadier General Joseph Finegan blocked his path at Olustee with 5000 troops. These forces clashed on February 20, 1864, in the only major engagement fought in Florida. The Federals were driven from the field with more than 1800 casualties; Finegan lost 900. This was the last major Federal attempt to gain control of Florida.

Soon after artillery and musket fire erupted about a mile away, wounded Federal soldiers began to appear at the field hospital set up in the shade of some stately Southern pine trees. Some of the wounded soldiers walked to the aid station; others were carried there on stretchers. The most severely wounded arrived in open ambulance wagons. They came "in single drops," recalled the chief surgeon, "then trickling, after a while in a steady stream, increasing from a single row to a double and treble, and finally into a mass."

For three hours, casualties mounted while the battle near Olustee, Florida, raged through the afternoon of February 20, 1864. Suddenly, "we heard from the front three lusty cheers and the firing ceased abruptly," wrote the chief surgeon. The eyes of wounded and doctors alike turned toward the silence for some sign of the battle's outcome.

The Battle of Olustee ended the only major military campaign waged in Florida during the Civil War. Led by Federal Brigadier General Truman Seymour, 5500 Federal troops had landed at Jacksonville, Florida, on February 7, 1864. Composed of three infantry brigades, including three regiments of black troops, a small brigade of cavalry, and 16 cannons, Seymour's force moved against Confederate defenses the next day.

Seymour had come to Florida to battle Confederate troops. But his small Union army was there for political as well as military reasons. President Lincoln's Proclamation of Amnesty and Reconstruction offered the possibility of statehood to Confederate states. This made Florida a potential source of votes for Lincoln and his opponents within the Republican party.

A Federal military invasion of Florida rested on the shoulders of Major General Quincy A. Gillmore, commander of the Department of the South. "I am expected to initiate, guide, and control such measures as may be necessary under the Presidential Proclamation," wrote Gillmore, "to restore the State of Florida to its allegiance." Accordingly, on February 5, from his base at Hilton Head, South Carolina, Gillmore placed Seymour's forces aboard ships for the voyage to Jacksonville.

Political motivations aside, sound military reasons to invade Florida did exist. Florida was an important source of beef and other supplies to the Confederacy. Great demand was placed on Florida's resources to fill food needs throughout the Confederacy. By invading Florida, Gillmore also wanted to "recruit my colored regiments and organize a regiment of Florida white troops."

To achieve his military goals in Florida, Gillmore planned to secure control of the Florida, Atlantic & Gulf Railroad, which ran west from Jacksonville across the northern end of the state. With this railroad and several key river crossings in his hands, Gillmore hoped to cut Florida off from the rest of the Confederacy.

On February 7, Federal General Truman Seymour landed with 5500 troops at Jacksonville against very light resistance and began marching west along the rail line. Opposing Seymour's advance were only about 2500 Confederate soldiers commanded by Brigadier General Joseph Finegan. Outnumbered more than two to one, Finegan sent a call out to neighboring states for reinforcements. While waiting for these reinforcements to arrive, Finegan's troops skirmished with Seymour's columns, slowing the Federal advance. "I will act cautiously until the plans of the enemy are more fully developed," Finegan wrote to Confederate authorities in Richmond.

While Finegan acted with caution, Union General Seymour did not. At first Seymour was hesitant to advance from Jacksonville—perhaps because of the exaggerated reports of Confederate strength. "This movement is in opposition to sound strategy," Federal General Gillmore wrote Seymour on February 11. "By all means, therefore, fall back to Jacksonville."

Just six days later, Seymour informed Gillmore that he had advanced well beyond the point designated in his original orders. Gillmore immediately sent Seymour a heated reply. "Your project," Gillmore wrote, "involves your command in a distant movement, without provisions, far beyond a point from which you once withdrew....It is impossible for me to determine what your views are with respect to Florida." It was also too late for Gillmore to stop Seymour's unauthorized advance.

On a clear, warm afternoon on February 20, 1864, Seymour ran head-on into Finegan's army. With 5000 men, including reinforcements from Georgia and the Carolinas, Finegan blocked Seymour's passage near Olustee, Florida. Located about 50 miles west of Jacksonville, Olustee was a small rail station set amid open pine barrens along the Florida, Atlantic & Gulf Railroad. The ground was flat and swampy.

Union and Confederate cavalry pickets opened the action while infantry and artillery battle lines deployed in the fields north of the rail tracks. Meanwhile, behind the Union line, Chief Surgeon Adolph Majer had his staff prepare "their instruments and appliances" in readiness for the wounded. About 3:00 P.M. Seymour flung his infantry at Finegan's line.

Hitting the Confederates with artillery and infantry fire in front, Seymour attempted to attack the Confederate left flank. Finegan shifted men to meet this Union threat and then ordered an advance of his own on the Federal center. Here a combination of confusing orders to raw Union troops resulted in chaos. "All semblance of organization was lost in a few moments," wrote a Federal officer. Small pockets of resistance held off the Confederates long enough for a Union regiment, the 8th U.S. Colored Infantry, to reinforce the broken line. Although never before in battle, the 8th stood firm for two hours "and to the best of their ability returned a fire which killed and wounded over half their number," observed a witness to the fighting. The 8th retreated only after its colonel was killed, the second officer in command was wounded, and three flag bearers were shot down. Low on ammunition, the Confederates were not able to follow up the Federal withdrawal.

Seymour replaced the 8th U.S. Colored Infantry regiment with the 54th Massachusetts Infantry, another black unit, and advanced again. "[I]n the hope of still effecting my original intention," Seymour recalled, "the First North Carolina [Union] was brought up." In the face of these Federal attacks, the Confederate line still held. The Confederates, meanwhile, had received more ammunition and proceeded to counterattack.

It was the beginning of the end for Seymour. The 1st North Carolina had been his last reserve. When the Confederates hit, according to observers, "with great vigor," the whole Federal line gave way. "Here all joined in the loud and defiant cheers which, started by the general," recalled one of Seymour's infantry officers, "rang along the whole line of our army, and showed that though defeated we were not routed or broken in spirit." These were the "lusty cheers" heard by Union Surgeon Majer and his patients.

By evening, Seymour was in full retreat toward Jacksonville, having lost 1861 men. Finegan had suffered 946 casualties. Although Jacksonville remained in Union hands, Florida remained part of the Confederacy.

THE FORT PILLOW MASSACRE
April 12, 1864

Major Lionel Booth, USA

Major General Nathan Forrest, CSA

Confederate Major General Nathan Forrest and 1500 of his cavalry attacked the Federal stronghold of Fort Pillow, defended by 557 Federals, including 262 black soldiers, under Major Lionel Booth. After several hours of intense fighting, the Confederates captured the fort. Charges soon arose that the Confederates had slaughtered many unarmed defenders as they attempted to surrender. The name of the fort became a rallying cry for the Federals.

The surrender ultimatum reached Federal Major William F. Bradford, commander of the Union garrison at Fort Pillow, Tennessee, under a flag of truce shortly after 3:00 P.M. on April 12, 1864. "Should my demand be refused," read the message from Confederate Major General Nathan Bedford Forrest, "I cannot be responsible for the fate of your command."

The presence of several Federal boats on the nearby Mississippi River within sight of the Confederate position, including a steamer "apparently crowded with troops"—possibly destined to reinforce the besieged Federal stronghold—prompted Forrest to give Bradford only 20 minutes to make up his mind. "If at the expiration of that time the Fort is not surrendered, I shall assault it," Forrest warned.

Two days earlier, Forrest embarked with his division from Jackson, Mississippi, on a raiding expedition aimed at Union operations in Tennessee and Kentucky. Fort Pillow was on his target list since, as he observed, "they have horses and supplies which we need."

Fort Pillow was originally a Confederate stronghold constructed early in the war. It was located about 40 miles north of Memphis, Tennessee, and sat on high bluffs overlooking the east bank of the Mississippi. Fort Pillow had a length of 125 yards and was enclosed on three sides by a moat six feet deep and 12 feet wide. The fort's packed dirt walls were four feet thick at the top and eight feet at ground level. Six cannons were mounted at embrasures cut into the walls. Rifle pits comprised an outer line of defense for the fort. The primary role of this Federal bastion was to protect navigation along the Mississippi River.

In spring 1864, Fort Pillow was garrisoned by 557 Federal troops, commanded by Major Lionel F. Booth. This force included 262 black soldiers of the 11th U.S. Colored Troops (6th U.S. Colored Artillery); Battery F, U.S. Colored Light Artillery; and 295 white soldiers of Major

Bradford's battalion of the 13th Tennessee Cavalry, enlisted from among the Unionist population of east Tennessee. Supporting the fort from the river was the U.S. Navy tin-clad gunboat *New Era*.

In the predawn darkness of April 12, 1864, 1500 hard-riding, veteran Confederate cavalrymen of General Forrest's command galloped up to the perimeter of Fort Pillow. Under the immediate leadership of Confederate Brigadier General James R. Chalmers—while Forrest raced from another mission to rejoin his command—the Confederates drove the Federal pickets back to the main line while dismounted sharpshooters fired into the fort from a series of low hills. Sheltered behind stumps and logs, the Confederate riflemen opened a desultory long-range firefight with the Union defenders that lasted into midmorning. At about 9:00 A.M. Federal Major Booth was killed by a sniper's bullet, and garrison command devolved on Major Bradford. Forrest arrived at 10:00 A.M. and reassumed control of his Confederate forces.

The aggressive Confederate leader was quick to act. His trained eye spotted weaknesses in Federal defenses, and Forrest maneuvered his soldiers to positions from which they could attack Fort Pillow without being exposed to counterfire from the garrison or the gunboat *New Era*. In fact, the construction of the fort itself worked to Forrest's advantage. In the words of a Confederate observer, "The width or thickness of the works across the top prevented the garrison from firing down on us, as it could only be done by mounting and exposing themselves to the unerring fire of our sharpshooters."

Another Confederate advantage was that Federal artillerists could not aim their guns low enough to blast attackers at close range. As the Confederate observer summed up, "we were as well fortified as they were; the only difference was that they were on one side and we were on the other of the same fortification." Forrest's

dispositions also protected his men from the heavy guns of the *New Era*.

At 11:00 A.M. General Forrest launched a general assault on the fort that netted him the barracks compound just south of the earthworks. From that position, Forrest's riflemen delivered a blistering fire at the fort's interior. During these actions, Forrest had three horses shot from beneath him, but he himself escaped serious injury.

The steady exchange of gunfire through the morning and early afternoon began to tell on the ammunition supplies of both sides. At 1:00 P.M. the *New Era*, its supply of canister and shrapnel shot exhausted, steered away from Fort Pillow to a resupply point down river. At about the same time Confederate fire slackened as their ammunition diminished and a resupply train failed to arrive. When the train finally reached the Confederate position at about 3:00 P.M., Forrest completed preparations for another attack and delivered his surrender ultimatum to Major Bradford.

While some members of the garrison confidently shouted taunts and profanities at their enemies, Bradford issued this succinct reply, "I will not surrender."

The end came swift and hard. As Confederate sharpshooters on the knolls outside the fort kept up a deadly cover fire, the bulk of Forrest's dismounted troopers lunged forward to attack the main fortification. Leaping into the ditch around the fort, the brawnier men hoisted comrades onto the steep earth walls. Virtually unexposed to Union fire in this position, the Confederates rallied at the foot of the parapets and then swarmed en masse up and over the embankments. Inside the fort, Federal defenders resisted against overwhelming odds. Except for scattered pockets of hand-to-hand combat, the Federal defense within the fort collapsed after a brief melee. The tumult spread beyond the confines of Fort Pillow as surviving bluecoats

broke and raced for the bluffs leading down to the landing at the river's edge. Like a blue wave, the Federals spilled down the slope.

From the bluffs above the landing, Forrest's men poured volley after volley into the fugitives below. As the fleeing Federals descended the cliff, their ranks were also torn by cross fire from Confederate units that had been shifted earlier into positions along the riverbank. Some desperate Federals dove into the water, only to drown or become easy targets for Confederate marksmen. Some tried to rescale the sheer face of the bluff, once again exposing themselves to Confederate rifles. Other Federals dropped their weapons and raised their arms in surrender.

At this point in the fight, a controversy arose that still rages today. Some Federal soldiers claimed that black soldiers attempting to surrender were gunned down in cold blood and that both black and white wounded Union soldiers were shot and killed where they lay, until Forrest and others managed to put an end to the killing. Confederates claimed that the losses were inflicted during the Federal retreat to the riverbank *before* any surrender signals were raised. Some Confederates also claimed that many of the blacks picked up weapons and attempted to fight after they had surrendered.

There are many unsubstantiated accounts of additional atrocities. Certainly racial and sectional animosities stirred the passions of Forrest's victorious Confederates. The lopsided casualty lists are evidence for legitimate concern about what transpired at Fort Pillow. While Confederate losses amounted to 14 killed and 86 wounded, the Federals tallied 231 killed, 100 wounded, and 226 captured. Only 58 of the 262 black soldiers engaged were taken prisoner.

Was there a massacre at Fort Pillow on April 12, 1864? The truth concerning what really happened that bitter spring afternoon atop the steep bluffs along the Mississippi remains as elusive today as it was more than a century ago.

BATTLE OF THE WILDERNESS
May 5-6, 1864

**Lieutenant General
Ulysses Grant, USA**

**General
Robert E. Lee, CSA**

Lieutenant General Ulysses S. Grant, General in Chief of all Federal armies, led more than 120,000 troops into an area of Virginia called the Wilderness, attempting to pass around the right flank of Confederate General Robert E. Lee's 66,000-man army. Lee struck the Federals in the thick underbrush, neutralizing Grant's manpower advantage. Two days later, some 17,600 Federal and more than 7500 Confederate troops were casualties. This was the first action in an 11-month campaign that would only end with Lee's surrender.

A Union officer and his 13-year-old son arrived in Washington, D.C., by rail on March 8, 1864. No one met the pair at the railroad station, so they made their way alone to Willard's Hotel.

Upon entering the hotel, the man and his son attracted no special attention. Many officers had passed through the inn's doors during the past three years. Even the man's major general status did little to set him apart from all the others. He was, as one bystander observed, an "ordinary, scrubby looking man with a slightly seedy look, as if he was out of office on half pay; he had no gait, no station, no manner."

However, once he signed his name to the register, "U.S. Grant and Son, Galena, Illinois," he became the major focus of attention of everyone lounging in the hotel's lobby. To most Northern citizens, the initials "U.S." were better

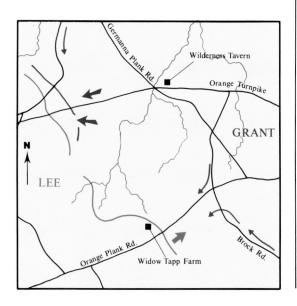

associated with the surrender terms Ulysses Simpson Grant had given to Confederate Brigadier General Simon B. Buckner upon the capture of Fort Donelson, Tennessee, in February 1862: "unconditional surrender."

During the two years since his capture of Fort Donelson, Grant's star had continually risen as his victory count in the western theater increased. Federal victories at Shiloh, Tennessee; Vicksburg, Mississippi; and Chattanooga, Tennessee, were evidence of Grant's successful ability to command and fight. By the time he arrived in Washington in March 1864, he was the most celebrated military personality in the North.

Grant's success in the west convinced President Abraham Lincoln that he had finally found the man with the strength of character to deliver the deathblow to the Confederacy. To better equip Grant for the task at hand, Lincoln, with the approval of Congress, appointed him to the rank of Lieutenant General of the Regular Army. In the past, this grade had been held only by the likes of George Washington and Winfield Scott. The President then named Grant General in Chief of all Federal armies. With his arrival on March 8, the new lieutenant general was making his first trip to the capital to officially assume his new responsibilities.

Grant left the capital for Cincinnati, Ohio, a little more than a week after his arrival. In Cincinnati, Grant met with Major General William T. Sherman, his closest confidant and the man Grant chose to replace himself as commander of Federal forces in the western theater. During this visit with Sherman, Grant began to develop his plan to strangle the life from the Confederacy. Grant understood that the Confederates were using their internal lines of communication to their greatest advantage by shifting troops and resources to the most

threatened areas while fighting holding actions on the other fronts. "Before this time," Grant later stated, "these various [Union] armies had acted separately and independently of each other, giving the enemy an opportunity, often, of depleting one command, not pressed, to reinforce another more actively engaged. I determined to stop this.... My general plan now was to concentrate all the force possible against the Confederate armies in the field." The new Federal commander resolved to launch all his major commands against the enemy at the same time to prevent the Confederates from shifting men and resources.

The primary commands in Grant's offensive scheme were those of Sherman and Meade. While Grant felt that Sherman had the ability to exercise independent command in the western theater, he did not have the same trust in Meade. Lincoln had been extremely disappointed in Meade's failure to follow up his great victory at Gettysburg, Pennsylvania, in July 1863. Since then, Meade had failed to initiate a successful campaign against the undermanned and ill-equipped Confederate army.

When Grant took command of the Federal armies, there was a great deal of pressure from the Federal War Department to replace Meade. But Grant decided to keep Meade in command of the army. Grant correctly ascertained that the problems in the east, where the war had been stagnant, could not be placed entirely on Meade's shoulders. "In the east," Grant later wrote, "the opposing forces stood in substantially the same relations toward each other as three years before, or when the war began.... Battles had been fought of as great severity as had ever been known in war... with indecisive results."

The new General in Chief determined that a much more aggressive, offensive campaign was

necessary to win the war in the east. Grant decided to establish his field headquarters with the Army of the Potomac to match his own wits against the wily Robert E. Lee. Throughout the remainder of the war, Meade was primarily the figurehead commander of the Army of the Potomac; Grant issued most of the orders. "To get possession of Lee's army was the first great object," Grant wrote. "With the capture of his army Richmond would necessarily follow."

The disastrous Gettysburg Campaign and the winter of 1863 had taken their toll on Lee's tired, hungry army. No one realized the seriousness of this situation better than Lee. "A regular supply of provisions to the troops in this army is a matter of great importance," Lee wrote in a January 1864 dispatch to Confederate Secretary of War James Seddon. "Short rations are having a bad effect upon the men, both morally and physically. Desertions to the enemy are becoming more frequent, and the men cannot continue healthy and vigorous if confined to this spare diet for any length of time. Unless there is a change, I fear the army cannot be kept effective, and probably cannot be kept together."

Lee realized that the appointment of Ulysses Grant as General in Chief of the Federal armies marked a change in Federal military policy. "The importance of [the spring campaign] to the administration of Mr. Lincoln and to General Grant," Lee wrote Jefferson Davis, "leaves no doubt that every effort and every sacrifice will be made to secure its success." By May 1864, Lee had no more than 66,000 men to oppose Grant's army of more than 120,000. The I Corps, commanded by Confederate Lieutenant General James Longstreet, had recently returned from winter campaigning in Tennessee. During Longstreet's absence, Lee's other two corps had maintained a line of defenses along

Mine Run and the Rapidan River that had proved too formidable for Meade's army during the Mine Run Campaign.

In planning his spring campaign, Grant decided not to attack Lee's well-entrenched army. Instead he would cross the Rapidan River and attempt to get around the Confederate right flank. Lee would be forced to abandon his works to prevent the Army of the Potomac from getting between his troops and Richmond.

To turn Lee's right flank, the Federal army would have to march through a dense forest of scrub pine and second-growth timber called the Wilderness. Both armies were very familiar with this area, having fought in this thick undergrowth during the Battle of Chancellorsville and during the Mine Run Campaign. "Do you know the scrub oak woods above Hammond's Pond," one Federal officer wrote to his wife, "a sort of growth that is hard for even a single man to force his way through for any great distance?... That is the growth of most of this country.... Along this region there are only two or three roads that can be counted on. These are the turnpike, the plank road south of it, and the plank road that runs from Germanna Ford. There are many narrow roads, winding and little known, that in good weather may serve for the slow passage of columns (though they are mere farmers' or woodcutters' thoroughfares); but a day's rain will render them impassable for waggons [sic] and artillery."

Grant was aware of the danger of ambush while passing through the Wilderness. The nature of the terrain would immobilize Federal artillery and cavalry and neutralize the overwhelming manpower advantage Grant held over Lee. All organization would be lost, as it would be impossible to deploy large bodies of troops in the dense underbrush. Grant hoped to escape unscathed through the impenetrable forest by forced marches. He hoped that by the time Lee discovered the movement and was able to mount an attack, the Federal army would be safely beyond the fringes of the Wilderness. As with so many past Federal commanders, Grant greatly underestimated the ability of his opponent.

Grant's force comprised three infantry and one cavalry corps of Meade's Army of the Potomac and an independent corps commanded by Major General Ambrose Burnside. Since Burnside outranked Meade, the former commander of the Army of the Potomac reported directly to Grant.

The Army of the Potomac began advancing shortly after midnight on May 4. By 6:00 A.M. Grant's troops were crossing the Rapidan River and entering the northern fringes of the Wilderness. The Federal V and VI Corps, commanded by Major Generals Gouverneur Warren and John Sedgwick respectively, crossed the river at Germanna Ford and proceeded southeast along the Germanna Plank

Road. The II Corps, under Major General Winfield Hancock, crossed at Ely's Ford and marched toward Chancellorsville. Grant directed Burnside's corps to remain behind to protect the railroad north of Rappahannock Station from Confederate raiders. Once across the Rapidan, Grant sent a message to the War Department in Washington. "The crossing of the Rapidan effected," the General in Chief wrote. "Forty-eight hours now will demonstrate whether the enemy intends giving battle this side of Richmond."

The Orange Plank Road in 1864, where Federal troops of Hancock's corps clashed with Confederate troops of A.P. Hill.

Grant did not have to wait long to learn Lee's intentions. Shortly after crossing the Rapidan, Grant was handed an enemy dispatch that had been intercepted and deciphered by a Federal signal station. The message sent to Confederate Lieutenant General Richard Ewell stated, "We are moving."

Lee learned of the Federal advance at about 9:00 A.M. on May 4. Not knowing Grant's intentions, Lee ordered his corps commanders to advance east along three different routes. He directed Lieutenant General Richard Ewell to advance his corps along the Orange Turnpike, the northernmost route, and Lieutenant General Ambrose P. Hill to march on the Orange Plank Road, parallel to and south of Ewell's line. Longstreet was directed to take his corps along the Catharpin Road, far south of Hill's path, toward Todd's Tavern. His army set in motion, Lee waited to see what they would find in the dense undergrowth of the Wilderness.

Although Grant hoped to have his army near the eastern fringes of the thick forest by nightfall, his advance bogged down when his wagons had difficulty along the narrow roads. As night fell, his V and VI Corps were strung out along the Germanna Plank Road and the II Corps was deployed near Chancellorsville. The terrain provided an eerie setting for the night's bivouac. Federal soldiers encountered many partially buried skeletons, which unnerved veteran and recruit alike. "We wandered to and fro," a veteran later recalled, "looking at the gleaming skulls and whitish bones, and examining the exposed clothing of the dead to see if they had been Union or Confederate soldiers."

During the night, Hancock was ordered to advance his II Corps south to form the left flank of the Federal line that would continue its southward movement. The Federal march began at dawn on May 5. To protect his right flank during the march, Federal General Warren, commander of the V Corps, sent a division west along the Orange Turnpike. Learning that Confederate troops were advancing east along the turnpike, Meade, who was closer to the Federal front than Grant, directed Warren to concentrate his troops along the turnpike and attack the enemy as soon as possible. Federal General Sedgwick, commander of VI Corps, was ordered to proceed to the turnpike to guard the Federal right flank.

Just after noon, the division Warren had deployed along the turnpike struck two divisions of Ewell's corps. The Confederate corps commander had been instructed not to bring on a general engagement until Longstreet's corps arrived within supporting distance, but the pressure of the Federal advance forced Ewell to commit his troops to battle. The two opposing lines deployed through the brambles and thick underbrush bordering the turnpike. With their vision limited by the darkness of the forest, the opposing lines stumbled upon each other. "Closing with the enemy," one Federal officer later recalled, "we fought them with bayonet as well as bullet. Up through the trees rolled dense clouds of battle smoke, circling about the green of the pines and mingling with the white of the flowering dogwoods. Underneath, men ran to and fro, firing, shouting, stabbing with bayonets, beating each other with the butts of their guns. Each man fought on his own resources, grimly and desperately." This description characterizes the manner of fighting during the next two days.

As soon as he realized that Lee's army was converging on his dispersed column, Grant issued orders to concentrate his three corps along a line running between the Orange Turnpike and Orange Plank Road. Of particular importance was the Brock Road-Orange Plank Road crossroad. If the Confederates should gain possession of that key

The tattered condition of the regimental colors of the 56th Massachusetts and the 36th Massachusetts indicate the brutality of the Battle of the Wilderness.

Confederate General James Ewell Brown ("Jeb") Stuart, one of Robert E. Lee's most reliable commanders.

intersection, the Federal II Corps would be cut off from the rest of Grant's army. Grant directed Hancock, commander of the II Corps, to proceed quickly to the crossroads, but when the lieutenant general realized that Hill's Confederate corps would arrive there before Hancock, the Federal commander ordered a division of the VI Corps to hold the position.

The Federal division sent by Grant to hold the crossroads arrived just in time to repulse the initial Confederate assault. The Federals held the position throughout the afternoon in the face of mounting Confederate pressure. Just as the Federal line was about to break, the leading elements of Hancock's corps arrived. The fighting continued in the confusion of the dense forest around the intersection until darkness finally arrived, answering the prayers of the soldiers on both sides.

Meanwhile, fighting had escalated along the Orange Turnpike between Ewell's corps and elements of the Federal V and VI corps. For hours, the opposing lines fought in the impenetrable Wilderness until darkness mercifully ended the blind slaughter. Numerous fires had erupted throughout the forest, ignited by the discharge of small arms and artillery pieces. Federal and Confederate soldiers staggered through the undergrowth, attempting to save the wounded before they were engulfed by flames. One Federal officer remembered how

he "stumbled, fell, and my outflung hands pushed up a smoulder of leaves. The fire sprang into flame, caught in the hair and beard of a dead sergeant, and lighted a ghastly face and wide open eyes. I rushed away in horror."

While Federal officers regrouped their scattered commands and prepared for the fighting that was sure to come the next morning, Lee sent orders to let his Confederate troops rest. He believed that Longstreet would arrive before daybreak to bolster the Confederate line. This almost proved to be the Confederate commander's most tragic mistake during the war.

That evening, Grant learned that Hancock's corps had almost broken through Hill's line before darkness put a stop to the fighting. Longstreet's Confederate corps was still several hours from the battlefield, and Grant hoped to soundly defeat Lee's other two corps before Longstreet arrived. Grant ordered his II Corps commander to resume the attack at dawn, drive Hill's troops back, and roll up the Confederate right flank while Warren's and Sedgwick's corps immobilized Ewell.

Lee realized his position was in jeopardy, and he directed Longstreet to march through the night to reach the embattled Confederate line. Lee also ordered Ewell to open fire at daybreak on the Federal line in his front in an attempt to relieve some of the pressure on Hill's position.

Hancock's men attacked at about 5:00 A.M. on May 6. Since Hill's officers had permitted their men to rest through the night rather than working to reform their lines, the Federals quickly overran the Confederate's disorganized position. Longstreet had not yet arrived and Lee's right flank was in danger of disintegrating. Federal infantrymen quickly pushed the mile to the clearing of the Widow Tapp Farm. Desperate Confederate counterattacks only slowed the Federal advance momentarily. One Federal officer wrote, "the roar of musketry was incessant and prolonged.... The whole forest was now one mass of flame."

Confederate artillery in the Tapp clearing opened fire with canister as the Federal troops charged forward, opening large, gaping holes in the blue-clad line. Union officers had just formed their men into an assault force to capture this last Confederate defense when a small group of Confederate soldiers came running down the Plank Road. They were the advance of Longstreet's corps. "Like a fine lady at a party," one cannoneer wrote, "Longstreet was often late in his arrival at the ball, but he always made a sensation... with the grand old First Corps, sweeping behind him, as his train."

The Confederates pushed the Federal II Corps back to the breastworks at Brock Road. After noon, as a lull settled over the battlefield, Longstreet rode forward to scout points in the Federal line to attack. Caught in a cross fire, he

was wounded in the throat and right shoulder by his own troops. It was almost a year to the day that "Stonewall" Jackson fell during the Battle of Chancellorsville, himself a victim of his own troops.

While Grant planned to renew the attack at 6:00 P.M., Lee, never one to allow the enemy to strike first, sent Hill's and Longstreet's men forward at 4:00 P.M. They succeeded in overrunning the Federal position on Brock Road. "At this moment," a Federal soldier later recalled, "orders were received by Colonel [Samuel S.] Carroll to charge the enemy and retake our breastworks; the men hurried into line at the command 'Fall in!' and when Colonel Carroll's stentorian voice rang out, 'Forward, double-quick, charge!' the brigade swept down the hill like an avalanche. A few minutes' bloody work and the rebels were routed, pursued to the edge of the woods, and several of our guns recaptured. Thus ended the battle of the Wilderness."

The opposing armies spent May 7 collecting their dead and wounded and catching up on well-deserved rest. The Federals had lost more than 17,000 men during the two days of bitter fighting, while Confederate losses amounted to more than 7500 soldiers.

Past Federal commanders, after such a great battle, usually retreated across the Rappahannock to regroup and plan future movements, but Grant was a different sort of leader and this was a different type of warfare. "Make all preparations during the day," Grant directed Meade on the morning of May 7, "for a night march to take position at Spotsylvania Court House." There would be no retreat for either army. For the next 11 months, the Federal Army of the Potomac and Confederate Army of Northern Virginia would be in constant contact. The fighting in the east would finally end at the tiny hamlet of Appomattox Court House, Virginia.

The thick, overgrown vegetation typical of the Wilderness. Soldiers fighting here were often on their own, as it was difficult to see very far or keep troops in any kind of organized line.

GRANT VERSUS LEE

Although the names of Ulysses S. Grant and Robert E. Lee will forever be associated with each other, the two men met only three or four times. During their second personal encounter, when the two came together at the McLean house at Appomattox Court House, Virginia, to discuss the terms of surrender for Lee's Army of Northern Virginia, Grant reminisced about the only previous time the two had met: during the Mexican War. "I met you once before, General Lee," Grant recalled, "while we were serving in Mexico, when you came over from General Scott's headquarters to visit Garland's brigade, to which I then belonged. I have always remembered your appearance, and I think I should have recognized you anywhere."

"Yes," Lee responded. "I know I met you on that occasion, and I have often thought of it, and tried to recollect how you looked, but I have never been able to recall a single feature."

While the two commanders met personally only a few times, their armies were inseparable from the moment Grant's command crossed the Rapidan River on May 4, 1864, until the Confederate surrender on April 9, 1865. The war of attrition Grant introduced with his ascendancy to army command called for constant pressure against Confederate armies on all fronts. Before the fighting ended on that April afternoon in 1865, Grant lost more than 90,000 men and Lee 44,000, almost as many men as the two commanders led into the Wilderness.

The savage hostility of the fighting between the troops commanded by these two men was in stark contrast to the civility and cordiality of their discussions at Appomattox Court House. A Federal staff officer, Horace Porter, recorded their meeting in his book *Campaigning With Grant*. The final sign of the respect these men had for each other is clear from Porter's account of their parting. "Lee signaled to his orderly to bring up his horse, and while the animal was being bridled the general stood on the lowest step, and gazed sadly in the direction of the valley beyond, where his army lay—now an army of prisoners. He thrice smote the palm of his left hand slowly with his right fist in an absent sort of way, seemed not to see the group of Union officers in the yard, who rose respectfully at his approach, and appeared unaware of everything about him....The approach of his horse seemed to recall him from his reverie, and he at once mounted. General Grant now stepped down from the porch, moving toward him, and saluted him by raising his hat. He was followed in this act of courtesy by all our officers present. Lee raised his hat respectfully, and rode off at a slow trot to break the sad news to the brave fellows whom he had so long commanded."

BATTLE OF SPOTSYLVANIA
May 8–18, 1864

Lieutenant General
Ulysses Grant, USA

General
Robert E. Lee, CSA

After the Battle of the Wilderness, Federal General Grant turned his Army of the Potomac southeast, trying to outflank General Lee's Confederate Army of Northern Virginia. But Lee blocked Grant at Spotsylvania Court House. For almost a fortnight the two forces faced each other. Finally, after nearly 17,500 Federal and 10,000 Confederate losses, Grant withdrew, again trying to outflank Lee in this bloody war of attrition.

Rain poured down in the darkness surrounding blue-clad troops moving quietly into formation for the attack. Just before daylight on May 12, 1864, three Union infantry divisions were tightly arrayed in lines and columns, creating an almost solid rectangular mass. Nearly 20,000 men, shivering in a chill morning fog, prepared to hurl themselves at the Confederate line near Spotsylvania Court House, Virginia.

At first light, after the mist cleared somewhat, the command to advance was given. "The whole corps stepped off at the same moment," recalled a Federal officer, "and...marched over the enemy's pickets, who were so astounded at our appearance...that they never fired a shot, nor did we, but moved right over them."

Just six days earlier, the course of the Civil War in the east had literally come to a fork in the road. On the night of May 6, two days of brutal combat at the Battle of the Wilderness ended. Having lost 17,600 soldiers, Federal Lieutenant General Ulysses S. Grant withdrew his force from the bloody battleground. Many Union veterans assumed that the Federal army would retreat to the north, as they had always done in the past after battling with Confederate General Robert E. Lee's Army of Northern Virginia. But this night was different; Grant had no intention of backing away from the enemy. Instead, he wanted to place his army between Lee and Richmond. So, at a dusty crossroads east of the Wilderness battleground, Federal forces took the highway leading south toward Spotsylvania. "Our spirits rose," a Yankee private wrote of the move. "The enlisted men understood the flanking movement."

Alert to Grant's flanking maneuver, Confederate General Lee quickly had his own army headed on a 12-mile trek to Spotsylvania. Marching all night by the shortest possible route, Lee's weary troops arrived first at the strategic crossroads village. Comprising a court house, a hotel, and several dwellings, Spotsylvania sat at a key intersection on the road to the Confederate capital. Having failed in his attempt to outflank Lee, Grant determined to force his way through the Confederate roadblock.

Confederate entrenchments around Spotsylvania were shaped like a blunt arrowhead pointing north. The tip of the earthworks formed a half circle the soldiers called the "Mule Shoe." Later, the position would earn the title "Bloody Angle." The five-mile-long Confederate lines were protected by about 50,000 men and 200 cannons.

The Battle of Spotsylvania began at about 8:00 A.M. on May 8 when the first of Grant's nearly 100,000 soldiers formed into battle lines west of the village. When the bluecoats advanced, Federal officers were surprised to find Confederate troops of Major General Richard Anderson's corps already well entrenched. Not all of Lee's army had arrived yet, however. "I was anxious to crush Anderson before Lee could get a force to his support," wrote Grant. As more of his troops arrived on the field, Grant directed a series of attacks throughout the afternoon, but all were effectively repulsed. By nightfall, both armies were in place and prepared to renew the contest the next morning.

On May 9, a single Confederate bullet caused Grant's army perhaps its greatest loss of the campaign. Major General John Sedgwick, commander of the VI Corps, rode out to inspect his line on the Federal right flank that morning. Near the center of his line he found soldiers cowering from Confederate sniper fire. Assuming a bold front to encourage his men, Sedgwick looked toward the distant enemy position and laughed. He told his men that the sharpshooters couldn't hit an elephant at that distance. The words were barely out of his mouth when he

toppled from his horse with a Confederate bullet through his forehead. "His loss was a severe one to the Army...and to the Nation," wrote Grant.

There was more action on May 10. Reports reached Grant that Lee had weakened the Confederate left flank. Launching several attacks in that direction, Grant found out too late that the reports were inaccurate. The piecemeal Union assaults withered under murderous gunfire. Lee's army, it turned out, was solidly entrenched along its entire line.

Undaunted by his failure to pierce Lee's left flank, Grant decided to strike heavily near Lee's center. About 6:00 P.M. a solid formation of 12 handpicked Union regiments attacked with bayonets. With a wild yell, the blue wave, 4000 men strong, emerged from tree cover and dashed madly at the Confederate breastworks. Deadly hand-to-hand combat flared along the earth wall. "The enemy," wrote attack leader Colonel Emory Upton, "sitting in their pits with pieces upright, loaded, and with bayonets fixed, ready to impale the first who should leap over, absolutely refused to yield the ground." The first Confederate line was broken, but Union attackers then faced a second enemy line about 100 yards behind the first. Federal reinforcements, though promised, never arrived. "Our position," Upton wrote, "without prospect of support, was untenable." Under cover of darkness, Federal survivors returned to their own lines.

"On the 11th," Grant later recalled, "there was no battle and but little firing." Instead, the two armies rested, replenished food and ammunition, and eyed one another warily from their trenches. To military leaders in Washington, Grant wrote that morning requesting reinforcements. Grant needed to replace his losses, writing that he proposed "to fight it out on this line if it takes all summer."

True to his word, Grant resumed the battle with a vengeance on May 12. He planned

another assault on the Confederate center. This time he would use 20,000 men, closely packed, instead of the 4000 used two days earlier. Having formed up in the pouring rain during the early hours of the morning, the massive attack struck the Confederate "Mule Shoe" about 4:30 A.M. A solid rectangular mass of screaming Federal soldiers stormed over the startled Confederate defenders. Within minutes, Union assault troops had captured about 4000 enemy soldiers and 20 cannons. The "Mule Shoe" collapsed and Lee's army, split in two, faced destruction. Union support troops then hit Confederate defenses right and left of the break.

Confederate reinforcements, personally led forward by General Lee, recovered the lost ground. The Federals, however, stood just outside the enemy breastworks. A thin wall of logs and fresh earth was all that separated the two armies. Fierce combat at point-blank range ravaged both forces. "Never since the discovery of gunpowder," wrote a Federal officer, "has such a mass of lead been hurled into a space so narrow." Lee drew back the center of his line a half mile to fortifications erected during the bitter fight at "Bloody Angle."

A lull settled over the battlefield for the next few days. Combat flared briefly at scattered points around Spotsylvania, but with little effect. A final Federal attempt to crack Lee's center died before the muzzles of massed Confederate artillery on May 18. Two days later, after repulsing a weak Confederate counterattack on May 19, Grant pulled his army away from the frightful carnage at Spotsylvania. More than 17,500 Federal soldiers and about 10,000 Confederates were victims of the bloody stalemate. Once again, Grant sidestepped east and south toward Richmond. "This is a hard campaign," wrote a Union officer as the armies parted on May 20, "putting in the shade all others."

BATTLE OF RESACA
May 14–15, 1864

Major General
William Sherman, USA

Federal Major General William Sherman, with 100,000 soldiers under his command, moved out of Chattanooga, Tennessee, and started his advance to Atlanta. Standing in his way were General Joseph Johnston's 60,000 Confederate troops. These armies clashed at Resaca, Georgia, and fought for two days. Sherman's clever tactics forced Johnston to abandon Resaca, leaving behind 5000 casualties. Following Johnston, Sherman, having suffered a loss of 6000, continued his long march to Atlanta.

General
Joseph Johnston, CSA

Awake most of the night of May 13, 1864, making his plans for the coming action, a weary Federal Major General William Tecumseh Sherman took a catnap beneath a tree. He was still there, along the line of march, early the next morning.

"Is that a general?" asked a passing soldier of the lone orderly accompanying Sherman.

"Yes," the orderly replied.

"A pretty way we are commanded when our generals are lying drunk beside the road!" the soldier said, disgusted.

Sherman suddenly jumped to his feet. "Stop, my man," he shouted. "I am not drunk. While you were sleeping last night, I was planning for you, sir; and now I was taking a nap."

Sherman had good reason to be tired. He commanded a force of 100,000 men poised to attack nearly 60,000 Confederate soldiers who were well entrenched on high ground outside the north Georgia town of Resaca. Sharp skirmishing had flared all day as Sherman aligned his men for a full-scale assault. He planned to attack Confederate General Joseph E. Johnston's army on May 14.

Located on the north bank of the Oostanaula River, Resaca sat along the tracks of the Western & Atlantic Railroad. This rail line was Johnston's vital supply link to Atlanta, Georgia. A few days earlier, Sherman had missed a golden opportunity to capture Resaca when it was defended by a small Confederate brigade. Now Sherman determined to bull his way into Resaca against Johnston's entire army.

The Federal advance on Atlanta began May 5, 1864, from camps outside Chattanooga, Tennessee. Leaving behind excess baggage and planning "to subsist on the chance food which the country was known to contain," Sherman moved under orders from Lieutenant General Ulysses S. Grant, commander of all Federal armies. Grant had instructed Sherman to "move

against Johnston's army, to break it up and get into the interior of the enemy's country as far as you can, inflicting all the damage you can against their war resources."

Sherman's force comprised the Army of the Cumberland (61,000 men) under Major General George Thomas, the Army of the Tennessee (24,000 men) under Major General James B. McPherson, and the Army of the Ohio (13,500 men) under Major General John M. Schofield. Opposing Sherman, Johnston had three army corps under Lieutenant Generals John Bell Hood, William J. Hardee, and Leonidas Polk, the last an Episcopalian bishop in uniform. Johnston was heavily outgunned and instead relied on the rugged, strongly fortified terrain of north Georgia to block Sherman's advance. Johnston hoped to entice costly Federal attacks against his entrenchments or, failing that, to withdraw slowly, forcing Sherman to stretch even further his vulnerable supply line from Nashville, Tennessee.

The first encounter between Sherman and Johnston came May 7 at Dalton, Georgia, about 25 miles southeast of Chattanooga, Tennessee, and about 14 miles from Resaca, Georgia. Confronted by strong Confederate fortifications, Sherman balked at a frontal assault. Instead, while Federal Generals Schofield and Thomas feinted attacks north and west of Dalton to hold Johnston in place, Sherman sent Federal General McPherson's army around Johnston's left. McPherson was to strike the Western & Atlantic tracks south of Johnston, forcing the Confederate leader to abandon Dalton. Schofield and Thomas would then fall on Johnston's rear "to catch our enemy in the confusion of retreat."

With the wooded slopes of Taylor's Ridge between his own army and Johnston's, McPherson marched south. Within a few miles of Resaca, McPherson met and repulsed a

Confederate cavalry brigade, and the Georgia rail station was at the mercy of McPherson.

The normally aggressive McPherson was stymied within a mile of Resaca, however, when he ran into stiff resistance from a single Confederate infantry brigade. Deep behind enemy lines, beyond close support, and unsure of the enemy strength he faced in fading daylight, McPherson halted his advance. "Such an opportunity does not occur twice in a single lifetime," Sherman lamented, "but at the critical moment McPherson seems to have been a little cautious."

Warned of the Federal threat at Resaca, Johnston at first thought it was a decoy for a larger attack at Dalton and remained in place. However, Johnston did divert to Resaca reinforcements originally destined for Dalton, and on May 11, 58-year-old Confederate "bishop-general" Polk arrived to command the defense at Resaca. Meanwhile, Sherman was shifting his forces toward Resaca. When Confederate cavalry patrols reported that Federal camps north of Dalton were nearly empty, Johnston evacuated the town. He arrived in Resaca on the morning of Friday the 13th. Sherman was up late the night of the 13th planning a general assault for the next day.

Schofield began the Federal attack at about noon on May 14. His infantrymen charged across an open field north of Resaca. One Union veteran recalled that the charge was met by "a roaring fire of artillery." The charge soon floundered when Schofield's men became entangled with Federal troops of Thomas's army meant to support Schofield's right flank. The confusion extended to the Federal left flank when Confederate General John Bell Hood's troops charged at a gap in the Union ranks. Only nightfall and the timely arrival of Federal reinforcements prevented a major Confederate breakthrough.

The battle north of Resaca and heavy skirmishing along the rest of the perimeter allowed Sherman to duplicate his tactics at Dalton. While Johnston's attention was diverted once again, McPherson was shifted south to get in Johnston's rear. McPherson established a temporary bridgehead on the Confederate bank of the Oostanaula River at Lay's Ferry, but McPherson recrossed the river at a report of a large Confederate force approaching. The report was false, but Johnston understood the real threat to his rear and prepared for the worst at Resaca. A single bridge was Johnston's only avenue of retreat; if the Federals broke his line west of the town, the bridge would be within easy range of Federal artillery.

Sherman struck at the Confederate line on the morning of May 15. Against a hail of Confederate cannon fire, elements of Schofield's and Thomas's armies hit a Confederate fort northwest of Resaca. "That 4-gun battery was playing on us fast as it could fire," recalled a Wisconsin soldier, "and did some frightfully wicked work." A bloody melee raged on the earthen ramparts after several Federal regiments rushed in to tip the scales to Union advantage. All around Resaca "the sound of cannon and musketry rose all day," Sherman later wrote, "to the dignity of a battle."

But the battle of Resaca was really decided about five miles south of town, where McPherson reestablished a strong bridgehead in Johnston's rear. The Federals again threatened to cut the Confederate rail artery to Atlanta. Johnston retreated from town that night over pontoon bridges east of Resaca that had been constructed earlier. He then guided his army south along the Western & Atlantic Railroad.

When Sherman and Johnston left Resaca, 5000 Confederate and 6000 Union casualties remained behind. Ahead lay months of bitter fighting leading to the trenches around Atlanta.

BATTLE OF COLD HARBOR
June 3, 1864

Lieutenant General
Ulysses Grant, USA

General
Robert E. Lee, CSA

At dawn, 50,000 Federal soldiers attacked the Confederates at Cold Harbor, Virginia. In less than 30 minutes, more than 7000 of these men fell. Robert E. Lee's Army of Northern Virginia took advantage of their strong entrenchments, sending death through the charging blue-clad ranks. Although he had personally ordered many assaults during the war, Ulysses Grant regretted this attack for the rest of his life.

Axes would have to do. Long columns of Federal infantry 10 lines deep had already emerged from the timber just a few hundred yards away. Raising a cheer, the neat blue ranks paraded steadily closer across the open, rain-drenched fields toward the Confederate works. "I ordered my men to take arms and fix bayonets," recalled Confederate Colonel William Oates, commanding the 15th Alabama Infantry. "Just then I remembered not a gun in the regiment was loaded." Oates quickly ordered his soldiers to load weapons, but he feared the Federals would be on top of his men before their guns were ready. To beat back enemy troops, who might appear on his line at any moment, Oates ordered his officers to stand ready—each with an ax in hand.

Throughout the previous night and well into the predawn hours of June 3, 1864, Oates's men had used the axes to build breastworks near the village of Cold Harbor, Virginia. For several miles to the right and left of the Alabama line, the rest of General Robert E. Lee's 50,000-man Confederate Army of Northern Virginia had done the same. Now, coming through thick ground fog against the first flush of dawn, 50,000 Union soldiers were about to test the strength of those Confederate labors.

In the late spring of 1864, the dust-choked roads from Spotsylvania Court House, Virginia, all led to Cold Harbor. Union Lieutenant General Ulysses S. Grant had ended the standoff at Spotsylvania after nightfall on May 20. He moved the Army of the Potomac to the east and south. Grant was repeating the tactics he had first used to end the Battle of the Wilderness, again trying to place Federal troops between Lee's army and Richmond.

Grant hoped to cross the North Anna River before Lee arrived on the opposite shore to block him. The river, with steep, wooded banks, was the first major geographic barrier crossing

Grant's path to Richmond. Grant and the corps of Federal Major Generals Winfield Hancock and Gouverneur Warren, about half Grant's army of 90,000, marched toward Hanover Junction, located two miles south of the North Anna River.

But Lee moved quickly. At the first sign of Union forces shifting around his right flank, Lee began to head south. "Lee's native genius," wrote a Confederate officer, "enabled him to place himself in Grant's position…to trace his marches…to mark on the map the points of future conflict…marking Grant's zigzag route to Richmond."

Lee, traveling by shorter routes, was strongly entrenched behind the North Anna River when Warren and Hancock reached the north bank on the afternoon of May 23. Lee had fortified his army in a compact, wedge-shaped position with its point on high ground west of the river's bridges.

After a brief halt, Warren's Federals forded the river upstream and approached Lee's left wing. Hancock, opposite Lee's right wing, faced a Confederate garrison of a small earthen fort located on the north bank and guarding the approaches to the bridge.

About 6:00 P.M. on May 23, both sides attacked the other's right flank. Warren, on the Federal right, held firm under the Confederate assault. Hancock's troops attacked the Confederate right and crossed to the south bank on the morning of May 24.

Once Grant had most of his infantry south of the North Anna River, he skirmished with Lee's defenses. Determining the shape of Lee's position, Grant realized the wily Confederate general had effectively cut the Federal army into three unequal parts. Wright's, Warren's, and part of Burnside's corps were south of the river and west of Lee. Burnside's remaining men were north of the river and opposite the nearly

impregnable tip of Lee's wedge. Hancock's lone corps, also south of the river, was isolated against Lee's right wing. Grant decided Lee's position was too strong to attack. Reuniting his army on the north bank after dark on May 26, Grant once again tried to get around Lee's right flank and cut the Confederate link with Richmond.

By June 1, Grant's move had carried his army to Cold Harbor, a small crossroads settlement only eight miles northeast of the Confederate capital. Lee was already waiting when Grant's troops arrived. Dug into a chain of low hills amid swampy flatlands near Cold Harbor, Lee's line stretched for seven miles across Grant's path. Both armies had received reinforcements since the North Anna operations. In sweltering heat and tired out by nearly a month of constant marching and bitter combat, Federal and Confederate soldiers prepared for battle on the very doorstep of Richmond.

Union assaults late on June 1 against both Confederate flanks gained some ground but failed to crack Lee's line. After Lee mounted fierce but futile counterattacks from each flank, Grant guessed his opponent must have weakened the Confederate center to do so. But an all-out Union attack on the middle of Lee's line, planned for June 2, fizzled. Hancock's troops, ordered to lead the main attack, got lost en route. "By some blunder we got on the wrong road," recalled a bluecoat, "became entangled in the woods,…mixed up in unutterable confusion…the heat was oppressive…the air thick with choking dust." With these troops too exhausted to do any good once they were in place, Grant postponed the attack until dawn the next morning.

Lee's troops, including Colonel Oates's ax-wielding Alabamians, worked all through the rainy night of June 2 to strengthen their earth and log barricades. Lee also shifted men from

his flanks to his center. When the nearly 50,000 blue troops appeared out of the fog at dawn on June 3, they were slaughtered.

"At every discharge of our guns," wrote a Confederate cannoneer, "heads, arms, legs, guns, were seen flying high in the air." To a Federal soldier, gunfire from the Confederate line was "more like a volcanic blast than a battle." "The army seemed to melt away like frost in the July sun," recalled another Federal veteran of the attack. Union survivors recoiled and slammed into Union battle lines still advancing behind them. "The crumbling ranks sank under the withering fire, unable to reach the goal, or retrace their steps to friendly shelter."

In less than 30 minutes, 7000 Federal troops fell. Lee lost fewer than 1500 men.

Unable to budge Lee's army, Grant's men dug in where they were, in many places within 50 yards of Confederate defenses. For the next nine sultry days, in filthy, bug-infested trenches near Cold Harbor, the killing continued. Some Federal officers even refused orders to renew attacks. "I will not take my regiment in another such charge," said one, "if Jesus Christ himself should order it." The only break from the killing occurred on June 7 during a brief truce to bury decaying corpses. "After they were through," a Union soldier recalled, "there was nothing left but stains of blood, broken and twisted guns, old hats, canteens…reminders of the death and carnage that reigned."

The death and carnage lasted until June 12, when both armies left Cold Harbor behind. The relentless Federal drive around Lee's right flank would continue all the way to Petersburg, Virginia. Despite what lay ahead, General Grant and thousands of Union and Confederate veterans never forgot Cold Harbor. Twenty years after the war, Grant wrote in his memoirs: "I have always regretted that the last assault at Cold Harbor was ever made."

BATTLE OF KENNESAW MOUNTAIN

June 27, 1864

General
Joseph Johnston, CSA

Confederate General Joseph Johnston repeatedly used the Georgia terrain to place his troops in a strong defensible position. But Federal General William Sherman always maneuvered around Johnston, forcing the Confederates to retreat closer to Atlanta. At Kennesaw Mountain, however, Sherman was forced to launch a frontal attack, sending 16,000 troops charging up the mountain. Four hours later, after losing more than 2000 men, Sherman halted the assault. The Confederates, losing perhaps 500, remained entrenched on the mountain, stalling Sherman's advance.

The young United States Army officer arrived at Marietta, Georgia, aboard a mail-coach and found lodging in a tavern. The year was 1844 and 24-year-old Lieutenant William Tecumseh Sherman was in town to perform clerical duties at the inspector-general's office. Sherman spent his off-duty hours riding about the surrounding countryside sightseeing. From two miles northwest of Marietta, he especially enjoyed the panoramic view of rustic woodlands and meadows seen from the 700-foot-high summit of Kennesaw Mountain. During his six-week assignment at Marietta in 1844, Sherman later wrote, "I repeatedly rode to Kennesaw Mountain."

In June 1864, Sherman returned to Kennesaw Mountain. This time he came as a major general in the U.S. Army, commanding more than 100,000 Union soldiers. The knowledge of the landscape he had gained 20 years earlier would prove invaluable.

Sherman's army had won a battle at Resaca, Georgia, on May 15, 1864, 50 miles north of Kennesaw Mountain. From Resaca, early on May 16, Sherman continued his campaign to capture Atlanta. Moving south along the tracks of the Western & Atlantic Railroad, Sherman pursued Confederate General Joseph E. Johnston's 60,000-man Army of Tennessee.

From the beginning of the Atlanta Campaign on May 5, 1864, Sherman had maintained his tactic of outflanking Johnston's defenses. Johnston, observed Sherman, still relied on "the natural strength of the country, in the abundance of mountains, streams and forests" to offset enemy strength and lure costly Federal attacks. At Kennesaw Mountain, Johnston had Sherman right where he wanted him.

After the Battle of Resaca, the armies entered a region of gentle hills and sparse woodlands,

land unsuited for Confederate defenses. Johnston gained a chance while in this area to split and perhaps defeat Sherman's force piecemeal near Cassville, Georgia. But, on the verge of springing the trap the morning of May 19, Hood suddenly spotted a Federal force threatening the right flank and rear of Johnston's army. Afraid of being cut off from Atlanta, Johnston called off his promising assault and entrenched his whole army just south of Cassville. When Sherman refused to attack his entrenchments there on May 20, Johnston resumed his stubborn retreat.

From Cassville, Johnston followed the Western & Atlantic tracks for 12 miles to Allatoona. At Allatoona the railroad snaked between steep ridges crowned with Confederate earthworks. It was a strong natural and man-made barrier to Sherman's advance. Here too, Sherman conjured up 20-year-old memories of his excursions from Marietta as a young army lieutenant. "I therefore knew," Sherman wrote, "that the Allatoona pass was very strong, would be hard to force, and resolved not even to attempt it." Instead, Sherman made a wide sweep 14 miles to the west of Allatoona, toward the road junction at Dallas, Georgia. A march east from Dallas would place Sherman between Johnston's army and Atlanta.

Alerted to this Union threat by his cavalry outposts, Johnston evacuated Allatoona Pass on May 23. By the next evening, Johnston had managed to stretch a gray curtain in front of Sherman. The Confederate line arched north and west of a Methodist meetinghouse called New Hope Church. Located in a hilly, densely wooded area midway between Dallas and the railroad, New Hope Church became the center of a ferocious but indecisive combat. "We have struck a hornet's nest at the business end," one

Federal wrote of the fighting. From New Hope Church, called "Hell Hole" by soldiers after a bloody week-long clash there, Sherman extended his line eastward. By the first week in June, Sherman's army was along the railroad again.

Sherman was satisfied with his progress. Since the start of the campaign at Chattanooga, a month earlier, "we had steadily driven our antagonist from...strong positions," wrote Sherman, "had advanced our lines [over] nearly a hundred miles of as difficult country as was ever fought over by civilized armies; and thus stood prepared to go on, anxious to fight, and confident of success."

Sherman would fight. His army faced Confederate entrenchments on Kennesaw Mountain by June 10. Day after day of drenching rains, however, had slowed the maneuvers of both armies. It wasn't until June 14 that the downpour slackened and Sherman began to hunt for a weak spot in the 10-mile long Confederate defenses north of Marietta. It was also on June 14 that Confederate Lieutenant General Leonidas Polk was killed by a Federal artillery blast.

Union progress continued for the next 12 days, as Sherman applied constant pressure to Johnston's line. By June 26, the Confederate left flank had been bent at a 90 degree angle from its center on Kennesaw Mountain. "We gain ground daily," Sherman informed the Federal War Department, "fighting all the time." Numerous Confederate counterattacks failed to push the Federals back.

Encouraged by his success elsewhere along the Confederate perimeter, Sherman determined on a frontal assault on Kennesaw Mountain. A 200-gun Union artillery barrage along the entire front opened the battle for Kennesaw at 8:00 A.M. on June 27. Thirty minutes later, under

blue skies and bright sunlight, Federal troops appeared. "[A]s if by magic," observed a Confederate officer, "there sprang from the earth a host of men, and in one long, waving line of blue the infantry advanced." Over rocks and fallen timber, 16,000 bluecoats surged up Kennesaw Mountain.

Union troops captured the first line of Confederate rifle pits after intense combat with bayonets and clubbed muskets. Several hundred yards higher, the confident Federal troopers ran into the main Confederate line. A Confederate private later recalled, "no sooner would a regiment mount our works then they were shot down or surrendered. Yet still the Yankees came." The Union assault came within 30 feet of the enemy's main line when the Federal troops "staggered and sought cover," the Confederate private continued, "as best they could behind logs and rocks."

Like human battering rams, two heavy columns of Federal troops had hit Kennesaw Mountain at different points hoping to breach the Confederate line. Instead, the massed blue troops made easy targets for the unexpectedly strong gray defenders. At one spot, while the battle still raged elsewhere, a truce was called so Federal soldiers could save wounded comrades caught in a brush fire that had flared between the lines. The killing resumed immediately after the truce had ended.

The temperature soared to nearly 100 as the bitter contest continued all morning with little headway. "By 11:30," Sherman later wrote, "the assault was in fact over, and had failed." Sherman had lost 2000 men on the familiar slopes of Kennesaw Mountain—Johnston about 500. Five days later, Sherman moved around Johnston's left flank and forced the Confederates off Kennesaw Mountain.

BATTLE OF ATLANTA
July 22, 1864

Major General
William Sherman, USA

Lieutenant General
John Hood, CSA

By mid-July, Federal Major General William Sherman's 100,000-man army was camped on the outskirts of Atlanta. Confederate General John Hood—newly appointed commander of the 60,000-man Confederate army—did not waste any time before launching several unsuccessful attacks against Sherman. The largest strike came on July 22, when Hood lost 7000 to 10,000 men to Sherman's 3700. Hood was forced to abandon Atlanta on September 1.

The band played outside Confederate General Joseph E. Johnston's Atlanta headquarters as darkness descended on the city. "Dixie," "The Bonnie Blue Flag," "The Homespun Dress," and other familiar favorites drifted lazily through the sultry air blanketing Atlanta. Lost in the music, listeners may have been able to forget about the heat and the 100,000 Union soldiers camped on the outskirts of town.

Inside his headquarters, Johnston was suddenly numb to the serenade and the heat. Even the tens of thousands of Federal campfires glowing north of Atlanta may have slipped from his mind. The commander of the Army of Tennessee instead focused his attention on a telegram he had just been handed. The message had originated with Confederate President Jefferson Davis at the Confederate capital in

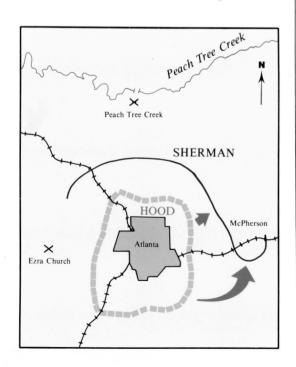

Richmond, Virginia. Dated earlier that day, July 17, 1864, it read in part: "...as you have failed to arrest the advance of the enemy in the vicinity of Atlanta, far in the interior of Georgia, and express no confidence that you can defeat or repel him, you are hereby relieved from the command of the Army and Department of Tennessee, which you will immediately turn over to General Hood."

"[Y]ou have failed to arrest the advance of the enemy...." Visions of battle at Resaca, "The Hell Hole" of New Hope Church, Kennesaw Mountain, and a score of other encounters must have flashed through Johnston's mind while these words tore at his heart. Certainly Confederate General Johnston had been compelled to withdraw slowly to Atlanta in the face of the Union army. With only 60,000 Confederate soldiers, however, Johnston believed he had done the best he could against Federal Major General William T. Sherman's much stronger force.

Johnston had successfully defended Kennesaw Mountain against Sherman for several weeks. The Confederates came down from the heights on July 2, after Federal troops had moved far around Johnston's left flank. Repeating the tactic he had used so often since the campaign opened, Sherman again threatened to cut Johnston's communications with Atlanta.

From Kennesaw Mountain, Johnston withdrew south about 10 miles to the Chattahoochee River, the last major natural barrier before Atlanta. Several pontoon bridges and the Western & Atlantic Railroad bridge spanned the river behind Johnston. Atlanta itself was within 10 miles of the bridge crossings. On July 4, retreating slowly along the railroad, Johnston took up a position of earthworks that formed a bridgehead on the north bank, "which proved one of the strongest

pieces of field-fortifications I ever saw," wrote Sherman. The Federal commander had a fine view of the river valley as he stood upon high bluffs on the north bank. "I could see the houses in Atlanta," Sherman wrote, "and...could observe the preparations for our reception on the other side."

After failing to dislodge the Confederate bridgehead by direct assault, Sherman looked for an easier crossing point. He found it a few miles east of the Confederate bridgehead, and by mid-afternoon on July 8, Union soldiers of Major General John Schofield's command were splashing across the Chattahoochee River. Crossing over a fish dam against little opposition, the Federals quickly secured the site. Pontoon bridges were assembled, and by nightfall Schofield was firmly planted on the south side of the river.

With his river line breached, Johnston abandoned the north bank defenses on July 9. Setting fire to the bridges as he withdrew, Johnston led his army into defenses already erected south of the river, concentrated along Peachtree Creek.

"This has been a sad day in our city," an Atlanta storekeeper wrote on July 10, after learning of the Confederate retreat. "[T]here is a great probability of Atlanta falling into the hands of the enemy, and the city has been in a complete swarm all day.... All Govt. Stores and Hospitals are ordered away and of course the citizens are alarmed, and many have left and others are leaving."

As the civilian exodus from Atlanta began, Sherman resupplied his army and waited. Sherman reinforced his foothold on the south bank but kept most of his force north of the river. Sherman wrote to Federal leaders in Washington, "we must maneuver some...but we shall cross in due time, and instead of attacking Atlanta direct...I propose to make a circuit, destroying all its railroads."

During the lull in fighting, Union and Confederate soldiers arranged a cease-fire at places along the Chattahoochee. "The men laid aside their guns," a Confederate lieutenant wrote his sister, "and are scattered up and down the river swapping canteens and hats and bartering one commodity for another. All day we lie in the shade of the banks and act very becomingly."

Johnston's inactivity along the Chattahoochee had Confederate President Davis fuming in Richmond. Never on good terms with Joseph Johnston on any occasion, Davis was especially upset now with the possibility that Atlanta would soon fall into Federal hands. Davis and other Confederate political and military leaders blamed Johnston's tactics of withdrawal for the situation. "If the Army of Tennessee was found to be unable to hold positions of great strength like those at Dalton, Resaca,...Kennesaw, and on the Chattahoochee," Davis wrote, "I could not reasonably hope that it would be more successful in the plains below Atlanta, where it would find neither natural nor artificial advantages of position."

Atlanta was second only to Richmond, Virginia, as an important rail, factory, and military supply center for the South. Loss of the city would be a crippling blow to the Confederate war effort. Acting on his own counsel, as well as the many demands from other officials, Davis decided to remove Johnston from command. "I realized how serious it was to change commanders in the presence of the enemy," Davis wrote. "I only overcame the objection...in the hope that the impending danger of the loss of Atlanta might be averted." Davis telegrammed Johnston, informing the beleaguered general that his army was to be turned over to General John Bell Hood.

Hood was a fighter and had openly sought Johnston's position. From early in the war,

Sherman's troops tearing up the railroad tracks in Atlanta, Georgia, marking the start of the "March to the Sea" that broke the back of the Confederacy.

army on the north bank of Peachtree Creek. On the afternoon of the 19th, Thomas crossed a part of his command over to the south side, "meeting," wrote Thomas, "with considerable resistance." By nightfall on the 19th, Sherman's army formed a broad crescent-shaped line north and east of Atlanta.

But Confederate General Hood noted that Thomas's force was divided by Peachtree Creek and that a two-mile-wide gap existed between Thomas's left flank and Schofield's right. "Feeling it impossible to hold Atlanta without giving battle," Hood wrote, "I determined to strike the enemy while attempting to cross the stream." Hood planned to hit Thomas with two of his three infantry corps. Hood's third corps and his cavalry would hold off McPherson and Schofield. The Confederate assault was set to begin at 1:00 P.M. on July 20.

Confusion in orders and poor staff work delayed Hood's attack nearly three hours. Thomas had most of his men south of Peachtree Creek by the time the Confederates finally struck his exposed left flank at about 4:00 P.M. "The first shot was followed by others in quick succession," recalled a Union sergeant, "then came the rattle of musketry, and with it the familiar 'Rebel Yell.' We knew then for a certainty that serious work was ahead of us." The Confederates "were charging by the acre," wrote another Federal witness to the charge. In places, the graycoats were six lines deep.

Thomas's left flank was bent back by Hood's charge. Observing the attack from north of the creek, Thomas saw that the Confederates threatened to capture a bridge in the rear of his troops. Loss of the vital span would trap the Federals south of the creek. Thomas rushed 12 Union cannons and four infantry regiments to defend the bridge. "They in turn broke," wrote a Federal soldier of the Confederate attackers, "then all went in wild disorder."

Fighting seesawed through ravines and woodlots for two hours as Hood tried desperately to win his first battle as a Confederate army commander. Thomas held firm on defense; at one point, a New York regiment even tore down a nearby house and used the lumber to build breastworks. The regiment's colonel wrote, "[T]his slight fortification in succeeding charges saved many valuable lives."

About 6:00 P.M. word reached Hood that McPherson's Union troops had advanced within cannon range of Atlanta. In fact, Federal artillery had already fired into the city. The first civilian casualty, a small girl, was killed by the first shot. Hood called off the Peachtree Creek attack to send troops to reinforce his right flank. The shift of troops to the Confederate right flank and the approach of darkness ended the day's battle. Hood had gained nothing for the 4800 casualties he suffered. Federal losses totaled only 1700.

Hood had built his reputation on battlefields from Virginia to Georgia. The battle-scarred 33-year-old Hood claimed he was "astounded" when he received the July 17 order to command the Army of Tennessee. "[O]verwhelmed... with [a] sense of responsibility," Hood wrote, "I remained in deep thought throughout the night." Early next day, Hood rode over to Johnston's sullen headquarters to officially accept command of the army.

While Hood may have been "astounded" by his new assignment, many Confederate soldiers were sorely disappointed by the change of commanders. "It came like a flash of lightning," wrote a Confederate private at news of Johnston's dismissal, "staggering and blinding everyone." A Confederate officer recalled, "Every man looked sad and disheartened at this information, and felt that evil would result from the removal of Johnston."

Sherman, on the other hand, seemed to relish the thought of Hood at the Confederate helm. Upon learning of the switch in command from a Union spy on July 18, Sherman later recalled how he "immediately inquired of General Schofield, who was a classmate at West Point, about Hood... and learned that he was bold

even to rashness." Sherman knew that the selection of Hood to command the Confederate Army of Tennessee was a sign that the Confederates were getting ready to fight. "This was just what we wanted," Sherman wrote, "to fight in open ground, on anything like equal terms, instead of being forced to run up against prepared entrenchments." Two days later, Sherman had his wish.

Sherman had begun his general movement against Atlanta on July 17. With little opposition, the three Union armies composing Sherman's force crossed the Chattahoochee River and descended on the city from the north and east. Beginning a clockwise "circuit" around the city, Federal Major General James McPherson's army, followed by John Schofield's army, advanced eastward and seized Decatur, Georgia. About five miles from Atlanta, Decatur was astride the Georgia Railroad tracks that were the first link in Atlanta's rail supply lines with the eastern seaboard and Virginia. From Decatur, McPherson and Schofield advanced toward Atlanta on July 19.

Meanwhile, directly north of Atlanta, Federal Major General George H. Thomas deployed his

MARCH TO THE SEA

Federal Major General William T. Sherman and his staff guided their mounts up the slope and along the column of wagons and marching soldiers that filled the road. Pausing on the hilltop, the Federal officers turned to look back at Atlanta. The city was in shambles. Where the torch had been applied, ruins still smoldered. Thick black smoke hung like a funeral shroud over the former Confederate stronghold. "Then we turned our horses' heads to the east;" Sherman wrote, "Atlanta was soon lost behind the screen of trees, and became a thing of the past."

On the morning of November 16, 1864, Sherman, with a force of about 60,000 men, started his march to the sea. Savannah, Georgia, an important Confederate port on the Atlantic coast, was his goal. Facing Sherman's Union army was a nearly 300-mile trek through the heart of the Confederacy. Unable to supply his army by conventional methods because of the distances involved, Sherman boldly planned to live off the land. "The skill and success of the men in collecting forage," recalled Sherman, "was one of the features of this march."

Sherman's hardy soldiers marched in parallel columns, wreaking destruction over an area 40 to 60 miles wide. "The order is to destroy all cotton gin factories & such other buildings as the General sees fit," recalled a Federal captain. Railroad tracks, bridges, and military storehouses were wrecked by the Federal army. Sherman's purpose was to split the South and cut the flow of supplies to Confederate General Robert E. Lee's army in Virginia. Sherman also wanted to bring the war to the Southern people and to break their will to continue their fight for independence.

The Federals faced little opposition during their march. Behind Sherman, Confederate General John Hood's army had invaded Tennessee in a futile effort to divert Sherman's army. In front of Sherman, weak Confederate militia units comprised of old men and young boys were no match for the veteran Union troops.

On December 10, Sherman reached Savannah. After a 10-day siege, the city surrendered. The North rejoiced at Sherman's message to President Lincoln on December 22: "I beg to present you as a Christmas gift the city of Savannah."

Hood's loss and the Union bombardment of Atlanta had a dramatic effect on the remaining residents of the city. "Trunks, bedclothing and apparel were scattered in every direction," wrote a Confederate officer. "People were stirring in every conceivable way to get out of town."

The smoke had hardly cleared from the Peachtree Creek battlefield before Hood was planning another assault on Sherman. Delay of any kind, Hood knew, would only give Sherman time to strengthen his grip around Atlanta.

Hood's next target was McPherson's army east of Atlanta. Confederate cavalry patrols had informed Hood late on July 20 that McPherson's left flank and rear were unprotected and open to attack. Hood planned to withdraw two Confederate corps back to Atlanta's shorter line of defenses to hold the city. Hood's remaining corps, commanded by Lieutenant General William Hardee, would sweep wide to the south and east of town. After an all-night march, Hardee would hit McPherson's weak left flank at daybreak on July 22. Following day-long skirmishes with Federal forces on July 21, Hood enacted his plans that night.

Early on the 22nd, Sherman was amazed to see that the outer line of Confederate earthworks in front of Schofield and Thomas had been abandoned. The Federal lines "were advanced rapidly close up to Atlanta," wrote Sherman. "For some moments I supposed the enemy intended to evacuate [the city]."

McPherson and his staff rode up as Sherman surveyed the Confederate defenses. The two Federal officers talked awhile until their attention was drawn to mounting gunfire from the direction of McPherson's army. McPherson "hastily called for his horse, his staff, and his orderlies," wrote Sherman of his subordinate's reaction to the ominous sounds of battle. As Sherman recalled, the handsome 34-year-old McPherson "jumped on his horse, saying he would hurry down his line and send me back word what these sounds meant." This was the last time Sherman saw the promising officer alive. Soon after departing, McPherson mistakenly rode into Confederate lines and was shot dead.

Because of lengthy, unexpected delays due to darkness and bad roads, Confederate General Hardee's column had made slow progress. Hours behind Hood's original timetable, Hardee finally struck a powerful blow at McPherson's left flank about noon. At first, the left half of Hardee's line made headway against the startled Federals. "This caused the Yankees to evacuate all the fortifications protecting their rear," wrote a Confederate captain. The Federal line stiffened, however, after the initial shock. The same Confederate captain later noted: "The Yanks reinforced and came back with a charge, and I thought it advisable to retire, which we did in hasty steps."

The rail depot for the Western & Atlantic Railroad through which many of Hood's supplies flowed. Atlanta was a major communication and transportation center for the South, making it vital for the Federals to capture the city.

The right half of Hardee's line smacked into a solid blue wall. By coincidence, several thousand Federal soldiers had been marching toward Atlanta when the men of Hardee's right emerged from trees to the left of the Union column. The long line of Union marchers "had only to halt," wrote Sherman, "face to the left, and was in line of battle; and this corps not only held in check the enemy, but drove him back through the woods."

At about 4:00 P.M., with Hardee's flank attack staggering, Hood ordered another Confederate corps to charge the front of McPherson's position. Hood hoped to draw some Federal soldiers away from Hardee. This new Confederate assault proved to be too little too late. The bitter combat raged east of Atlanta until evening but only added to the total of 7000 to 10,000 Confederate killed, wounded, and captured. Federal losses totaled about 3700. "The enemy had retired during the night," Sherman observed the next day, "and we remained masters of the situation outside."

For a month after the Battle of Atlanta, Federal earthworks were strengthened and extended, placing Atlanta under virtual siege. Heavy Union artillery bombardments devastated the city, and several Union cavalry raids struck deep behind Confederate lines but with little success. Federal infantry pressure was relentlessly shifted from east to west of Atlanta. Gradually, Sherman pressed to the southwest of town to cut the two remaining railroads that supplied Hood's army.

Two Confederate counterattacks failed to halt Sherman's massive flank movement. The first of the two Confederate attacks came July 28 at Ezra Church, just west of Atlanta. Hood suffered a staggering 5000 casualties in yet another defeat, compared with less than 1000 Federal losses. After the Battle of Ezra Church, Sherman recalled how his soldiers "spoke of the affair...as the easiest thing in the world; that, in fact, it was a cannon slaughter of the enemy."

Hood's final attempt to break the Union siege occurred at Jonesboro, a village on the Macon Railroad about 15 miles south of Atlanta. The Federal advance reached Jonesboro on August 31. For two days, about half the Confederate army made a desperate attempt to stop the Federals from gaining control of this last rail line into Atlanta, but the Federals proved much too strong. "We did our best to get up a fight," wrote a Confederate infantryman, "but it was no go, any way we could fix it up." A Federal officer observed, "They seem to know they are beaten." The futile effort cost 1700 Confederate and 200 Federal losses. The greatest Confederate loss on September 1 was the city of Atlanta itself. The fall of Jonesboro had cut the last remaining supply line to the city. Late that night, Hood destroyed supplies his army could not carry off and marched out of Atlanta.

Sherman later wrote in his memoirs, "as the news spread to the army, the shouts that arose from our men, the wild hallowing and glorious laughter, were to us a full recompense for the labor and toils and hardships through which we had passed on the previous three months." To President Abraham Lincoln and the anxious Northern public, Sherman telegraphed: "Atlanta is ours, and fairly won."

WILLIAM TECUMSEH SHERMAN

Named for a famous Shawnee Indian chief, Tecumseh, Federal General William Tecumseh Sherman became a renowned warrior himself, despite serious setbacks early in his career.

Sherman was born in Lancaster, Ohio, on February 8, 1820, the third of 11 children. After his father's death in 1829, Sherman went to live with the neighboring Thomas Ewing family, where he was baptized with the name William.

An influential lawyer, businessman, U.S. Senator, and later in his career Secretary of the Treasury, Thomas Ewing secured an appointment to West Point for 16-year-old William. After graduating from the military academy in 1840, ranking sixth in a class of 42 cadets, young Sherman served at army posts throughout the South. During the Mexican War, Sherman served as an artillery officer in California, where he saw little action. "I feel ashamed," Sherman had written his future wife, Ellen Ewing, "having passed through a war without smelling gunpowder."

Soured on the army by the low pay, little opportunity for promotion, and his lack of combat experience, Sherman resigned from military service in 1853. But subsequent endeavors in banking, law, and investment ventures provided no success. "I am doomed to be a vagabond, and shall no longer struggle against my fate," Sherman wrote.

Fate took Sherman to Louisiana in 1859. Here he finally found success as superintendent at a private military academy until the Civil War began in April 1861. Returning to the North, Sherman headed a St. Louis, Missouri, streetcar company until he reentered the army in May 1861.

Sherman rose from colonel to major general within a year. The next three years featured a string of battlefield successes for the aggressive Sherman that was capped by his unprecedented march through Georgia and the Carolinas. By the war's end, only Lieutenant General Ulysses S. Grant's fame as a Union military leader exceeded Sherman's.

Sherman's achievements continued in the postwar army. By 1869 he had attained the rank of general of the army and held that post for 14 years. Sherman was active in veteran affairs until his death in 1891. After retiring from the military in 1883, Sherman entered New York society. A former Union officer wrote of Sherman: "In whatever circle he moved, he was the center; at whatever table he sat, he was the head. The nation had lifted him to the highest military rank; Congress had presented him with votes and thanks.... There were no more public honors to bestow, and now he was receiving the courtesies and attentions of private life in a manner which gave the sweetest solace to the veteran's declining years."

BATTLE OF WINCHESTER
(OPEQUON CREEK)
September 19, 1864

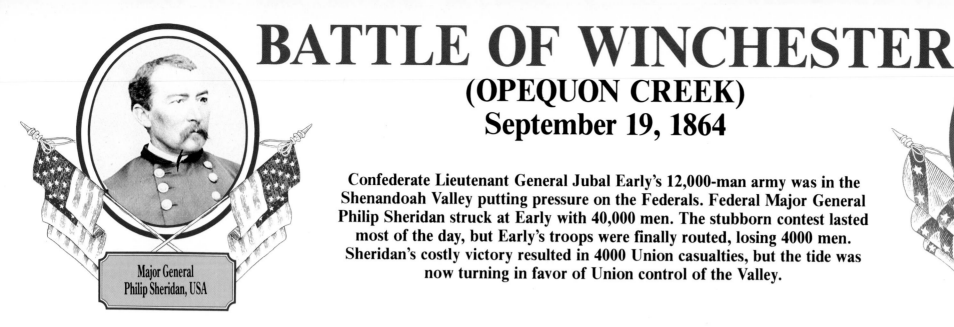

Major General
Philip Sheridan, USA

Lieutenant General
Jubal Early, CSA

Confederate Lieutenant General Jubal Early's 12,000-man army was in the Shenandoah Valley putting pressure on the Federals. Federal Major General Philip Sheridan struck at Early with 40,000 men. The stubborn contest lasted most of the day, but Early's troops were finally routed, losing 4000 men. Sheridan's costly victory resulted in 4000 Union casualties, but the tide was now turning in favor of Union control of the Valley.

A note from the young Quaker schoolmarm, smuggled behind the Federal lines on September 16, 1864, by a black messenger, confirmed Federal Major General Philip H. Sheridan's suspicions. The Confederate force at Winchester, Virginia, was "much smaller than represented." The Winchester schoolteacher, Miss Rebecca Wright, had learned this valuable information from a Confederate officer who had visited her parent's home the night before. He had innocently remarked that a dozen cannons and a few thousand Confederate infantrymen were being sent from Confederate Lieutenant General Jubal A. Early's Army of the Valley District back to General Robert E. Lee's Confederate army at Petersburg, Virginia.

Sheridan had solicited information from Miss Wright because he had heard that she was loyal to the Union. Miss Wright at first was hesitant to participate in such a dangerous venture, but her report was invaluable to the Union commander. With the news in hand, Sheridan decided to attack Early's army at Winchester.

Early had originally come to the Shenandoah Valley from Petersburg in June 1864 with 14,000 Confederate troops. Lee had hoped that, combining these 14,000 soldiers with the small force already in the Valley, Early could duplicate the success of Confederate Lieutenant General "Stonewall" Jackson's Shenandoah Valley Campaign of 1862. In the spring of 1862, Jackson's brilliant success in the Valley against superior Union forces had helped ease Federal pressure on Richmond, Virginia. In the spring of 1864, with Union forces on the doorstep of the Confederate capital once again, Lee sent Early's corps to the Valley to repeat Jackson's feat.

Early did repeat Jackson's success. By mid-summer, Early had cleared the Valley of Federal troops and marched within sight of the capitol dome in Washington, D.C. As Lee had hoped, Grant dispatched an entire army corps under

Phil Sheridan, almost 20,000 men, from Petersburg to deal with Early. From the Federal supply base at Harpers Ferry, West Virginia, at the northern tip of the Shenandoah Valley, Sheridan led his army of 40,000 men against Early on August 10.

Early, with roughly 18,000 men, retreated slowly ahead of Sheridan. The smaller Confederate force skirmished almost daily with the Federals but did not risk a major battle. Early eventually halted and dug into a strong defensive position on Fisher's Hill, about 45 miles southwest of Harpers Ferry. Sheridan advanced his command to within a few miles of the Confederate line. Skirmishing continued while both sides waited for reinforcements.

But Sheridan was far from his base at Harpers Ferry. He grew concerned as his supplies dwindled. When raids on supply wagons by Confederate Colonel John Mosby combined with word of the approach of Confederate reinforcements, Sheridan withdrew to a more defensible position closer to Harpers Ferry, where he awaited the reinforcements promised by Grant. Following the Federal withdrawal, Early advanced his own army to positions near Winchester, within 20 miles of the Federal army.

Sheridan remained relatively cautious through the end of August and the first two weeks of September. While blue and gray infantry units occasionally clashed during this time, "[t]he cavalry," wrote Sheridan, "was employed a good deal...skirmishing—heavily at times—to maintain a space about six miles in width between the hostile lines...so that...I could move my men into position for attack without the knowledge of Early." After receiving Rebecca Wright's valuable intelligence report on September 16 that a few thousand Confederate troops had departed Early's army, Sheridan prepared to attack.

Meanwhile, at Winchester, Early was content to be a thorn in the side of the Federal government. His army prevented tens of thousands of Federal troops from joining Grant at Petersburg, maintained pressure on the important Baltimore & Ohio Railroad, and protected the valuable resources of the Shenandoah Valley.

Since the Federals remained inactive along his front, Early felt confident enough to divide his army on September 17. He moved three of his four divisions several miles to the north toward the Baltimore & Ohio Railroad, leaving only one division east of Winchester, along Opequon Creek, facing the Federal camps. According to Early, Sheridan was overcautious, "which amounted to timidity."

Far from timid, Sheridan was making final preparations on September 17 to pounce on Early and, according to a Confederate officer, "devour him piecemeal, a division at a time." Sheridan planned his main attack against the lone Confederate division east of Winchester. He would sweep it aside, capture the town, and block the road behind Early's other three divisions. At the same time, a large Federal cavalry force would hit the three divisions from north of the town. At about 2:00 A.M. on September 19, Sheridan's army marched against the unsuspecting Confederates.

At first the Federal attack floundered. Advancing on a single, narrow road that ran between steep, wooded slopes, thousands of Union troops and supply wagons took hours to get through. This delay allowed the single Confederate division to hold off Sheridan's army long enough for Early's other three divisions to swiftly march back to Winchester. By mid-morning, Early had formed solid lines north and east of town.

Though heavily outnumbered, momentum shifted to Early because Union assaults were

uncoordinated. By 11:00 A.M., Confederate troops counterattacked into a gap that suddenly appeared in Sheridan's battle line east of town. The open fields, orchards, and wooded ravines swirled with combat. Confederate artillery was used with deadly effect, and it was not long before the center of Sheridan's line caved in. Panic gripped the fleeing Federal troops, but Sheridan quickly plugged the hole with reserves. Once the Union line was restored, a lull settled over the battleground east of Winchester.

North of the town, two Federal cavalry divisions swooped down on Early's left flank at about 4:30 P.M. Joined by solid Union infantry formations, these Federal troops, in the words of a Federal infantry officer, "surged forward with a yell that lasted for minutes." The charging Federals hit the Confederate line with devastating impact. Union cavalrymen burst upon the Confederate foot soldiers, "showering saber blows on their heads and shoulders," recalled a Federal officer, "trampling them under, and routing them in droves in every direction." Following on Confederate heels, the Federals overwhelmed a last-ditch stand in Confederate earthworks in the suburbs of Winchester. One Confederate captain wrote, "our scattered troops...retreated rapidly and in disorder through the city." Only a desperate rearguard action by Confederate horsemen south of Winchester prevented Sheridan from blocking the remnants of Early's army.

At sunset, Early's battered survivors disappeared into the lengthening shadows to the south with almost 4000 fewer men. Some 4000 bluecoats paid the cost for Sheridan's victory. The Federal commander did not rest on his laurels, however. While Early was reforming his army on Fisher's Hill, 20 miles from Winchester, Sheridan was already planning his next attack against the battered Confederate army.

BATTLE OF CEDAR CREEK
October 19, 1864

Major General
Philip Sheridan, USA

Lieutenant General
Jubal Early, CSA

Confederate General Jubal Early detected a weak spot in the Federal lines and attacked the 30,000-man Federal army at dawn, but the Confederate army, numbering about 18,000, missed a golden opportunity to completely rout the Federals. Federal General Philip Sheridan, absent at the time of the surprise attack, rode down the Valley Turnpike, rallied his troops, and launched a counterattack. When the smoke cleared, 5600 Federals and 2900 Confederates were casualties. This battle marked the Confederacy's last attempt to keep control of the Shenandoah Valley.

Within minutes of first hearing the rumble of distant cannon fire at dawn on October 19, 1864, James E. Taylor was mounted and galloping south from Winchester, Virginia, toward the sound of the guns. He was armed with pencil and sketch pad only. As special artist for *Frank Leslie's Illustrated Newspaper,* Taylor had been assigned in August 1864 to cover the progress of Federal Major General Philip H. Sheridan's Shenandoah Valley Campaign. Since then, the talented young artist had pictured decisive Union victories at the battles of Winchester and Fisher's Hill as well as numerous skirmishes.

Confederate Lieutenant General Jubal A. Early's Army of the Valley District had suffered severe losses in those two major defeats in September. Many Union authorities, including Sheridan, believed the Valley campaign was over. James Taylor may also have believed that his assignment was drawing to a close—until the boom of heavy cannon fire caught his ear the morning of October 19. The battle sounds were coming from the direction of Sheridan's army camped along Cedar Creek, about 15 miles away.

A few minutes behind Taylor, Phil Sheridan himself galloped along the Valley Turnpike. Sheridan later wrote, "there burst upon our view the appalling spectacle of a panic-stricken army...all pressing to the rear in hopeless confusion." En route back to his Army of the Shenandoah after two days of strategy meetings in Washington, Sheridan, like Taylor, had passed the night in Winchester. He too had been quickly drawn to the gunfire from the south.

Until that October morning, the Shenandoah Valley had been relatively quiet for nearly a month. Sharp encounters flared daily between Federal and Confederate troops, but no major

battles had occurred since the Union victory at Fisher's Hill on September 22, which had been Sheridan's second victory over the Confederate army in the space of three days.

Sheridan, meanwhile, continued to carry out his original instructions from Grant, supreme commander of all Union armies, "for desolating the Shenandoah country," recalled Sheridan, "so as to make it untenable for permanent occupation by the Confederates." Throughout the Shenandoah Valley, Union troops systematically destroyed crops, burned barns and mills, and drove off livestock. "Many...are without a pound of meat, bread, or anything to live on," wrote a Valley resident.

The Federal destruction of food supplies forced Early to decide "to move back for want of provisions and forage, or attack the enemy in his position with the hope of driving him from it." Despite reinforcements drawn from General Robert E. Lee's army in Petersburg, Virginia, Early's army was still less than half the size of Sheridan's. Nonetheless, Early determined to attack, relying on the element of surprise to make up for his army's lack of strength. Early's chance came on the morning of October 19.

Reconnoitering from a mountain peak near the Confederate camps located just five miles from Sheridan's army, Confederate officers on October 17 detected a weak spot in the Union position. The Federal left flank, resting about where Cedar Creek joined the North Fork of the Shenandoah River, was lightly defended. Sheridan and his corps commanders had felt that the terrain along this portion of their line was defense enough and therefore concentrated their strength on the right side of their line at the expense of their left. Seizing on this Federal mistake, Early directed two infantry divisions to strike the Union front, while his three remaining

infantry divisions were to hit Sheridan's weak left flank.

Marching, often in single file, in darkness by a narrow path between the waterways and the mountainside, the three Confederate flanking divisions were in place before first light on the 19th. Jubal Early, with the other two divisions opposite Sheridan's front, recalled, "We got in sight of the enemy's fires at half-past three o'clock." At 4:30 A.M. the troops with Early forded Cedar Creek and formed a line of battle under cover of darkness and fog.

The three Federal army corps lay quiet and unsuspecting behind light entrenchments on a string of low hills north of Cedar Creek. Divided by the Valley Turnpike, two corps camped east of the road and the other on the west.

About 5:00 A.M. the Confederates rolled forward. "[L]ike a resistless sea driven by the tempest," a Confederate officer later wrote, "poured a steady stream of gray-jackets over the works and into the Union camp." Hardest hit were the two Union corps east of the turnpike.

Startled from their sleep, Federal soldiers sprang from their tents. Some collected in small groups and managed to fire a volley or two before being engulfed in the Confederate rush. Most Union troops fled in panic toward Middletown, Virginia, or beyond. "Large numbers were captured," wrote Confederate General John Gordon. "Many hundreds were shot down as they attempted to escape.... Across the fields they swarmed in utter disorganization, heedless of their officer's commands." Only some courageous Federal artillerymen, firing their cannons blindly into the fog in the direction from which the Confederates came, were able to slow the Confederate advance. This was the cannon fire that brought

James Taylor and Federal commander Phil Sheridan galloping to the front.

Sheridan, waving his hat, pounded along the turnpike toward Cedar Creek, rallying his broken troops. Individually, in squads, and finally en masse, the terror-stricken Federal soldiers flocked back to the wooded slopes northwest of Middletown. Here, remnants of the Union Army of the Shenandoah formed a solid front around the lone corps posted west of the turnpike. From behind a barrier of rock fences, the bloodied but determined Federal army beat back repeated Confederate attacks.

By noon, Early's assault had stalled. The Confederate troops were disorganized by their morning onrush and distracted by the tempting spoils found in the abandoned Union camp. The "open tents displayed a scene almost enchanting to the eyes of the Southern soldier," wrote Gordon, "costly blankets, overcoats...hats... boots." Many hungry Confederates broke ranks to plunder food as well as clothing. Early's army never recovered its momentum.

Sheridan's troops, in the meantime, had recovered despite extensive casualties suffered that morning. About 4:00 P.M. the dynamic Sheridan led a powerful counterattack. James Taylor observed, "the enemy make but feeble resistance, and we are quickly over their line of entrenchments." Once broken, the Confederate line crumbled. Union cavalry led the onslaught, and by dusk the Confederates were completely routed, losing some 2900 men and scores of cannons. Sheridan suffered almost 5600 casualties, most a result of the initial attack.

Early didn't regain control of his beaten army until their stampede ended at New Market, Virginia, 25 miles south of Cedar Creek. The Confederacy, however, never regained control of the vital Shenandoah Valley.

BATTLE OF FRANKLIN
November 30, 1864

Major General
John Schofield, USA

Federal Major General John Schofield made a mistake that gave Confederate General John Hood's 38,000-man army a chance to crush Schofield's 28,000 troops. Their backs to the Harpeth River, the Federals had to beat back Hood's attack until bridges over the river could be repaired. Despite a cost of 6200 Confederate soldiers, Hood failed to stop Schofield from marching to reinforce the Federal garrison at Nashville, Tennessee. Although suffering 2300 casualties, Schofield managed to save his army.

Lieutenant General
John Hood, CSA

Band music announced the Confederates' arrival. Strains of "Dixie" and "The Bonnie Blue Flag" drifted across the open meadows. From hilltops, the Federals surveying the scene below waved signal flags as Confederate infantry came into view. Tattered red battle flags waved in abundance over the gray-clad troops; a line of glistening bayonets and musket barrels stretched from left to right as far as the eye could see. In perfect alignment, the battle line drew steadily nearer. "It looked to me," recalled a Union artilleryman in the path of the advance, "as though the whole South had come up there and were determined to walk right over us." Confederate General John Bell Hood, the impetuous commander of the Army of Tennessee, intended to do just that. Hood, previous battle wounds having taken his right leg and rendered his left arm lifeless, had determined to bull his way into Franklin, Tennessee, on the afternoon of November 30, 1864, forcing the Federals "into the river in their immediate rear."

Driven from Atlanta, Georgia, by Federal Major General William Sherman's army three months earlier, Hood had moved his weakened force 40 miles southwest of the city to rest and refit. After a strategy conference with Confederate President Davis, it was agreed that Hood should advance north toward Chattanooga, Tennessee, to strike Union supply lines and lure Sherman into battle. The diversion distracted Sherman only temporarily, however, and he eventually turned eastward, embarking on his "march" through the South. Hood proceeded north and west to attack Sherman's lines of communication and to begin an operation that he hoped could lead to an invasion of Tennessee and Kentucky.

Sherman countered Hood's move by sending Major General George H. Thomas with a small force to Nashville, Tennessee, to raise an army from various detached units to oppose Hood's

Confederates. Supporting Thomas with a force of less than 30,000 men was Major General John Schofield at Pulaski, Tennessee, 70 miles south of Nashville. Schofield was blocking the main highway to the Tennessee capital.

After a costly delay of about three weeks at Tuscumbia, Alabama, while awaiting the arrival of 6000 soldiers of Confederate Major General Nathan Bedford Forrest's command to join his army of about 32,000, Hood finally launched his advance on Nashville on November 19. He hoped to wedge his army between Schofield and Thomas, defeating them piecemeal. Halfway between Nashville and Pulaski sat Columbia, Tennessee, on the south bank of the Duck River. Columbia was the site of vital rail and road bridges in Schofield's rear. With the crossing in his hands, Hood knew Schofield would be trapped. Hood rapidly marched his men toward Columbia.

Alerted to his peril by his cavalry scouts, Schofield rushed two of his five divisions ahead to secure Columbia. Schofield also scuttled his pontoon wagon train to lighten his load. The absence of this pontoon equipment proved nearly fatal to Schofield a week later.

Skirmishes flared along the Federal line of march as Forrest's Confederate cavalry attempted to slow the Union advance. When Forrest reached Columbia, he found Brigadier General James H. Wilson's Federal cavalry already there. Schofield's entire force reached Columbia on November 24.

With his back to the river and Forrest's horsemen threatening to turn his flanks, Schofield withdrew to the north bank of the Duck River on November 27. But Forrest's cavalry crossed about 10 miles upstream the next day and pushed north. Hood then sent two corps across the Duck River and toward Spring Hill, the next stop on the road to Nashville, while Confederate Lieutenant General Stephen

D. Lee distracted Schofield with a loud cannonade. Warnings of a possible Confederate sweep around his left prompted Schofield to send two divisions toward Spring Hill, but he kept the bulk of his force at Columbia.

With Forrest out front and his infantry marching closely behind, Hood felt sure he had the drop on Schofield. But Schofield's two divisions reached Spring Hill moments before Forrest hit from the east and north. Twice Forrest charged, twice he was repulsed under blazing fire. Confederate infantry arrived just before dark, but their lethargic attacks failed to drive the Federals from the hamlet. With darkness at hand, the Confederates suspended operations for the day. Hood intended to crush the Federals the next morning.

Aware of the danger in his rear, Schofield abandoned his position along the Duck River and hastily advanced north. Throughout the night, Schofield's entire force flowed undetected along the road to Franklin, past Hood's unsuspecting command. Hood would later lament, "The best move in my career as a soldier, I was thus destined to behold come to naught."

By noon on November 30, Schofield had fortified his army around Franklin, Tennessee, which was located on the south bank of a bend in the Harpeth River, 10 miles north of Spring Hill. Without the pontoons he had jettisoned at Columbia, Schofield was forced to hold Franklin until the bridges there were repaired and his 800 wagons were safely across. At 3:00 P.M., after most of the wagons had crossed the river, Hood's massive battle line suddenly advanced on the town.

Hood had been furious when he learned that the Federals had escaped his trap. By 1:00 P.M. Hood and his corps commanders were surveying the Federal position from Winstead's Hill, about three miles south of the town. Over the heated protests of several subordinates,

including Forrest, Hood decided to launch a direct attack against the Union line.

Stretching nearly two miles from flank to flank and numbering 20,000 to 27,000 men, Hood's ranks swept forward. Astride the turnpike and a half mile ahead of the main Union line, a V-shaped earthwork manned by two brigades took the brunt of the initial strike. This suicidal stand ended with a single volley before the Federals broke and ran for the main line. The Confederates came screaming on their heels, shouting "Go in with them." When the charging Confederates reached the main Union line, a Federal regiment gave way. Fearful of hitting their comrades, Federal units adjacent to the break held fire, and vicious hand-to-hand combat raged over the breastworks. "The standards of both armies were upon them at the same time," wrote a participant. The crack in the Federal line expanded as more Confederates plunged into the gap.

The Union line stiffened when Federal Brigadier General Emerson Opdycke's brigade sealed the break behind the main line. Federal artillery then began to turn the tide, plowing great furrows in Confederate formations maneuvering over the open meadows. Hood was unable to match Union firepower since most of his artillery was still en route from Columbia and Spring Hill when the attack opened. Six Confederate generals were shot down in the maelstrom at the Federal works. Darkness finally ended the battle and the bloodshed. More than 6000 Confederate casualties littered the Tennessee countryside. Federal losses added another 2300.

Two hours after the fighting ended, Schofield abandoned Franklin and steered his army north toward the safety of Thomas's Nashville fortifications. With his beaten and bleeding army, Hood pursued the next day.

BATTLE OF NASHVILLE
December 15–16, 1864

Major General
George Thomas, USA

Lieutenant General
John Hood, CSA

Despite prodding from the Federal high command and outnumbering General John Hood's less than 30,000-man Confederate Army of Tennessee almost two to one, Federal Major General George Thomas had hesitated to attack. Finally, on December 15, 1864, Thomas struck and all but destroyed Hood's army. Suffering some 3000 casualties, the Federals routed the Confederates and ended any threat to the control of Tennessee and Kentucky.

Before retiring to his hotel room for the night, the Federal general left word at the front desk that he be awakened at 5:00 the next morning, December 15, 1864. Major General George H. "Pap" Thomas didn't want to be late for the assault he had so meticulously planned. Jump-off was set for 6:00 A.M.

For the first two weeks of December 1864, Thomas's 50,000- to 55,000-man Union army had cowered in dismal trenches around Nashville, Tennessee, confronted by a Confederate army barely half its size. Officials in Washington, D.C., prodded Thomas to attack, and Lieutenant General Ulysses S. Grant, General in Chief of all Union armies, was on the verge of sacking Thomas in favor of a more aggressive officer. Still, Thomas had refused to budge.

A stickler for detail and sincerely concerned for the welfare of his men—hence the nickname "Pap"—Thomas answered his critics by requesting enough horses and equipment to build a cavalry force sufficient to contend with Confederate Major General Nathan Bedford Forrest's horsemen. Until then, Thomas contented himself with preparing for the day he would sally forth against the enemy entrenchments overlooking Nashville.

General John B. Hood's Confederate Army of Tennessee occupied itself by fortifying earthworks south of the city. Hood knew his poorly equipped and underfed force of less than 30,000 men was no match for Thomas. A brutal toll exacted on his troops at the November 30, 1864, Battle of Franklin had all but crushed the offensive strength of his army. When Union Major General John Schofield's 25,000-man force reached the safety of the Nashville defenses after the Federal victory at Franklin, Hood followed in light of his plan to invade Tennessee and Kentucky. Hood hoped to lure recruits and stop or slow down Federal Major

General William T. Sherman's invasion of Georgia. A bloodless stalemate in the frigid trenches around Nashville ensued.

Too weak to attack or besiege the city and too near the enemy position to maneuver— fearful of exposing his flank or rear to the superior Federal force—Hood contented himself with launching Forrest's cavalry against Union supply lines. Expecting reinforcements from the Trans-Mississippi area, the Confederate commander hoped to lure Thomas out of the safety of his earthworks and then, after repulsing a Union assault, break through the Federal defenses around Nashville. But while Hood waited for Thomas to take the offensive, the Federal commander was being assaulted on several other fronts.

For months, the Federals had enjoyed nothing but success in the west. Confederate forces had been in almost constant retreat under the relentless pressure of Sherman's army. In October, however, Hood had sidestepped Sherman and pushed north against the Federals' lines of communication, in hopes of halting the Union advance through Georgia. This proved only a temporary distraction in Sherman's march to the sea. The Federal commander sent three corps to Nashville to join Thomas, who was gathering troops from throughout Tennessee and neighboring states to create an army to meet Hood. By the time Schofield's command joined Thomas, the Federal high command felt that Thomas's force was more than equal to the task of defeating Hood's army. The Federal general, however, still awaited the arrival of a sufficient number of horses to mount his cavalry force.

But the Federal authorities were not as patient as Thomas. The thought of a large Confederate force operating north of Sherman's army, threatening both Tennessee and Kentucky, concerned the Federal high

command, including Grant. Irked by Thomas's failure to take immediate advantage of his superior numbers despite repeated urgings from Washington as well as his own City Point, Virginia, headquarters, Grant wired Thomas: "Attack Hood at once and await no longer the remount of your cavalry." Stirred by Grant's rebuke, Thomas hurried his preparations for an attack on December 10.

The weather suddenly turned miserable on the 10th. Temperatures plunged and sleet and snow swept over the prospective battlefield. For the next four days "everything was covered with ice an inch thick, as far as the eye could reach," a Federal sergeant observed, "and walking was still extremely difficult and dangerous." The unexpected weather stopped Thomas's planned attack before it got started. Grant fumed at word of the delay. Disregarding the weather excuse, he dispatched Major General John A. Logan to replace Thomas. Grant then boarded a train for Washington, en route to Nashville for a firsthand look at the situation there.

A thaw arrived on December 14, before either Union general could reach Nashville, and Thomas quickly set the attack for 6:00 the following morning. "I am sure my plan of operations is correct," Thomas told a Federal General, "and we shall lick the enemy, if he only stays to receive our attack." Then Thomas retired for the night to his room at Nashville's St. Cloud Hotel.

With the thaw, a dense ground fog settled around Nashville on the morning of December 15. Delayed for two hours while his soldiers groped through the haze into position, Thomas finally launched his assault at about 8:00 A.M. His well-planned attack—"a perfect exemplification of the art of war," Schofield claimed—worked to perfection. Striking first at Hood's right flank, which was anchored on the tracks of the Nashville and Chattanooga Railroad, Thomas

diverted attention away from his main thrust against the Confederate left. Schofield then attacked at 9:00 A.M. while Federal cavalry curled around Hood's left rear. Acres of mud and stout Confederate resistance made for slow going at first, but as the Federal troops gained momentum, the already thin Confederate defense line reached the breaking point. "On we rushed," an Indiana infantry sergeant recalled, "shouting, loading, yelling."

Hood's meager line gave way under the fierce pressure, and he conducted a fighting retreat to a last-ditch line on a low range of hills two miles south of his original position. Darkness ended the fighting for the day, but Hood was determined to renew the combat the next day.

A devastating Federal artillery bombardment on Hood's compact battle line opened the fight on December 16. The keys to Hood's position were Shy's Hill on his left and Overton Hill on his right. Thomas aimed his attack at these two heights. With orders to "halt for nothing, but to gain the works at a run," Federal troops climbed the slopes of Overton Hill at 3:00 P.M. Hood managed to beat back this assault but was forced to draw reinforcements from his left flank to bolster his center and right. This tactic proved fatal when a heavy Union attack engulfed the weakened Confederate position on Shy's Hill. It was the beginning of the end for the Army of Tennessee. Retreat quickly degenerated into rout, ending any form of organized resistance. "Wagon trains...artillery, cavalry and infantry were all blended in inextricable confusion," recalled a Confederate private.

Thomas lost about 3000 men. Confederate reports failed to list casualty figures, but Federal authorities estimated the number captured at more than 4000 Confederates. An entire Confederate army practically ceased to exist as a fighting unit. The war in the west was nearly at an end.

CAPTURE OF FORT FISHER
January 15, 1865

Major General
Alfred Terry, USA

Major General
William Whiting, CSA

Following incredible bungling by an inexperienced Federal general, Federal Brigadier General Alfred Terry assumed command and led 10,000 men on an assault against the 1900 defenders of Confederate Fort Fisher. After eight hours of vicious hand-to-hand combat, the Confederates surrendered. Although the Federals lost more than 1300 men to the Confederates' 500, the capture of Fort Fisher led to the fall of Wilmington, North Carolina, a month later, and closed the last gap in the Federal naval blockade.

It must have looked as if the whole Federal fleet had suddenly emerged from the depths of the Atlantic Ocean. As the Confederate soldiers arrayed on the lofty ramparts of Fort Fisher watched at twilight on January 12, 1865, Union admiral David Dixon Porter's vessels appeared in stages along the eastern horizon. Mastheads appeared first, dim and indistinct and topped with banners that shifted with the sea breeze. Then came the slender smokestacks merging into dark hulls as mighty frigates came into full view. Next, the low bulk of ironclad monitors hove into sight between the larger men-of-war. The ships grew in size as the distance narrowed between them and the anxious Confederate warriors in the fortress. For the second time in less than three weeks, Fort Fisher was about to be attacked by Federal forces. Fort Fisher guarded the entrance to the Cape Fear River, water avenue to the important Confederate port city of Wilmington, North Carolina.

Fort Fisher became the focus of Union military planners in the winter of 1864. Capture Fort Fisher, reasoned the planners, and Wilmington would fall, eliminating the last Confederate bastion for blockade runners who imported tons of vital products and munitions. The capture of Fort Fisher and Wilmington would also provide a convenient base for supplying Federal Major General William T. Sherman's army as it advanced northward from Georgia.

It was not until Christmas Eve 1864, however, that a Federal attack was launched against Fort Fisher. A combined Federal assault force of 60 vessels of Admiral Porter's fleet and 6500 army troops under Major General Benjamin Butler faced the imposing target of Fort Fisher.

The massive L-shaped fortress was located north of the channel entrance on the southern tip of a peninsula called Confederate Point.

(The peninsula had been known as Federal Point before the war.) Of 50 artillery pieces, the fort boasted 16 heavy caliber cannon at embrasures cut into earth. The fort's timber walls stretched for three-fourths of a mile along the ocean front and then turned 90 degrees to the west and ran almost a quarter mile toward the inland shore. The sod-covered parapets averaged 20 feet in height—eight feet wide at the top and 25 feet wide at the base. A wooden palisade fronted by a wide minefield protected the open, northern end of the fort.

Before exposing his troops to Fort Fisher's guns, General Ben Butler, an eccentric, unorthodox political appointee, devised a plan to blow up the fort on Christmas Eve. An obsolete gunboat, *U.S.S. Louisiana,* was packed with 215 tons of gunpowder. Detonators and fuses were set, and the boat was towed to within 500 yards of the fort during the night. It exploded with a dull boom, producing a towering sheet of flame and smoke, but the explosion had little effect on the Confederate fort other than to rattle the nerves of some of the 500 men in the garrison. Eighty percent of the powder had been defective and failed to explode. Several hours later, Federal Admiral Porter began the war's heaviest naval bombardment to date while Butler's troops prepared to storm the fort.

But Porter's barrage failed to inflict much damage on the giant fort. This did not deter Butler's plans, however, and at 1:30 P.M. on Christmas Day, 2200 of his infantrymen came ashore. Shifting weather conditions and reports of a strong Confederate force advancing on his rear from Wilmington compelled Butler to abandon the attack. In his haste to return to sea, Butler left about 700 men stranded on the shore. The Federal soldiers were finally rescued by the U.S. Navy on December 27.

Confederate Major General William Whiting, the district commander, waived his rank and turned command of the fort to Colonel William Lamb. Lamb reported the results of Butler's actions, "This morning, December 27, the foiled and frightened enemy left our shore." If any good came to the Union camp from the fiasco, Admiral Porter expressed it best: "If this temporary failure succeeds in sending General Butler into private life, it is not to be regretted." Lieutenant General Grant concurred. "Please hold on where you are," he told the admiral, "and I will endeavor to be back again with an increased force and without the former commander." Grant relieved Butler and replaced him with Brigadier General Alfred Terry.

With 8000 troops under his command, Terry joined Porter in another attack against Fort Fisher. Porter's armada dropped anchor just beyond range of the fort's guns on the evening of January 12. At dawn the next morning, Porter's fleet opened fire. "All day and night on the 13th and 14th," Confederate Colonel Lamb wrote, "the navy continued its ceaseless torment." Terry, meanwhile, established a beachhead about five miles north of the fort on the afternoon of the 13th. He posted two brigades to guard his rear against a possible Confederate attack from that quarter. He then prepared his main force to strike Fort Fisher. Terry's soldiers were joined in the assault by a volunteer force of 2000 sailors and marines armed with rifles, revolvers, and cutlasses. Porter instructed his men to "board the fort in a seaman-like way." In the meantime, the fort had been reinforced to a total strength of 1900 men.

The Federal admiral preceded the assault with a point-blank cannonade on the fort in the morning and early afternoon of January 15. At about 2:30 P.M., the naval barrage lifted and the

charge was sounded. "Packed like sheep in a pen"—not in orderly columns as had been planned—the sailors-turned-foot-soldiers struck the northeast quarter of the fort. Met by well-directed blasts of small arms and artillery fire, the hapless bluecoats were shot to pieces and retreated in disorder.

Porter's sailors and marines did manage, however, to create enough of a diversion within the fort for Terry's infantry, who struck the western salient. Terry's men surged over the wall and engaged in brutal hand-to-hand combat with the Confederates atop the parapets. In successive assaults, the attackers captured one gun emplacement after another. The fighting raged until 10:00 P.M., when the fort was surrendered.

Almost 1300 Union casualties mingled with about 500 Confederate killed, wounded, and captured amid the bloody sand dunes. "If hell is what it is said to be," a Federal sailor wrote afterwards, "then the interior of Fort Fisher is a fair comparison." With the Cape Fear estuary firmly in Federal hands, Wilmington fell a month later.

A fair comparison to hell: the "Pulpit" inside Fort Fisher after the fort's capture by Federal forces.

BATTLE OF FIVE FORKS
April 1, 1865

Major General
Philip Sheridan, USA

Confederate General George Pickett was caught napping when Federal Major General Philip Sheridan's 27,000 soldiers descended on the 10,000 Confederates guarding Five Forks, a crossroads vital to the Confederate position at Petersburg, Virginia. The Confederates were routed. Sheridan lost about 1000 men while the Confederates suffered more than 4500 casualties. Five Forks fell into Federal hands, sealing the fate of the Confederate Army of Northern Virginia.

Major General
George Pickett, CSA

Fried fish was not much of a meal for a general, but by April 1, 1865, a meal of any kind was something the Confederate officers and enlisted men near Petersburg, Virginia, were thankful for. The soldier with a handful of parched corn in his pocket was lucky to have any ration at all. The Confederate army's breadbasket in the Shenandoah Valley had been destroyed by Federal troops the previous fall. General Lee's army then had to depend on two worn-out railroads to carry meager food supplies into Petersburg, where it was engaged in trench warfare with the Federals.

Confederate Major Generals George Pickett and Fitzhugh Lee, nephew of Confederate General Robert E. Lee, welcomed their invitations to a fish bake on April Fools' Day. Their friend and fellow major general, Thomas Rosser, had caught the fish himself two days earlier. He planned to serve the fish on the afternoon of April 1 at his headquarters, which was located two miles behind the Confederate line and guarded the crossroads at Five Forks, Virginia.

"Some time was spent over the lunch," Rosser recalled, "during which no firing was heard, and we concluded that the enemy was not in much of a hurry to find us at Five Forks." The lack of gunfire caused the generals to discount several reports of a Federal advance. Continuing their meal, the trio of Confederate officers, in the words of Fitz Lee, "were not expecting any attack that afternoon."

Then the unexpected happened. A burst of rifle fire from nearby woods interrupted the fish bake. Suddenly, in plain view of the startled Confederate generals, a long line of bluecoats appeared, coming right at them.

A junction of five roads set in flat, thickly wooded terrain 17 miles southwest of Petersburg, Five Forks was the key to Lee's entire defense of the strategic Southern city. If Petersburg fell, Richmond and the whole Confederate cause was doomed. On March 29, 1865, 53,000 Federal infantry and cavalry started marching toward the crossroads. The target of the massive Union advance was the Southside Railroad, which ran just three miles behind Five Forks. The railroad was the last link between Petersburg and that part of the Confederacy not yet in Federal hands. With about 19,000 troops, almost one-third of the Army of Northern Virginia, under their joint command, Generals Pickett and Fitz Lee were ordered to hold Five Forks at all costs.

Overall command of the Federal force deployed around Five Forks was in the hands of Major General Philip H. Sheridan. The conqueror of the Shenandoah Valley had arrived at Petersburg on March 27. Ordered by Grant to "turn the right flank of Lee's army," Sheridan marched far to the west of the city on March 29 with 10,000 cavalry in the lead.

To counter the Federal movement, Lee extended his already thin line to the breaking point. A three-mile-wide gap opened between Lee's right flank and Pickett's left. The breach in the line was unavoidable if Pickett was to remain between Sheridan and the Southside Railroad. Pickett's only ally was heavy rain, which turned roads to muddy soup, slowing Sheridan's columns.

Lead elements of the Union and Confederate armies clashed as the flank maneuver progressed on March 29 and 30. On the 31st Sheridan's troops were concentrated near Dinwiddie Court House, and he sent his cavalry ahead a few miles to Five Forks. Pickett was ready and waiting. Charging boldly from the timber, Pickett's men pushed the Federals all the way back to Dinwiddie. Federal artillery fire finally stopped Pickett's rush.

The Federal advance had been slowed; Confederate resistance had been stubborn.

Sheridan, however, had Pickett right where he wanted him—far from Petersburg. "If I am cut off from the Army of the Potomac," Sheridan told a Federal staff officer, "[Pickett's] force is cut off from Lee's army, and not a man of it should be allowed to get back to Lee." On April 1 Sheridan made sure of that.

Warned of a large Federal unit approaching his left flank, Pickett retreated from Sheridan's front by 2:00 A.M. on April 1. "Regret exceedingly your forced withdrawal," a disappointed Robert E. Lee telegrammed Pickett, "and your inability to hold the advantage you had gained." With Lee's message came the order to hold Five Forks, "at all hazards." Complying with this directive, Pickett constructed an irregular breastwork of dirt and logs. The hastily built Confederate line stretched for two miles east and west of Five Forks.

Sheridan advanced on the Confederate roadblock from the south before sunrise on April 1. He hoped to strike Pickett before the Confederates became entrenched. Slow movements by one of his subordinates, however, delayed Sheridan's plan. Sheridan fumed as the hours ticked away, and it was well past noon before about 27,000 Federal troops were ready for the assault.

It was during this lull that Pickett and Fitz Lee were invited to the fish fry. Hungry and perhaps overconfident from their victory the day before, the two Confederate generals left the front line shortly after noon. In the process, Pickett failed to appoint someone to command in his absence.

Unlike Pickett, Sheridan was prepared. Once his troops were in place, Sheridan planned to attack Pickett's entire line. Union cavalry would hit the Confederate center and right flank. Sheridan's infantry would strike the main blow in the gap against Pickett's left flank and rear. At a signal, Sheridan's men stormed Pickett's

leaderless command about 4:00 P.M. Begun with spirit, Sheridan's infantry assault staggered somewhat because of faulty map work that sent some units away from the Confederate position. Redirected by Sheridan himself—"the very incarnation of battle," wrote a witness—the stray bluecoats hit hard with the rest of their comrades.

After running a gauntlet of Federal musketry from the fish fry back to the front line, Pickett could do little. "Their cavalry, charging at a signal of musketry from the infantry," wrote Pickett, "enveloped us front and right and, sweeping down upon our rear, held us in a vise." Charging in overwhelming numbers, Federal forces tightened their grip on Pickett's line as daylight faded.

Sheridan was in the forefront of the Federal attack. Flag in hand, he jumped his horse over a Confederate breastwork and helped capture a group of Confederates. "Drop your guns," Sheridan ordered the disheartened enemy soldiers, "you'll never need them anymore." Pickett, attempting to rally his crumbling line, tried a similar feat. With a Confederate banner thrust into his hands by a wounded flag bearer, Pickett waved it and "called to my men to get into line to meet the next charge," he wrote, "overpowered, defeated, cut to pieces, starving, captured as we were." Pickett's effort, and a last-ditch defense by Confederate cavalry, bought just enough time for Confederate survivors to "melt into the darkened woodland."

Pickett lost more than 4500 men at Five Forks, compared with Sheridan's 1000 casualties. Completely cut off from Petersburg, many more Confederates were captured as they fled. A shadow of Pickett's former command battled at Five Forks on April 2, but they surrendered with the rest of Robert E. Lee's army seven days later at Appomattox Court House, Virginia.

FALL OF PETERSBURG

April 2, 1865

Lieutenant General
Ulysses Grant, USA

General
Robert E. Lee, CSA

For 10 months Petersburg had been under siege by Federal Lieutenant General Ulysses Grant's 110,000-man army. When the last rail line supplying Confederate General Robert E. Lee and his Army of Northern Virginia, numbering 55,000, fell into Federal hands, Lee was forced to abandon the town. Although a valiant and bloody stand by 300 Confederates in Fort Gregg saved Lee's army from complete destruction, the war in the east lasted only seven more days.

After charging headlong across the open field, several Federal soldiers struggled to the summit of Fort Gregg's steep eastern wall near a cannon embrasure. Lunging forward with their muskets at the ready, the Federals came face-to-face with a lone Confederate artilleryman whose hand was closed around the lanyard of a 3-inch field gun. He was about to pull the cord and blast a double charge of canister into Federal troops massed outside the fort.

"Drop the lanyard, or we'll shoot!" the Yankees demanded.

"Shoot and be damned!" the Rebel gunner yelled back as he pulled the cord.

It was just past 1:00 P.M. on April 2, 1865, and Fort Gregg sat directly in the path of a massive Federal assault on Petersburg, Virginia. With its back to the rain-swollen waters of the Appomattox River and overwhelming numbers of Union troops closing in on its other three sides, the fate of Confederate General Robert E. Lee's Army of Northern Virginia rested with the garrison of Fort Gregg. If the fort fell, Petersburg would be lost and Lee's army doomed.

By April 1865, the armies of Lee and Grant had battled one another for nearly 10 months across a necklace of stout earthworks that ringed the city of Petersburg. Located on the south bank of the Appomattox River about 23 miles south of the Confederate capital at Richmond, Petersburg was a supply and transportation center vital to the Confederate war effort. In the spring of 1864, its capture became a main goal of Union military planners. If Petersburg were captured, the collapse of Richmond and the Confederacy would follow.

Beginning in May 1864, Lieutenant General Ulysses S. Grant embarked the Federal Army of the Potomac on a campaign to destroy Lee's army in combat. After more than a month of almost continual combat across the face of eastern Virginia, Grant finally drove Lee to the

outskirts of Richmond in mid-June 1864. Rather than assault the solid defenses around the city, however, Grant decided to isolate the Confederate capital by capturing the vital railroad and communication center at Petersburg. On June 15, he slipped two corps across the James River on a 2200-foot-long pontoon bridge and struck the lightly defended Virginia city. Several feeble attempts to capture Petersburg were repulsed by a hastily gathered defense force under Confederate General Pierre G.T. Beauregard. During the next three days, Federal assaults failed to break the Confederate line, which was bolstered by reinforcements from Lee. Realizing that further direct attacks would be costly and ineffective, Grant prepared for siege warfare.

A 10-mile-long chain of trenches, breastworks, and redoubts that were constructed around Petersburg in 1862–1863 was the foundation of Lee's defenses. The earthworks were anchored by the Appomattox River east and west of the city.

Starting east of Petersburg with an outer line of works captured in his mid-June assaults, Grant began constructing a network of fortifications opposite Lee's army. The Federal commander's plan was to gradually push his works south and west of the city to sever the dozen or so highways and railroads that linked Petersburg with the rest of the Confederacy. Grant's first push to the southwest, at the Weldon Railroad, ended in defeat when Lee counterattacked on June 21–23, inflicting 2300 Union casualties. On June 25, Grant continued his assault. A regiment of Pennsylvania coal miners began tunneling a shaft beneath Confederate lines east of Petersburg. Although skeptical of the scheme, Grant approved the effort to blow a huge hole in the Confederate lines and charge through the gap into Petersburg. Explosives were detonated on July

30, 1864; the result was a Federal bloodbath. Bumbling Federal leaders and stiff Confederate resistance virtually annihilated an entire Federal division in the fight.

As the scorching summer wore on, disease, boredom, and constant skirmishing took their toll on both armies. Grant's trench works steadily edged westward. While Grant failed to inflict a decisive blow against Lee's army, the resulting war of attrition stretched Confederate manpower to the limit. By October the Weldon Railroad was in Federal hands. Lee was left with a single, rickety rail line to supply his army and Petersburg through the bitter winter months.

By March 1865, Lee could muster only 55,000 hard-pressed soldiers to oppose Grant's 110,000 in the trench maze that had grown to over 30 miles in length. Remaining idly in place would be slow suicide for the Confederates, who could not replace losses suffered from disease, desertion, and battle. With this in mind, Lee gambled on one last grand offensive in an attempt to break the Federal stronghold on Petersburg and perhaps lift the siege. If the attack failed, Lee at least hoped to force Grant to contract his lines, thus easing the pressure on Confederate defenses.

At 4:00 A.M. on March 25 Lee sprang his surprise. Grant's line at Fort Stedman, about a mile east of Petersburg, was punctured, and Lee momentarily verged on achieving his goal. Recovering quickly, the Federals counterattacked, recaptured Fort Stedman, and so fiercely raked the path of retreat with gunfire that thousands of Confederates surrendered rather than risk the suicidal withdrawal to the safety of their own lines.

In the aftermath of this success, Grant planned an offensive to capture the one remaining open rail line out of Petersburg. With the Southside Railroad in Grant's control, Lee would have no recourse but to abandon both

Petersburg and Richmond. The resulting Battle of Five Forks on April 1 ended in the defeat and rout of nearly a third of Lee's remaining troops. More importantly, it opened the door for control of the Southside Railroad. That night, Grant unleashed a powerful artillery bombardment all around Petersburg, and early the next morning a massive infantry assault on the city followed.

By noon on April 2, Lee's entire outer line west of Petersburg had crumbled except for Fort Gregg and a smaller neighboring earthwork called Fort Whitworth that sat on the crown of a treeless ridge about three miles west of Petersburg. The "salvation of Lee's army is in your keeping," an officer shouted to the 300-man garrison of Fort Gregg. If they could hold the fort for an hour or two, Lee would be able to evacuate his army from Petersburg at nightfall.

About 1:00 P.M. thousands of Federal troops surged against the fort in the face of intense rifle and artillery fire. "By the time our men reached the moat," recalled a Federal observer, "the slope was strewn with bodies." Brutal hand-to-hand combat raged around the dirt and timber ramparts for over an hour. Toward the end, a Confederate witness recorded, "There were so many Federals coming over the parapet…we could not shoot them all."

The slaughter was frightful on both sides—256 of the 300-man garrison of Fort Gregg were killed or wounded, and 720 Federal casualties sprawled about the grounds. The Confederate sacrifice had only served to prolong the agony of this long and costly war. The fighting at Fort Gregg allowed Lee to save his army from destruction at Petersburg. The few starving, exhausted survivors of the once great Army of Northern Virginia took one last march together to their surrender at Appomattox Court House, Virginia, seven days later.